Strategic Environmental Assessment in Action

Riki Therivel

London • Sterling, VA

First published by Earthscan in the UK and USA in 2004
Reprinted 2006

ISBN-10: 1-84407-042-5
ISBN-13: 978-1-84407-042-8

Typesetting by MapSet Ltd, Gateshead, UK
Printed and bound in the UK by Cromwell Press Ltd
Cover design by Danny Gillespie

For a full list of publications please contact:

Earthscan
8–12 Camden High Street
London, NW1 0JH, UK
Tel: +44 (0)20 7387 8558
Fax: +44 (0)20 7387 8998
Email: earthinfo@earthscan.co.uk
Web: www.earthscan.co.uk

22883 Quicksilver Drive, Sterling, VA 20166-2012, USA

Earthscan publishes in association with the International Institute for
Environment and Development

A catalogue record for this book is available from the British Library

Library of Congress Cataloging-in-Publication Data

Therivel, Riki, 1960-.
    Strategic environmental assessment in action / Riki Therivel.
        p. cm.
    Includes bibliographical references and index.
    ISBN 1-84407-042-5 (pbk. : alk. paper) — ISBN 1-84407-041-7 (hardback :
alk. paper)
    1. Environmental impact analysis. 2. Strategic planning—Environmental
aspects. 3. Environmental policy. I. Title
TD194.6.T48 2004
333.71'4—dc22

                                                                    2003021890

This book is printed on elemental chlorine free paper

Contents

Part I: Introducing
Strategic Environmental Assessment

Part II: The SEA Process

Part III: Assuring SEA Quality

Appendices

List of Figures, Tables and Boxes

Figures

Tables

Boxes

Acknowledgements

This is my first solo book, so I have not had a co-author to share in the joys and pains of writing it. Instead I have had the assistance of many people who contributed ideas, case studies and other support.

Roger Levett, my business partner, took on more than his share of work to keep our company afloat while I wrote this book, and has been a fantastic source of inspiration, ideas and support over the years. He wrote the sections of the book that discuss how sustainability and the environment interrelate, and suggested rules for how not to carry out SEA. My colleagues at Oxford Brookes University, particularly Elizabeth Wilson, John Glasson, Graham Wood and Stewart Thompson have been unfailingly generous and helpful. Students on my SEA unit at Oxford Brookes University's MSc in Environmental Assessment and Management, and participants on various SEA training courses that I have run have contributed ideas, examples and enthusiasm.

I am also grateful to many other people for their support, advice and ideas. Many are fellow SEA practitioners who have contributed in major ways to the evolution of SEA; others are forward-thinking government officials responsible for administering and implementing SEA. They include (in alphabetical order) Charles Aston, Joan Bennett, Nick Bonvoisin, Jean-Denis Bourquin, Clare Brooke, Lex Brown, Helen Byron, Cheryl Cowlin, Jenny Dixon, Ric Eales, Chris Fry, Halldora Hreggviðsdóttir, Simon Hooton, Emma James, Norman Lee, Phill Minas, Peter Nelson, Jeremy Owen, Maria Rosario Partidario, Stephen Pickles, David Saul, Deb Seamark, Nick Simon, Chris Smith, Steve Smith, Roger Smithson, Asdis Hlokk Theodorsdottir, Paul Tomlinson, Ben Underwood and Chris Wood. The International Association for Impact Assessment's 2002 conference was particularly helpful.

The examples used in this book are all based on real-life situations. I am grateful to the authorities – named and anonymous – that have provided these examples.

I am grateful to Chris Wood for permission to use Figure 2.3; Maria Partidario for permission to use Figure 5.3; Friends of the Earth and the New Economics Foundation for permission to use Figure 6.3; Oxfordshire County Council for permission to use Figure 7.3; the Council for the Protection of Rural England for permission to use Figure C.1; the European Environment Agency for permission to use Figure C.2; and John Lee, Stewart Thompson and others for permission to use Figure C.3.

Finally, as always, I owe much of my sanity and happiness to Tim O'Hara.

List of Acronyms and Abbreviations

Art.	article
CEC	Commission of the European Communities
DEFRA	Department of Environment, Food and Rural Affairs
DETR	Department of Environment, Transport and the Regions
DfT	Department for Transport
DoE	Department of the Environment
DTP	district transport plan
EAGGF	European Agricultural Guidance and Guarantee Fund
EC	European Commission
EIA	environmental impact assessment
EU	European Union
GDP	gross domestic product
GIS	Geographical Information Systems
ha	hectare
IEMA	Institute of Environmental Management and Assessment
ISEW	Index of Sustainable Economic Welfare
IUCN	International Union for the Conservation of Nature
km	kilometre
LCA	life cycle analysis
LGMB	Local Government Management Board
MCA	multi-criteria analysis
NGO	non-governmental organization
NIMBY	not in my back yard
ODPM	Office of the Deputy Prime Minister
QoLC	Quality of Life Capital
RDA	regional development agency
RES	Regional Economic Strategy
RPG	Regional Planning Guidance
RSS	Regional Spatial Strategy
SAC	Special Area of Conservation
SDC	Sustainable Development Commission
SEA	strategic environmental assessment
SEA Directive	European Union Directive 2001/42/EC
SPA	Special Protection Area
UDP	Unitary Development Plan
UK	United Kingdom
UN	United Nations
UNECE	United Nations Economic Commission for Europe
WCED	World Commission on Environment and Development

Part I

Introducing Strategic Environmental Assessment

Chapter 1

Introduction

Strategic environmental assessment (SEA) is a process that aims to integrate environmental and sustainability considerations in strategic decision-making. It has the potential to make the world a greener and more liveable place. It also has the potential to be a dreary and resource-intensive formality, applied in a grudging minimalist fashion by people who just *hate* having to do it, adding still further to some great useless administrative burden paid for by hapless taxpayers.

This book is intended to help people to set up good SEA systems and carry out effective, efficient SEAs: it is a manual for SEA. It presents straightforward SEA approaches and techniques that achieve the objectives of SEA – green, equitable – but with a minimal burden. The book focuses in particular on the implementation of the European Union Directive 2001/42/EC 'on the assessment of the effects of certain plans and programmes on the environment' (known as the SEA Directive) and the United Nations Economic Commission for Europe (UNECE) Protocol on SEA, but the approaches it explains are applicable to SEAs worldwide.

Book structure

Part I of this book introduces SEA generally and the SEA Directive and Protocol in particular:

- Chapter 2 explains what strategic actions and SEA are, and the benefits and constraints of SEA.
- Chapter 3 discusses the SEA Directive's history, requirements and issues that it raises. Appendix A presents the Directive in full. It also summarizes the SEA Protocol, which is presented in full at Appendix B.
- Chapter 4 presents an example of SEA to explain how the whole process hangs together. It considers what bits of SEA are crucial and less crucial. It also presents a quality assurance checklist for SEA.

Part II discusses techniques, approaches and issues related to different stages of SEA:

- Chapter 5 discusses the context in which SEA is carried out: what strategic actions require SEA, how SEA links with decision-making and other assessment requirements, and who should be involved in SEA.
- Chapter 6 explains how to describe the baseline environment, identify links between the strategic action and other strategic actions, and identify relevant environmental problems.
- Chapter 7 considers different types of alternatives to a strategic action, how they can be identified, and which can be eliminated from further consideration.
- Chapter 8 is a long chapter on how to predict, evaluate and mitigate impacts, and how to decide on what prediction and evaluation techniques to use in SEA. Many of the techniques themselves are summarized in Appendix C.
- Chapter 9 explains how the SEA process can be documented, and approaches to monitoring the environmental impacts of strategic actions.

Part III contains a final chapter which revisits the concept of SEA quality and how to assure it. Chapter 10 discusses how long SEA takes and what resources it requires. It concludes with ideas for SEA capacity building.

Some chapters and appendices will be more applicable to some readers than others. Table 1.1 summarizes which might be of most use to different reader groups.

Table 1.1 *Parts of the book likely to be of particular relevance for specific readers*

For	Particularly relevant parts of the book
People who write SEA regulations and guidance	Chapter 3 Chapters 5 and 10 Appendices A and B
People who carry out SEAs and students of environmental management	Chapters 2–10
People who want to influence strategic actions, or are responsible for SEA quality assurance	Chapters 2, 3 and 10 Chapter 4 checklist
Environmental lawyers and law students	Chapters 2 and 3 Appendices A and B

Background to the book

This book is based on my experience of the early days of implementing the SEA Directive in Europe – and more specifically the United Kingdom (UK) – and particularly two projects I was involved in during 2002/2003.

The first was the development of guidance for the Office of the Deputy Prime Minister (ODPM) on how to apply the SEA Directive to English regional and local land use plans (ODPM, 2003). This involved writing a short report about key issues in translating the Directive into guidance, which was commented on by about two dozen SEA experts and government officials; writing draft guidance (ODPM, 2002) which was put out for full public consultation in autumn 2002; analysing the 140 consultation responses to the draft guidance; and revising the draft guidance to take account of those responses. During autumn 2002, I also coordinated a small team of consultants who tested aspects of the draft guidance on seven pilots, and two groups of MSc students from Oxford Brookes University who carried out full SEAs based on the draft guidance in spring 2003. Information from these pilots and case studies helped to refine the guidance, and provides much of the material in Part II of this book.

The second project was a two-stage research project that Roger Levett, Phill Minas and I carried out for the South West Regional Assembly. The first stage (Levett-Therivel, 2002) examined existing SEA practice in the UK: how it met the requirements of the Directive; what its links were with sustainability appraisal, health impact assessment and 'appropriate assessment' under the Habitats Directive; and possible barriers to implementation. This was based on a literature search, questionnaire survey and an experts workshop. The second stage (Levett-Therivel, 2003a) tested techniques and approaches to implementing the SEA Directive using five sectoral plans and programmes from South West England. This involved reading and analysing the relevant documents, and interviewing key people responsible for the development of the plans and programmes.

Some of the case studies in this book are based on my participation, as a consultant, in several dozen SEAs, and the many training courses I have conducted for planners on SEA.

The book also builds on studies by other organizations. A team of international SEA experts (ANSEA Team, 2002) have devised a new 'Analytical SEA' approach which focuses on identifying 'decision windows' when decision-makers are open to influence, and injecting sustainability ideas during those windows. Several UK government bodies are promoting the Quality of Life Assessment approach which focuses on, and manages for, the benefits that people receive from the environment (Countryside Agency et al, 2002). A leading UK centre for transport research (TRL, 2002) has studied baseline data and cumulative impacts in SEA.

Strategic Environmental Assessment in Action is my third book published by Earthscan, and is an evolution from the previous two. *Strategic Environmental Assessment* (Therivel et al, 1992) was an early analysis of the need for, and status and applicability of, SEA. In retrospect, some of the techniques discussed in that book are too heavily based on project environmental impact assessment (EIA), and not cognizant enough of the uncertainties and short timeframes inherent in strategic decision-making. *The Practice of Strategic Environmental Assessment* (Therivel and Partidario, 1996) compiled good practice SEA case studies from around the world. It identified a range of good techniques and approaches to SEA, including the need to fit with decision-making timeframes and involve the right people. This book aims to go beyond the previous two by discussing how to *do* SEA: not enough SEA examples existed in 1992 and 1996 to allow for the kind of practical information covered here.

This background means that the book has a particular slant. It focuses on the European SEA Directive (and, to a lesser extent on the UN Protocol on SEA), and does not give equal weight to the many other exciting SEA developments that are happening worldwide. It is based primarily on the UK system of SEA and on UK case studies (though with understanding of the SEA and planning systems of many other countries), so the focus is on a single European Member State, albeit one with a long history of SEA and the first one to put out guidance on the SEA Directive. The book includes many personal opinions which are not necessarily shared by other SEA practitioners or academics. The references listed at the back of this book help to redress these biases.

The practice of SEA is evolving incredibly quickly. I suspect that in a few years much of this book will need updating. Until then, I hope that it will contribute to the evolution of an exciting and useful discipline.

Chapter 2

Strategic Environmental Assessment: An Overview

This chapter provides a background for the rest of this book. It explains:

- the aims and principles of SEA;
- what strategic actions are and what they look like; and
- the benefits and problems of SEA.

It talks about SEA generically, not the specific form of SEA required by the European SEA Directive or the UNECE Protocol on SEA that will be discussed in Chapter 3. Readers who are familiar with SEA may wish to skip this chapter and go directly to Chapter 3.

Aims and principles of SEA

The ultimate *aim of SEA* is to help to protect the environment and promote sustainability. Of course there are many ways of doing this, but SEA contributes to this by helping to integrate environmental (or sustainability) issues in decision-making:

> *SEA is a systematic process for evaluating the environmental consequences of proposed policy, plan or programme initiatives in order to ensure they are fully included and appropriately addressed at the earliest appropriate stage of decision making on par with economic and social considerations* (Sadler and Verheem, 1996).

There are many other definitions of SEA (eg Therivel et al, 1992; Partidario and Clark, 2000), but they are all essentially variants on this theme.

Just how environmental concerns should be integrated in strategic decision-making is the subject of many guidance documents and regulations worldwide, and of Part II of this book. However, there is general agreement on some basic *principles of SEA* (Hales, 2000), which in turn start to suggest SEA stages and techniques.

First, SEA is a tool for *improving the strategic action*, not a post-hoc snapshot. The strategic action may well be changed as a result of the SEA, with different objectives, different means of achieving these objectives, and different forms of implementation. This suggests that the SEA should be started early, be integrated in the decision-making process, and focus on identifying possible alternatives and modifications to the strategic action. The decision-maker should be involved in the SEA process in an active capacity, to ensure that the SEA findings are fully taken into account in decision-making.

Second, SEA should *promote participation of other stakeholders* in the decision-making process. Essentially, SEA aims to expand the decision-maker's focus to include issues that go beyond their main area of concern – sustainability and environmental issues. This is illustrated in Figure 2.1. As such, SEA should involve a range of stakeholders, normally including the public. It should also document what has been done, why decisions have been made, and assumptions and uncertainties.

Third, to fit into the timescale and resources of the decision-making process, SEA should *focus on key environmental/sustainability constraints*, thresholds and limits at the appropriate plan-making level. It should not aim to be as detailed as project environmental impact assessment (EIA), nor be a giant collection of baseline data which does not focus on key issues. A scoping stage is always important to sort out what the key issues are.

Fourth, SEA should help to *identify the best option* for the strategic action. It should thus help to identify and assess different plan options, for instance the Best Practicable Environmental Option which meets demands but minimizes damage, and options for demand management – modifying forecast demand rather than accommodating it.

Fifth, SEA should aim to *minimize negative impacts, optimize positive ones, and compensate for the loss of valuable features and benefits*. SEA should apply the precautionary principle: if the value of development and its impacts are uncertain there should be a presumption in favour of protecting what exists. Impact mitigation in SEA often takes other forms than end-of-pipe technology: it could include changing aspects of the strategic action to avoid the negative impact, influencing other organizations to act in certain ways, or setting constraints on subsequent project implementation.

Finally, SEA should *ensure that strategic actions do not exceed limits beyond which irreversible damage from impacts may occur*. This requires identification of such limits. It requires prediction of the effects of the strategic action; comparing the likely future situation without the strategic action – the baseline – against the situation with the strategic

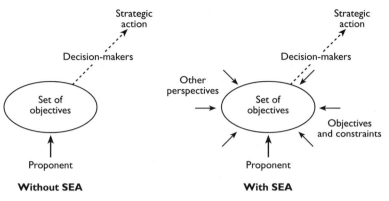

Note: The proponent is often also a decision-maker.
Source: adapted from Therivel and Brown (1999)

Figure 2.1 *SEA as decision-making process that takes on board a broader range of perspectives, objectives and constraints*

action. It also requires a judgement about whether the effect is significant and whether it will cause environmental limits to be exceeded.

Strategic actions

So far, the discussion has been about strategic actions generally. However, this term covers a huge range of activities. Strategic actions can involve land use or development plans for an area, financial allocations, management of a particular sector such as agriculture or energy, or clusters of related projects. Strategic actions include (Therivel and Brown, 1999):

- legislation: national, regional, local; international treaties;
- Green and White Papers;
- economic policies, budgets, fiscal planning, eg structural adjustments, privatization, subsidies, taxation, trade agreements;
- integrated/development plans: national, regional/territorial, local/town; multi-project programmes; conservation areas (World Heritage, national parks);
- sectoral policies, plans and programmes at a wide range of scales, eg for agriculture, transport, waste;
- policies, plans and programmes for management of a specific resource at a wide range of scales, eg coastal management, forest management, water management; and
- policies, plans and programmes to achieve social ends, eg employment development, equitable access to transport, international aid.

Strategic actions are normally developed by public agencies such as land use planning departments or energy planning agencies. However, they can also be developed by private or semi-private companies. For instance, telecommunications or water companies will have programmes for where to site their infrastructure.

All strategic actions are composed of one or more *objectives* plus more detailed *statements* about how the objective(s) will be implemented. The objective can also be called an aim, vision, strategic policy, etc; and the statements can also be called actions, measures, implementation plan, policies, etc. But roughly an objective will look like this:

> *This plan aims to secure within an available level of expenditure that motorists, those without cars, pedestrians and commercial vehicles are given the maximum freedom of movement and parking compatible with the achievement of convenient and prosperous conditions for all in Tooton Rush and an acceptable quality of environment.*

(This is not a good objective, as we will see in Chapter 4, but it is typical). The statements – and there may be hundreds of these in a single strategic action – will look roughly like this:

> *New housing developments will provide at least as many car parking spaces as there are bedrooms in the house.*

As airy-fairy as the objective looks, it is very important because it sets the tone for the rest of the strategic action. Consider, for instance, the two objectives of Box 2.1, both based on real-life examples (Sustainable Development Commission (SDC), 2001). Both objectives read like motherhood and apple pie, but what very different activities they would lead to on the ground! Objective A would lead to statements promoting large-scale agri-business, large food distribution and retailing centres, use of herbicides and fertilizers to ensure optimal productivity, trade liberalization, and responsiveness to consumer demands. Objective B would lead to statements promoting small-scale farms and abattoirs, promotion of local foods via farmers' markets and farm shops, reduced use of herbicides and fertilizers, and education of consumers to promote more sustainable consumption. These different activities and projects would in turn have very different environmental, social and economic impacts. The role of SEA is to identify these impacts early on, and suggest ways to minimize negative and maximize positive impacts.

Strategic decision-making

Strategic actions arise for various reasons. In some cases organizations are legally required to produce them. In other cases they evolve out of

---

Box 2.1 Two examples of objectives for a national policy on farming and food

Objective A

The UK farming and food sector should be profitable, able to compete internationally, and responsive to consumer demands. It should provide:

- choice of a range of fresh produce all year round;
- high-quality convenience foods at stores that provide a wide range of foods under one roof; and
- value for money and low prices, in keeping with the trends of the last ten years.

Objective B

The farming and food sector should provide sustainability, health and livelihoods for UK citizens. In doing so it should, at worst, not undermine the provisions of the same for other countries, and at best, contribute to achieving these goals for other countries. Elements of such a system include:

- natural genetic diversity in farmed plants and animals, to reduce vulnerability to diseases, preserve the heritage and enrich diets;
- careful husbandry of non-renewable natural resources and reduced reliance on fossil fuel;
- a food supply that is nutrient-dense and fibre-rich;
- access to the best quality food for the most vulnerable in society;
- jobs in the food and farming sector that provide a living wage; and
- direct links between primary food producers and purchasers.

Source: adapted from SDC (2001)

---

a perceived need, or a political manifesto, or simply because there is a tradition of devising such strategic actions. Sometimes a decision is made to stop producing them, for instance where there is no longer a need for them.

Strategic actions do not emerge fully fledged from a bureaucrat's or politician's brain. They evolve over time from vague glimmer to final strategy through brainstorming, discussions and 'negotiations' (aka arm-twisting, wrangling, horse-trading). For instance John Major may have woken up one morning with the idea of privatizing Britain's railways, but the details of how to do this will only have emerged over months of studies and discussions – and adjustments are still being made, years after privatization occurred. Much of this decision-making process is nebulous and hard to predict. The 'decision windows' (ANSEA Team, 2002) may be in the form of formal meetings informed by scientific reports, but they may just as easily come through discussions in the ladies room or café.

Figure 2.2 shows the broad stages of strategic decision-making. Once the strategic action's objective is decided on, alternative ways of achieving the objective are considered. These can be either–or alternatives such as different approaches to the international food trade (liberalize completely, liberalize with some environmental and animal welfare safeguards, 'fair trade' only, focus on regional self-sufficiency etc); or mix-and-match statements (promote farmers' markets, promote 'fair trade' foods, give subsidies to farmers to help them to compete internationally); or broad alternatives leading to a choice of preferred alternatives, in turn leading to more detailed statements of how the preferred alternative will be implemented. Once a preferred alternative and/or more detailed statements have been drafted, they are fine-tuned until a final strategic action is agreed, announced, implemented and monitored.

Of course, in reality this model seldom holds true. Decision-makers often start with some idea of a preferred alternative and then write the objective around it. Other alternatives may only be considered where someone makes a truly compelling case for them. The action may not be monitored. Any SEA system needs to be able to operate under these conditions as well as under the more idealized ones.

Policies, plans, programmes and tiering

The SEA literature often refers to strategic actions as 'policies, plans or programmes'. Wood and Djeddour's (1991) definition of these terms is still the best one around:

> *a policy may ... be considered as the inspiration and guidance for action, a plan as a set of co-ordinated and timed objectives for the implementation of the policy, and a programme as a set of projects in a particular area.*

Policies, plans and programmes are jointly called 'strategic actions' in this book for the sake of efficiency, and also to reduce confusion over whether something is a policy, a plan or a programme.

For instance, a policy on food and farming with Objective A (Box 2.1) might focus on improving the efficiency and competitiveness of the agricultural sector; related plans might focus on developing networks of efficient large-scale food storage, processing and distribution centres built to the highest international specifications, and effective ways of marketing UK products abroad over the next decade; and a related programme might be for the construction of large abattoirs in region X (note that the same players are not responsible for all of these policies, plans and programmes). A policy with Objective B might emphasize diversity, local provenance and nutrition; related plans could promote the establishment of producer–consumer

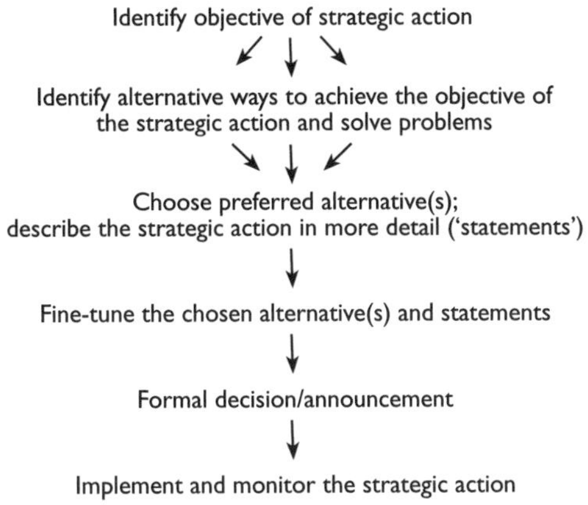

Identify objective of strategic action

Identify alternative ways to achieve the objective of
the strategic action and solve problems

Choose preferred alternative(s);
describe the strategic action in more detail ('statements')

Fine-tune the chosen alternative(s) and statements

Formal decision/announcement

Implement and monitor the strategic action

Figure 2.2 *Idealized model of strategic decision-making*

networks and labelling schemes; and related programmes in area Y could be for the establishment of weekly farmers' markets, conversion of farmland to organic status, and schools which procure all their food from within 20 kilometres of the school.

The definitions above suggests that there can be a *tiering* of strategic actions, from policy, to plan, to programme and finally to project. There can also be a tiering of assessments, from policy SEA down to programme SEA and project EIA: this is shown at Figure 2.3. In theory, aspects of decision-making and SEA carried out at one level do not need to subsequently be revisited at 'lower' levels, so that tiering of decision-making and SEA can save time and resources.

Of course the reality, again, is not so clear-cut. Strategic decision-making often skips stages: for instance there are no steps between the European Commission's Common Agricultural Policy which determines levels and rules for agricultural subsidies, and the activities of farmers at individual sites. Many strategic actions are not called what they are (for instance UK local 'plans' include sub-component 'policies'), or combine aspects of policy, plan and programme all in one strategic action. Sectors overlap, for instance transport and energy, or minerals and waste, so that strategic actions for one cannot be neatly disentangled from strategic actions for the other. However, the concept of 'tiering' is an important one, particularly in terms of what information is presented in what SEAs: this is discussed in Chapter 8.

Stages of SEA

The SEA principles discussed earlier, and particularly the need for SEA to feed into the whole of the decision-making process, suggest

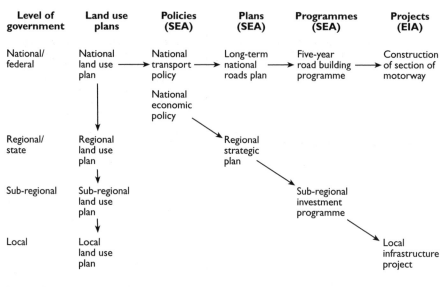

Level of government	Land use plans	Policies (SEA)	Plans (SEA)	Programmes (SEA)	Projects (EIA)
National/ federal	National land use plan	National transport policy	Long-term national roads plan	Five-year road building programme	Construction of section of motorway
		National economic policy			
Regional/ state	Regional land use plan		Regional strategic plan		
Sub-regional	Sub-regional land use plan			Sub-regional investment programme	
Local	Local land use plan				Local infrastructure project

Source: adapted from Lee and Wood (1987)

Figure 2.3 *Tiering of policies, plans and programmes*

particular stages and approaches to SEA. Figure 2.4 shows the basic steps of SEA and how they feed into various stages of decision-making. Note all of the arrows from right to left: the aim throughout is to ensure that environmental/sustainability considerations (Chapter 6 discusses which of these should be the focus of SEA) are taken on board at each stage of decision-making. Table 2.1 gives an indication of possible SEA outputs. The example SEA in Chapter 4 gives more detail on these SEA stages.

Advantages of SEA

Why is SEA needed? What is its 'value added' over project EIA or other systems of environmental management, footprinting or standards?

First, SEA gets in earlier. Strategic actions lead to and shape projects, so appraising the strategic actions offers the chance to influence the *kinds* of projects that are going to happen, not just the details after projects are already being considered.

Second, SEA deals with impacts that are difficult to consider at the project level. It deals with cumulative and synergistic impacts of multiple projects, for instance the traffic implications of the redevelopment of an entire area. This is very difficult to address at a project-by-project level. Box 2.2 gives an example of cumulative impacts addressed in SEA. Similarly, SEA can deal with larger-scale

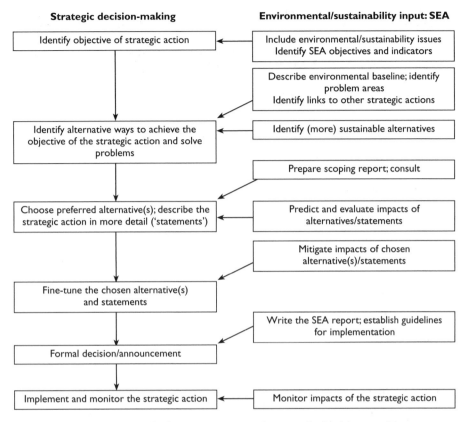

Figure 2.4 *Links between SEA and strategic decision-making*

environmental impacts such as those on biodiversity or global warming more effectively than can individual EIAs.

SEA promotes a better consideration of alternatives. By the time most projects are proposed, many alternatives have already been closed off because of higher-level decisions. For instance, renewable energy developments are unlikely to get built in a region whose energy strategy promotes gas-fired power stations. SEA affects the decision-making process at a stage where more alternatives are available for consideration, including reducing demand (reducing the need to travel, promoting accessibility rather than mobility). Box 2.3 gives an example of this.

SEA incorporates environmental and sustainability considerations in strategic decision-making. Using the example above, SEA would inform decision-makers about the environmental and sustainability implications of energy efficiency versus renewable energy versus fossil fuel power generation. These implications could then be considered alongside financial, technical, political and other concerns. SEA thus adds an additional dimension to the decision-making process.

Table 2.1 *SEA outputs*

SEA stage	What to decide	What to record
1. Identify SEA objectives, indicators and targets	What environmental and sustainability objectives, targets and/or indicators to test the plan options and statements against	List of SEA objectives, indicators and targets where relevant
2. Describe environmental baseline, including future trends; identify environmental issues and problems	What environmental and sustainability issues and constraints to consider during decision-making	Data on the baseline environment; list of relevant environmental and sustainability issues and constraints
3. Identify links to other relevant strategic actions	What other strategic actions influence the strategic action in question and how	List of relevant strategic actions, their requirements, and any constraints or conflicts with the strategic action in question
4. Identify (more) sustainable alternatives for dealing with the problems and implementing the strategic action objective	What alternatives or options to consider	List of alternatives or options
5. Prepare Scoping Report; consult	What to include in the Scoping Report	Results of stages 1–4; agreed written statement of how to proceed with subsequent SEA stages
6. Predict and evaluate impact of alternatives/ statements; compare alternatives; mitigate impacts of chosen alternative(s)/statements	What are the effects of the alternatives/options and statements on the environmental/ sustainability objectives and indicators; what are the preferred alternatives; what mitigation measures to include	Summary of effects of alternatives/options and statements on the environment and sustainability; list of preferred alternatives; explanation of why these are preferred; mitigation measures proposed
7. Write the SEA report; establish guidelines for implementation	How to present the data from stages 1–6	Prepare the SEA report
8. Consult	Whom to consult; how to respond to consultation results	How consultation results were addressed
9. Monitor the environmental/ sustainability impacts of the strategic action	How to deal with any negative impacts of the strategic action	How the strategic action's impacts will be monitored and significant effects dealt with

---

Box 2.2 Example of cumulative impacts identified as part of SEA

A local authority wants to protect its countryside and ensure that its town centres are vibrant. Many of its plan statements are phrased something like this: 'Development of type Y in rural areas will only be allowed where it fulfils [very stringent conditions]', with no similar conditions for urban areas. However, an SEA for the plan shows that, cumulatively, this could have the effect of too much inappropriate development in urban areas. The plan strategies are rewritten to include similar conditions appropriate for urban areas.

SEA facilitates – in theory, even if often not in practice – public participation in strategic decision-making. Traditionally, strategic actions have been developed with limited public input. At minimum, SEA provides one opportunity for the public to comment on a strategic action before it is formally agreed. At best, it allows the public to be actively involved throughout the strategic decision-making process.

All of these factors make the decision-making process more transparent and robust. SEA helps to ensure that the strategic action will be implemented effectively and that no unintended impacts will result from the strategic action. It also helps the strategic action to be approved more quickly by any inspectors or auditors. As a side effect, SEA helps decision-makers to better understand their plan, feel more confident about it, and learn about sustainability.

Finally, because of tiering, SEA has the potential to promote more streamlined decision-making, where decisions taken at one planning stage (using SEA at that stage) may not need to be revisited at subsequent stages of decision-making (and their SEA or EIA). It could obviate, for instance, the need for lengthy project-level inquiries that consider strategic-level issues, though in practice it is rarely possible to fully separate the strategic and project levels.

Box 2.3 Example of strategic alternatives identified as part of an SEA

A draft regional development plan aims to improve quality of life for the region's residents but still maintain the region's rural character by permitting the construction of homes in rural areas as long as housing density is less than one per hectare. The SEA identifies that this will have impacts on the landscape, traffic and on infrastructure, which will be more expensive to provide for such low-density developments. It suggests several alternatives: promotion of development in rural towns rather than scattered across the countryside, provision of specific levels of services in towns of a certain size, and/or requirements that low-density rural development should be self-sufficient in some forms of infrastructure.

In sum, SEA can help achieve clearer, more environment-friendly and more publicly acceptable strategic actions that are approved more quickly.

Problems with SEA

On the other hand, SEA has some limitations.

First, it takes time and resources. Just how much time and resources are needed depends on the type of strategic action and how efficiently the SEA is carried out. Arguably much or all of this could be recouped in easier, faster approval and implementation of the strategic action. Nevertheless, it is an up-front cost which is normally incurred just when planners are particularly busy and there are already other costs (eg feasibility or capacity studies). And if SEA is done badly, all of the costs can be incurred with no benefits at all in terms of an improved strategic action.

Second, SEA is still a relatively new process. Appropriate baseline data may not be available. Mechanisms for public consultation may not be set up. Planners may need to go through the learning curve associated with any new decision-making tool. In most countries, special SEA resourcing and capacity building will be needed.

SEA needs to cope with a huge range of decision-making situations, from the broadest international policy down to almost project-level local detail. Strategic actions cover large areas with many potential projects. They can last for many years with associated uncertainties about what will happen during that time: droughts? sharp changes in petrol prices? technical changes? (In the UK alone, 1999–2001 brought severe floods, foot and mouth disease, a huge increase in the use of mobile phones and email, protests over petrol prices, and large-scale trials of genetically modified organisms.) In many cases the decision-making process will not be neatly charted out, and some decisions may be made very quickly. SEA thus needs to be responsive, adaptable and quick. This often means that SEA cannot be as robust, detailed and 'scientific' as one might like.

Finally, after all the hard work and agony put into SEAs, they still end up being only one input into the decision. Often the decision will be made for reasons that the decision-takers find compelling but that are unconnected with, or opposed to environmental/sustainability principles. At that point, the SEA practitioner has to pick themselves up, dust themselves off, and move on to the next strategic action.

But there are also times when, in the midst of filling in an SEA matrix, the decision-maker comes up with a new, elegant approach to a problem. Or where a doubtful politician is convinced to take a more sustainable option because of the findings of an SEA. Or where the decision-maker starts approaching their strategic action in a different way because the SEA made them explicitly aware of an environmental problem that they had only been vaguely aware of before. Those moments, in my mind, make it all worthwhile.

Conclusions

If there is only one thing that the reader learns from this book I would wish it to be this: SEA is meant to improve – change – the strategic action. This concept carries with it all of the other stuff about timing, whom to involve, techniques to use etc.

This has been a very condensed overview of SEA. Further information can be found at, for instance, Partidario and Clark (2000), Sadler and Verheem (1996) and Therivel and Partidario (1996). Chapter 3 discusses two specific SEA systems. Chapter 4 gives an example of SEA in action.

Chapter 3

The European Union SEA Directive and UNECE SEA Protocol

By late 2003, about 20 countries worldwide had established legal requirements for SEA, and others had adopted SEA guidelines. This book does not aim to discuss these systems, excellent as many of them are. More information on specific countries is available elsewhere, for instance:

- internationally: Dalal-Clayton and Sadler (2003); International Association for Impact Assessment et al (2002);
- European countries: Kleinschmidt and Wagner (1998);
- countries in transition: Verheyen and Nagels (1996);
- francophone countries: Secretariat Francophone (2000); and
- early SEA systems: Sadler and Verheem (1996) and Therivel and Partidario (1996).

This chapter discusses two emerging SEA systems: the European Union's Directive 2001/42/EC – the 'SEA Directive' – and the UNECE's SEA Protocol. It does so for several reasons. Both the Directive and the Protocol apply to a wide range of strategic actions, with many different types of impacts. They apply to many countries, and represent the efforts of many countries to agree on a single SEA system. At the time of writing, the Directive had been agreed (July 2001) but not yet made operational (July 2004); and the SEA Protocol was recently adopted. So they are also interesting examples of some of the problems faced by bureaucrats when they attempt to make a regulation operational.

This chapter presents:

- a brief history of the SEA Directive;
- the Directive's requirements, first as an overview and then in more detail;
- good and bad points of the Directive; and
- an overview of the SEA Protocol.

Readers with no interest in the Directive or Protocol may wish to go directly to Chapter 4.

History of the SEA Directive

Discussions about a Europe-wide SEA Directive started at the same time as discussions about an EIA Directive, in about 1975. It was initially intended that one Directive would cover both projects and strategic actions, but by the time that the EIA Directive was approved in 1985 (Commission of the European Communities (CEC), 1985), its application was restricted to projects only (Wood, 1988).

In the absence of a Europe-wide SEA requirement, several European Member States established SEA systems starting in the late 1980s. For instance, the Netherlands required SEA for certain plans and programmes and an abbreviated 'e-test' for Cabinet decisions. Denmark required SEA of government proposals under an administrative order. In the UK, good practice guidance for local planning authorities essentially required an abbreviated form of SEA, 'environmental appraisal', to be carried out for all local and regional development plans (see Box 3.1).

This country-by-country approach meant that SEA systems could be responsive to the specific context of each country. However it did not encourage the 'level playing field' – establishment of reasonably similar economic conditions throughout Europe – that is a hallmark of European economic policy, nor did it provide the robust environmental protection advocated under successive European Commission Action Programmes on the Environment.

The European Commission's Directorate General XI (Environment) released an initial proposal for an SEA Directive in 1990. This was discussed and refined extensively between the Member States, primarily in terms of the types of strategic actions that the Directive should apply to. An official proposal for a Directive (CEC, 1997a) was made public in December 1996. Whereas earlier versions had applied to 'planning processes' or 'decision making processes', the proposal was restricted to 'certain land use plans and programmes', but confusingly included some sectoral plans and programmes under this heading. This version of the Directive is discussed in depth by, eg, von Seht and Wood (1998) and Feldmann (1998).

The proposal was considered by EC committees on the environment, economic and social affairs, and the regions in 1997, and by the European Parliament in October 1998. An amended proposal which took on board 15 of the Parliament's 29 proposed amendments was published in February 1999 (CEC, 1999). This proposal expanded the objective of the Directive from protecting the environment to also promoting sustainable development; distinguished clearly between

Box 3.1 UK environmental/sustainability appraisal system pre-Directive

In the UK, local development frameworks (formerly 'development plans') regulate development in a local authority area. In 1992 the government recommended that local authorities carry out 'environmental appraisal' of their development plans (Department of the Environment (DoE), 1992). In 1993 it published guidance on how they should do this (DoE, 1993), recommending a three-stage process:

1   identify environmental components (eg air quality, urban liveability) that could be affected by the development plan;
2   ensure that the plan is in accordance with government environmental and planning advice; and
3   determine whether the plan's objectives/policies are internally consistent, using a policy compatibility matrix (see Appendix C); and assess the policies' likely effects on the environmental components, using a policy impact matrix (see eg Table 4.2).

The guidance suggested that appraisal can be carried out at any stage of plan-making. It assumed that the process would be carried out in-house, and recommended consultation with outside groups. Although it implied that the plan could be changed in response to the appraisal findings, this was not a key message (DoE, 1993).

In 1999, the government produced guidance on how regional authorities should carry out 'sustainability appraisal' of their regional planning guidance (now Regional Spatial Strategies) which sets the framework for development plans (Department of Environment, Transport and the Regions (DETR), 1999a). The guidance suggested that sustainable regional planning guidance objectives should be developed first, then indicators which test whether strategic options achieve the objectives: in other words, it promoted a full integration of objectives for regional planning guidance and for sustainability.

The government also revised its guidance on development plans (DETR, 1999b). It recommended that environmental appraisal could also encompass economic and social issues. It suggested that the appraisal should begin with an 'awareness' by the local authority of the nature of the environment in the plan area, and that alternative policies, proposals and locations for development should be evaluated wherever possible. It noted that the appraisal should be subject to public consultation at key stages of plan preparation, and that involvement of outside bodies 'can help to validate the whole appraisal process'.

By 2001 the great majority of the UK's 400-odd local authorities had carried out at least one appraisal of their development plan. On average these took about 30 person-days. All eight of the English regions had carried out sustainability appraisal of their regional planning guidance (Therivel and Minas, 2002; Smith and Sheate, 2001a, 2001b).

In sum, SEA in the UK before the Directive was rapid, subjective and in-house. Over time, it had evolved from a mostly environmental focus to also take on board social and economic issues; from a stand-alone 'environmental test' to an approach that aimed to integrate sustainability and plan-making; and from a minimal approach into a slightly broader process that sometimes included public participation, description of the baseline environment, and consideration of sustainable alternatives to the plan.

town and country plans and other sectoral plans; and included robust requirements for the consideration of alternatives to the proposed plan.

This proposal was discussed by the Member States during 1999, and a common position by the Council was adopted in March 2000. Negotiations took place between the European Parliament and the Council during 2000 and 2001, and a final jointly adopted Directive was published on 21 July 2001 (Dalkmann, 2001; Feldmann et al, 2001).

The Directive must be implemented in all the European Member States – either instead of or in addition to any existing Member State SEA systems – by 21 July 2004. It does not have direct effect in the different European Member States; instead it will need to be interpreted into regulations in each Member State. In September 2003, the European Commission (2003) published guidance on how to interpret the Directive's requirements.

The Directive's requirements

Appendix A gives a full copy of the adopted Directive (CEC, 2001). The Directive's title – 'on the assessment of the effects of certain plans and programmes on the environment' – already gives a clue about many aspects of its requirements:

- It requires not an appraisal but an 'assessment'. For instance, compared with the existing UK system of sustainability appraisal (Box 3.1) it requires greater rigour, more quantitative analysis, and more collection of baseline data.
- It applies to 'certain' plans and programmes, and so does not apply to certain others. It has exclusions.
- It does not apply to policies.
- It considers effects on the 'environment', not sustainability (though its objective refers to sustainable development and its definition of environment is quite wide).

The Directive is quite a concise and well-structured document with five main clusters of requirements:

- the initial justification and Article 1, which explain the Directive's objectives;
- Articles 2–4 and Annex II which explain what strategic actions the Directive applies to, when SEA should be carried out, and some basic definitions;
- Articles 5–7 and Annex I which explain the key SEA inputs to the decision-making process: the environmental report, consultation

with the public and 'authorities', and consultation with other Member States where appropriate;

- Articles 8 and 9 which require the information arising from Articles 5–7 to be taken into account in decision-making and explain how this needs to be documented; and
- Articles 10–15 which deal with miscellaneous other requirements.

The first four of these are now considered one by one. Box 3.2 summarizes, for a given plan or programme, what the SEA Directive requires.

Objective of the Directive

The initial justification to the Directive (the bit with the 'having regard to' and 'whereas' paragraphs, also known as the 'substantive' part of the Directive) lists a range of objectives that the Directive tries to achieve, including preservation and improvement of the environment, protection of human health, the prudent use of natural resources, integration of environmental considerations into plan-making, provision of common procedural requirements for different Member States (and implicitly a more level economic playing field), and support of other environmental regulations and conventions.

Article 1 in the main part of the Directive notes that:

> *The objective of [the] Directive is to provide for a high level of protection of the environment and to contribute to the integration of environmental considerations into the preparation and adoption of plans and programmes with a view to promoting sustainable development, by ensuring that ... an environmental assessment is carried out of certain plans and programmes which are likely to have significant effects on the environment* (Art. 1).

The requirements of the rest of the articles aim to help achieve this objective.

However Article 1 already immediately raises an issue which affects the rest of the Directive, namely the link between the environment and sustainable development. Just how does protecting the environment promote sustainable development? Does the environment need special legislation to give it extra 'weight' in decision-making compared to social and economic concerns? This is not helped by the Directive's implicit definition of the environment as 'biodiversity, population, human health, fauna, flora, soil, water, air, climatic factors, material assets, cultural heritage ..., landscape and the interrelationship between the above factors' (Annex I(f)), which clearly includes some social factors such as human health and cultural heritage, and economic factors such as material assets. These issues, which have

Box 3.2 Summary of SEA Directive requirements for a given plan or programme

Preparation of an environmental report in which the likely significant effects on the environment of implementing the plan or programme (the term 'plan' is used hereafter to denote both), and reasonable alternatives are identified, described and evaluated. The information to be given is (Art. 5 and Annex 1):

a)   the contents and main objectives of the plan, and its relationship with other relevant plans and programmes;
b)   the relevant aspects of the current state of the environment and the likely evolution thereof without implementation of the plan;
c)   the environmental characteristics of areas likely to be significantly affected;
d)   any existing environmental problems which are relevant to the plan;
e)   environmental protection objectives which are relevant to the plan, and the way those objectives and any environmental considerations have been taken into account during its preparation;
f)   the likely significant effects of the plan on the environment;
g)   proposed ways of mitigating any significant adverse environmental effects;
h)   the reasons for selecting the alternatives dealt with, and a description of how the assessment was undertaken;
i)   proposed monitoring measures; and
j)   a non-technical summary of the above.

The report must include the information that may reasonably be required, taking into account current knowledge and methods of assessment, the contents and level of detail in the plan, its stage in the decision-making process and the extent to which certain matters are more appropriately assessed at different levels in that process in order to avoid duplication of the assessment (Art. 5.2).

The environmental reports should be of a sufficient standard to meet the requirements of the SEA Directive (Art. 12.2).

Consultation

•   of environmental authorities when deciding on the scope and level of detail of the information which must be included in the environmental report (Art. 5.4);
•   of environmental authorities and the public, who must be given an early and effective opportunity within appropriate timeframes to express their opinion on the draft plan and the accompanying environmental report before the plan's adoption (Art. 6.1, 6.2);
•   of other EU Member States where the plan's implementation is considered likely to have significant effects on the environment of those States (Art. 7).

The environmental report and the results of the consultations must be taken into account in decision-making (Art. 8)

Provision of information on the decision

When the plan is adopted, the public, the environmental authorities and any EU Member State consulted under Art. 7 must be informed and the following items made available to them:

- the plan as adopted;
- a statement summarizing how environmental considerations have been integrated into the plan and how the environmental report of Art. 5, the opinions expressed pursuant to Art. 6 and the results of consultations entered into pursuant to Art. 7 have been taken into account in accordance with Art. 8, and the reasons for choosing the plan as adopted, in the light of the other reasonable alternatives dealt with; and
- the measures decided concerning monitoring (Art. 9).

Monitoring of the significant environmental effects of the plan's implementation (Art. 10)

---

bedevilled early UK attempts to write guidance on how to implement the Directive, are discussed further in Chapter 5.

Plans and programmes that require SEA

Understanding what plans and programmes require SEA under the SEA Directive requires a careful reading of the 'and's and 'or's below. Strategic actions that require SEA are plans and programmes that:

1 are subject to preparation and/or adoption by an authority (Art. 2(a)); *and*
2 are required by legislative, regulatory or administrative provisions (Art. 2(a)); *and*
3 are likely to have significant environmental effects (Art. 3.1) as determined by using the criteria set out in Annex II of the Directive; *and*
4a are prepared for agriculture, forestry, fisheries, energy, industry, transport, waste management, water management, telecommunications, tourism, town and country planning or land use *and* set the framework for development consent of projects listed in the EIA Directive (which are similar, though not identical to, those in Annexes I and II of the SEA Protocol; see Appendix B)(Art. 3.2(a)); *or*
4b in view of the likely effect on sites, require an appropriate assessment under the Habitats Directive (Art 3.2(b)); *or*

4c are other plans and programmes determined by Member States to set the framework for future development consent of projects (Art. 3.4); *and*

5 are begun after 21 July 2004 or are adopted after 21 July 2006 (Art. 13.3).

This is summarized in Figure 3.1.

Member States can also require SEA for other plans and programmes that set the framework for development consent of projects *and* are likely to have significant environmental effects (Art. 3.4).

Strategic actions that do not require SEA under the Directive are plans and programmes:

6 that determine the use of small areas at local level or are minor modifications to plans and programmes that would otherwise require SEA *and* that are unlikely to have significant environmental effects (Art. 3.3); *or*

7 that are financial or budget plans or programmes (Art. 3.8); *or*

8 whose sole purpose is to serve national defence or civil emergency (Art. 3.8); *or*

9 that are begun before 21 July 2004 *and* are adopted before 21 July 2006.

Some examples of these rules in action might be helpful. Land use management plans prepared by voluntary bodies (for instance for land held by an environmental charity) would not require SEA because such an organization is not an 'authority' (1 above). Many plans and programmes prepared by private companies will not require SEA because the companies are not 'authorities', although plans and programmes prepared by some privatized companies that perform public services as part of their statutory duties (eg water or electricity provision) may require SEA. A local authority's voluntary tourism strategy would not require SEA because the strategy is not 'required' (2 above), whereas its mandatory land use plan would require SEA. Many national-level plans and programmes are also likely to be exempt from SEA because they are not 'required'. Plans that are very strategic – for instance a regional strategy on how to deal with genetically modified organisms – do not require SEA because they do not set the framework for development consent of projects (4a above). Neither do plans for war (8). However, plans for the management of military training grounds may need SEA where such land is used for recreational as well as military purposes.

There are still obvious areas of uncertainty, and individual Member States will need to decide exactly what the Directive means for their strategic actions. The issue of what is meant by an 'administrative

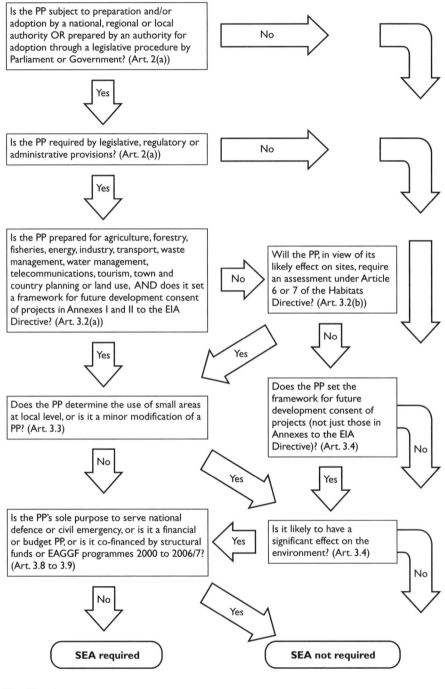

Note: PP = plan or programme
Source: ODPM (2003)

Figure 3.1 *Screening under the SEA Directive*

provision' is proving to be particularly contentious in the UK. Land use plans, which are the types of plans that SEA has most often been applied to in Europe to date, will continue to require SEA as before. But the Directive will clearly also apply to many other plans and programmes for which no SEA has been required before.

Key SEA inputs to the decision-making process

The Directive requires three major SEA inputs to be taken into account in decision-making: the environmental report, the consultation responses of the public and 'authorities', and the consultation responses of other Member States where appropriate.

An *environmental report* must be prepared which identifies, describes and evaluates 'the likely significant effects on the environment of implementing the plan or programme, and reasonable alternatives taking into account the objectives and the geographical scope of the plan or programme' (Art. 5.1). The information that the environmental report must cover is (Annex I):

a) *an outline of the contents, main objectives of the plan or programme and relationship with other relevant plans and programmes;*

b) *the relevant aspects of the current state of the environment and the likely evolution thereof without implementation of the plan or programme;*

c) *the environmental characteristics of areas likely to be significantly affected;*

d) *any existing environmental problems which are relevant to the plan or programme including, in particular, those relating to any areas of a particular environmental importance, such as areas designated pursuant to Directives 79/409/EEC and 92/43/EEC;*

e) *the environmental protection objectives, established at international, Community or Member State level, which are relevant to the plan or programme and the way those objectives and any environmental considerations have been taken into account during its preparation;*

f) *the likely significant effects* on the environment, including on issues such as biodiversity, population, human health, fauna, flora, soil, water, air, climatic factors, material assets, cultural heritage including architectural and archaeological heritage, landscape and the interrelationship between the above factors;*

g) *the measures envisaged to prevent, reduce and as fully as possible offset any significant adverse effects on the environment of implementing the plan or programme;*

h) *an outline of the reasons for selecting the alternatives dealt with, and a description of how the assessment was undertaken including any difficulties (such as technical deficiencies or a lack of know-how) encountered in compiling the required information;*

> i) a description of the measures envisaged concerning monitoring in accordance with Article 10;
>
> j) a non-technical summary of the information provided under the above headings.

* These effects should include secondary, cumulative, synergistic, short-, medium- and long-term, permanent and temporary, positive and negative effects.

Member States are required to ensure that environmental reports are of a sufficient quality of meet the Directive's requirements (Art. 12.2), although there is no indication of how they should do this.

Several aspects of this are noteworthy. First, a)–e) provide a clear context for the development of the plan or programme by requiring an analysis of related plans and programmes including environmental ones, a description of the baseline environment with a greater focus on areas likely to suffer significant impacts, and an identification of environmental problems. Arguably b)–e) can be done relatively independently of the plan or programme, and the results can be used for several plans in one area. Second, there is a clear emphasis on alternatives: they are mentioned several times, and the Directive does not distinguish between the level of analysis needed for the plan or programme and its alternatives (EC, 2003). This is a clear improvement on the EIA Directive, which requires only 'an outline of the main alternatives studied by the developer' (CEC, 1997b), and no identification and evaluation of the alternatives' environmental impacts. Third, the SEA Directive includes a requirement for monitoring of effects, which is also absent in the EIA Directive.

Clearly, the Directive's requirements have the potential to be extremely onerous and to lead to encyclopaedic environmental reports. Article 5.2 sets bounds on the level of detail needed:

> *The environmental report ... shall include the information that may reasonably be required taking into account current knowledge and methods of assessment, the contents and level of detail in the plan or programme, its stage in the decision-making process and the extent to which certain matters are more appropriately assessed at different levels in that process in order to avoid duplication of the assessment.*

This and Article 4.3 suggest that, where data have been provided and analyses carried out in other SEAs, they do not need to be repeated in the SEA in question: SEAs can be tiered.

The 'authorities' need to be consulted when the environmental report's scope and level of detail is decided (Art. 5.4). Member States can determine which authorities must be consulted. They are those authorities which, 'by reason of their specific environmental responsibilities, are likely to be concerned by the environmental effects of implementing plans and programmes' (Art. 6.3). In the end, what exactly will need to be included in an environmental report in practice will be decided by trial and error, precedent and the lawyers. But first some environmental reports need to be written!

Once the environmental report has been prepared, it and the draft plan or programme must be made available for *consultation*. The documents 'shall be made available to the authorities [of Art. 6.3] and the public' who must 'be given an early and effective opportunity within appropriate time frames to express their opinion on the draft plan or programme and the accompanying environmental report before the adoption of the plan or programme' (Art. 6.2). Again, Member States can determine which members of the public should be consulted. Other Member States that are likely to be significantly affected by the plan or programme must also be consulted. Table 3.1 summarizes the consultation requirements of the Directive.

In practice, it is still unclear which authorities and which members of the public must be consulted. Clearly the Directive's consultation requirements involve a balance between the comprehensiveness and transparency of wide coverage and the resource implications that such requirements have on the authorities involved. It is also unclear what an 'early and effective opportunity within appropriate time frames' means. For instance, would this be met where a draft plan and its SEA are made public, but consultation comments go to an inspector who decides on changes needed to the draft plan rather than to the plan-making authority?

Taking the SEA information into account in decision-making

The environmental report and the consultation comments from the authorities, public and other Member States where appropriate 'shall be taken into account during the preparation of the plan or programme and before its adoption' (Art. 8). To ensure that this is done properly, the following items must be made available to the authorities, public and other Member States afterwards:

(a) *the plan or programme as adopted;*
(b) *a statement summarising how environmental considerations have been integrated into the plan or programme and how the environmental report [and consultation opinions] have been taken into account ... and the reasons for choosing the plan or programme as adopted, in the light of other reasonable alternatives dealt with, and*
(c) *the measures decided concerning monitoring* (Art. 9.1).

This is a significant step forward from the EIA Directive, which requires only an explanation of 'the main reasons and considerations on which the decision is based'. It should help to improve the transparency of

Table 3.1 *Summary of the SEA Directive's consultation requirements*

Stage of SEA	Mandatory requirements	Additional requirements where the plan/programme is likely to have significant transboundary effects
Determination if a plan or programme requires SEA	Consultation of authorities (Art. 3.6) Information made available to the public (Art. 3.7)	
Decision on the scope and level of detail of the SEA	Consultation of authorities (Art. 5.4)	
Environmental report and draft plan or programme	Information made available to authorities and the public (Art. 6.1) Consultation of authorities and the public (Art. 6.2)	Consultation of authorities and public in the Member State likely to be affected (Art. 7.2)
Adopted plan or programme; statement on how the SEA information has been taken into account in decision-making (Art. 9.1b); monitoring measures	Information made available to authorities and public (Art. 9.1)	Information made available to the consulted Member State (Art. 9.1)

Source: adapted from EC (2003)

decision-making and ensure that the SEA findings are properly taken into account, not just in a symbolic or superficial manner.

Significant environmental effects of the implementation of the plan or programme must be monitored 'in order, inter alia, to identify at an early stage unforeseen adverse effects, and to be able to undertake appropriate remedial action' (Art. 10).

Good and bad points of the Directive

The SEA Directive is, in my view, much better than it could have been, particularly given its inauspicious beginnings and the lengthy wrangling it went through. It is a great improvement on earlier versions and on the EIA Directive (CEC, 1985). It covers a wide range of sectors. It also rightly emphasizes the entire SEA process, not just the preparation of a report. Its emphasis on alternatives should help to ensure that decision-makers do not limit the SEA to an exercise of fine-tuning a plan once key decisions have already been made. It requires monitoring of the plan's actual effects, which will help to improve subsequent SEAs. Article 9 provides a real incentive to decision-makers to take the SEA findings into account.

The Directive sets a minimum baseline which all European Member States will need to reach. As such, it sets up an SEA system for those countries that did not have one before, including accession countries. For those Members States who already had SEA systems, it applies to a wider range of plans and programmes than before. It will lead to many more SEAs being carried out, with consequent improvements in SEA experience and development of SEA techniques. It will probably inspire the establishment of SEA systems elsewhere.

The Directive's biggest limitations are in the types of strategic actions that it does not cover. It does not apply to policies, which set the framework for plans and programmes: as such, SEAs are required for strategic actions whose predecessors do not require SEA, with all the possible inconsistencies and conflicts this raises. Initial indications are that many national-level plans and programmes will also not be subject to SEA because they are not 'required'. The Directive's 'and/or' rules for deciding which strategic actions require SEA are very complex. Many lawyers and environmental assessment practitioners will be employed for many years in sorting out what is an administrative provision, what is a minor modification, what is a significant effect on the environment, etc.

The Directive's definition of the environment is also problematic. For instance, in practice, what is the distinction between flora, fauna and biodiversity? What exactly are material assets? Why are some social and economic factors included in this 'environmental' Directive but not others? Many of these aspects relate to the Directive's origins as an extension to project environmental impact assessment.

Many aspects of the Directive still remain to be interpreted, and much of this will have to wait until individual cases emerge which require judgement through the courts or through precedent. Issues include which authorities must be consulted, what level of detail is needed in the SEA, and what alternatives are 'reasonable'.

The UNECE Protocol on Strategic Environmental Assessment

The United Nations Economic Commission for Europe's SEA Protocol (UNECE, 2003) – shown in full at Appendix B – is a rather longer and more daunting document than the Directive, made to cope with a more daunting implementation process. The Protocol supplements the 1991

Convention on Environmental Impact Assessment in a Transboundary Context (the Espoo Convention) and acknowledges the 1998 Convention on Access to Information, Public Participation in Decision-making and Access to Justice in Environmental Matters (the Aarhus Convention). It was developed by a UN ad hoc working group, finalized in January 2003, and formally adopted and signed by 35 countries in Kiev on 23 May 2003. States may ratify the Protocol as of 1 January 2004. It will come into force 90 days after the 16th State has ratified, though it may be several years before this occurs. Although negotiated under the UNECE (which covers all of Europe, the USA and Canada, the Caucasus and Central Asia), the Protocol is open to all UN members.

The Protocol's requirements are broadly similar to, and compatible with, those of the Directive. Broadly the same types of plans and programmes require SEA under the Protocol (Art. 2.5 and 4, Annexes I–III) as under the Directive. The Protocol requires an environmental report to be prepared (Art. 7, Annex IV) comprising very similar information to that required in the Directive, although it requires transboundary effects to be more explicitly addressed. Similar rules (Art. 7.2) determine the level of detail needed in the report. The type of consultation with authorities and the public required (Art. 6, 8 and 9) is broadly similar, but the authorities explicitly include health authorities, and the public's involvement is specifically mentioned (though not required) in the scoping stage. 'Due account' should be taken of the results of the SEA report and consultation results (Art. 11.1), and the reasons for the decision should be made public (Art. 11.2) as in the Directive. Monitoring of significant effects (Art. 12) is also required.

The main differences between the two documents are that:

- the Protocol is less explicit in its definition of the 'environment' but more explicit (and droningly repetitious) about the fact that it perceives the environment as 'including health'. This reflects the involvement of the World Health Organization in its development;
- the Protocol is more explicitly a document for public participation than the Directive is, with more reference to the public in its preamble and general provisions, reference to the possible role of the public in scoping (Art. 6), and a requirement for public consultation arrangements to be formally determined and made public (Art. 8.5), including a complete annex (Annex V) on how to do so. This reflects its links to the Aarhus convention;
- although the Protocol only requires SEA of plans and programmes, it also addresses policies and legislation; and
- the Protocol includes many more requirements about ratification, integration, implementation, modification, etc, reflecting the large

number of countries with very different judicial systems that it applies to (Art. 14 is particularly overwhelming).

Conclusions

Over the coming years we can expect dozens, if not hundreds of SEA regulations, administrative provisions, and associated guidance documents to be developed worldwide, both in response to the Directive and Protocol and independently. Hopefully they will be interpreted with flair and innovation, keeping in mind the SEA principles discussed in Chapter 2, rather than in a *de minimis* manner which aims to stay just on the right side of the law. The former approach does not have to be more resource-intensive than the latter, especially taking into account the time and legal resources required to justify a grudging, minimal approach.

In Part II, Chapters 5–9 provide a range of approaches for carrying out SEA in general, and the requirements of the SEA Directive and Protocol in particular. They cover, in turn, the context for SEA; the baseline environment and links to other strategic actions; alternatives; prediction, evaluation and mitigation of impacts; and SEA documentation and decision-making. Chapter 4 gives an example of the SEA process using a hypothetical case study.

Chapter 4

The SEA Process as a Whole

This chapter aims to give an understanding of the SEA process as a whole – how it affects the strategic action, what the SEA outcomes are, and what to look out for. It considers the application of SEA to a hypothetical district transport plan, then considers which aspects of SEA are an essential minimum and which are best practice or applicable only in some cases. It concludes with a quality assurance checklist for SEA. Chapters 5–9 in Part II explain the reasoning behind some of the approaches used, variants on these approaches, and pitfalls to avoid.

Example of SEA: Tooton Rush District Transport Plan

Tooton Rush is an imaginary but typical English district council with one main town, Standstill, and two smaller towns, Rushmore and Walkerton. A very brief district transport plan (DTP) has been in place for many years. Box 4.1 shows this DTP. It consists of a broad objective and three more detailed statements of how the objective will be implemented (in real life there would probably be dozens of detailed statements).

The new, bright chief transport planning officer, Wanda Duright, wants to get her team to rewrite the DTP, integrating SEA into the plan-making process. She has already noted that the old DTP objective gives little weight to the environment, is unwieldy, and is not in keeping with current government advice on reducing the need to travel. She has also noted that two of the detailed statements are potentially contradictory (improve roads but give priority to pedestrians), and one is vague (which of the district's roads are in the proposed primary network?). The SEA will hopefully help to clear up these problems and ensure that the new DTP is as sustainable as possible, but where should she start?

The following sections give a brief explanation of how SEA could be carried out for Tooton Rush's DTP (although other approaches

---

Box 4.1 The bad old District Transport Plan for Tooton Rush District

Objective: This DTP aims to secure, within an available level of expenditure, that motorists, those without cars, pedestrians and commercial vehicles are given the maximum freedom of movement and parking compatible with the achievement of convenient and prosperous conditions for all in Tooton Rush and an acceptable quality of environment.

T1. Improvements will be made to a primary network of high quality roads which will serve as the major routes for through and lorry traffic.

T2. New housing developments will provide at least as many car parking spaces as there are bedrooms in the house. New industrial, shopping and employment development will provide enough parking for current and likely future demand.

T3. In Standstill priority will be given to pedestrians and public transport. Appropriate comprehensive local policies for service areas will be sought.

---

would be possible too). It is structured according to the main SEA stages that are covered in more detail in the next five chapters:

1 set the context: determine who should be involved in the SEA and how it fits with other assessment requirements;
2 describe the baseline environment, identify environmental problems, identify constraints and objectives set out by other strategic actions, revise the old objective;
3 identify sustainable options for achieving the (new) plan objective;
4 identify, assess and evaluate the likely environmental impacts of the options, choose the preferred option(s), mitigate significant negative impacts; and
5 document the process and monitor the impacts.

Set the context

Wanda has a small and relatively inexperienced team of planners. She decides to involve all of them in the SEA, to help ensure that they all understand the links between transport and sustainable development. There is already an established form of public consultation on DTPs, which she plans to expand to include consultation on the SEA. The DTP is not subject to other forms of assessment.
Tip: SEA can be an educational process, not just an administrative procedure.

Describe the baseline environment, identify environmental problems, identify constraints and objectives set by other strategic actions

The point of describing the baseline environment is to get a feel for what the area's environmental problems are, and to provide a basis for future impact predictions and monitoring. A straightforward way of doing this is through a matrix which shows, for various aspects of the environment, current baseline levels, comparators, targets and trends. An analysis of the baseline and likely future trends against the comparators and targets, and discussions about this with planners who have experience of the area or with local residents, will give an indication of what the area's environmental problems are.

A first question, though, is what aspects of the environment should be analysed. In Tooton Rush's case, a straightforward approach would be to use the UK SEA guidance shown in Table 6.1, adapted to the transport planning context. This provides the first column of Tooton Rush's baseline environment in Table 4.1. Wanda gets one of her planners to spend a week collecting data from various websites and documents, and organizing it in the matrix cells.

About half of the data needed for the table – which is based on a real case study – is not available. In particular, many trends cannot be determined because there is no time-series data. There is no time in this planning cycle to collect more baseline information, but Wanda's team decide to carry out a survey of local residents and an analysis of Tooton Rush's planning files before the next plan-making cycle to collect the outstanding data.

Tip: Not all the baseline data must be available for an SEA to proceed. The first SEA can be seen as a way of identifying what needs to be monitored in the future.

Wanda's team review existing higher-level (national and regional) strategic actions relating to their plan. They note that the government is now focusing on promoting transport choice and reducing the need to travel. They also refer to a recent local residents' visioning process which shows that residents' priorities in terms of travel are speed, comfort and safety.

The team then identify environmental problems. They look, in Table 4.1, at where Tooton Rush is worse than its targets or other comparators and likely to get worse: a high percentage of journeys in Tooton Rush are made by car, long distances are travelled by car, and services in rural areas are not particularly accessible. Wanda presents the team's findings at a meeting of the local elected representatives who identify two further problems: future problems likely to result from developments on the edge of Standstill that have been given planning permission but have not yet been built, and that many people without cars have problems getting to essential services such as shopping and the doctor.

Tip: The views of planners and others who are familiar with the area are invaluable in SEA. Use 'expert judgement' liberally.

By now, Tooton Rush's planners have three sets of information which should help them to rewrite their DTP objective: the government's emphasis on transport choice and reducing the need to travel; the results of the local resident visioning process that emphasizes speed, comfort and safety; and the environmental baseline that suggests that residents' health and accessibility are being negatively affected by the over-emphasis on car use, and that this in turn is affected by land use planning decisions which makes it difficult for many people to get around without a car. They re-assess the DTP objective (parentheses denote their thought processes).

This DTP aims to secure within an available level of expenditure (This objective puts economics symbolically first: we must change that to emphasize our sustainable development agenda)...

that motorists, those without cars, pedestrians and commercial vehicles (Hm. The focus on different user groups is good, but what strange overlaps! Commercial vehicle drivers are motorists, and pedestrians are people without cars. And what about cyclists or public transport users, whom we should be trying to encourage?)...

are given the maximum freedom of movement and parking (Emphasize accessibility, reducing the need to travel, and speed, comfort and safety instead: focus on the ends rather than the means)...

compatible with the achievement of convenient and prosperous conditions for all in Tooton Rush and an acceptable quality of environment (Just a last grudging mention of the environment. This has to be made stronger and be linked to sustainable development).

They develop a new objective which deals with these problems:

This DTP aims to optimise accessibility to jobs and services for all in an efficient, comfortable and safe manner whilst maintaining or enhancing environmental conditions in the district.

Whereas the original objective inherently implied the construction of roads and parking lots, the new one describes the outcomes desired unencumbered by assumptions about how best to achieve them. This has three benefits: it facilitates public consultation about what policy should try to achieve; enables implementation options to be compared

Table 4.1 *Baseline data for Tooton Rush*

Topics/indicators	Quantified data	Comparators and targets	Trend
Water			
River and canal quality (very good and good)	Biology 57% (2000) Chemistry 65% (2001)	Tooton Rush: Bio 29%, Chem. 20% (1990) England: Bio 66%, Chem 66% (2000)	Improving sharply (comparison 1990–2000)
Air and climatic factors			
Distance travelled per person per year by mode of transport (miles)	walking 165, cycling 51, car 6156, public transport 648	England: walking 189, cycling 39, car 5713, public transport 874 Target: double cycling levels by 2012	More car use than national average. Car use going up, walking and cycling down
Number of days of air pollution	Standstill: 18	England & Wales: average 26	
CO_2 emissions	5.8 million tonnes (1997)	UK target: reduce by 20% of 1990 levels by 2010	
Biodiversity, flora, fauna			
Achievement of conservation objectives	No district level data available		
% tranquil areas	No district level data available	England: 74% (early 1960s); 56% (early 1990s)	Getting worse (national trends)
Human health			
Transport accidents/billion passenger kilometres	No district level data available	UK: bus 0.3; car 2.8; rail 0.4; pedestrian 47 (2000)	
% population without minimum level of healthy exercise	No district level data available		
Public concern over noise	21% 'very worried' about noise (2000)	30% of UK respondents affected by traffic noise (1999)	Getting worse (planners' perceptions)

Topics/indicators	Quantified data	Comparators and targets	Trend
Social inclusiveness			
% development within x minutes walk of frequent public transport service	No district level data available		
Ease of access to various services with and without a car	No district level data available		
Access to services for disabled people	No district level data available	GB: difficulty in: shopping 29%; using bank 6%; going to pub/restaurant 15%	Getting better (planners' perceptions)
Cultural heritage, landscape			
% land designed for particular quality or amenity value	Area of Outstanding Natural Beauty 3.3%; Green Belt 5%	England: Area of Outstanding Natural Beauty 16%; Green Belt 13%	No change
% of population living < 200 metres from parks and open spaces	No district level data available		
Economics and access			
Existing and committed key land uses in town centres/ edge of centre/out of town/rural areas	No district level data available		
Access to key services	% rural households < 4 kilometres from service: supermarket 81%; primary school 93%; secondary school 74%; bank 70%; doctor 87%	England: supermarket 79%; primary school 92%; secondary school 76%; bank 76%; doctor 87%	

Note: This table is not comprehensive, it is for example purposes only.
GB = England, Wales and Scotland   UK = GB plus Northern Ireland.

Box 4.2 Brainstormed options for achieving Tooton Rush DTP's new objective

Reduce the need to travel

a   Provide schools, shops, etc close to where people live; and build new houses close to existing schools, shops, etc.
b   Congestion charging in Standstill.
c   Provide school buses to obviate the need for parents to drive their children to school.
d   Double the cost of petrol.
e   Reduce the number of parking spaces in towns.
f   Require businesses to prepare travel plans which aim to reduce commuting.
g   Encourage farm shops and locally produced foods.

Alternative modes of travel

h   Pedestrianization of Standstill, Rushmore and Walkerton town centres.
i   Park and Ride system for Standstill.
j   Improved bus fleet with wheelchair access.
k   Separate cycle-only lanes running parallel to each road.
l   Increase safety on footpaths perceived to be unsafe.
m   Tunnel under Standstill, Rushmore and Walkerton to carry through-traffic.

Note: The options given are for example purposes only. The list is not comprehensive.

---

empirically and objectively, increasing the chances that what the council finishes up doing will help to achieve what it wants; and provides more room to manoeuvre to allow these transport-related objectives to be reconciled with other objectives.

Identify sustainable options for meeting the (new) plan objective

Traditionally at this stage Tooton Rush's transport planners would have identified locations where accidents were particularly bad or where other improvements were necessary; and then they would have written plan statements that tried to improve transport conditions in those areas. Instead, Wanda encourages them to brainstorm possible alternative ways of meeting the plan objective: to be proactive rather than reactive. Following good SEA practice, they try to focus particularly on the more strategic issues – reducing the need to travel and broad approaches for dealing with the remaining travel demand. Box 4.2 shows the results.

 The team then determine which of these are clearly not feasible (m) and not within its control (a, c, d, g, j, l). Some of these are within the remit of other local authority departments: for instance school buses are the remit of the education department and the encouragement of farm shops that of the economic development department: the transport planners decide to discuss these issues with the responsible departments. Others options, like petrol charging, are clearly outside the local authority's control and they decide not to take them further (though this should inform the council's response to national policy consultation). The team takes the rest of the options forward for further analysis.

Tip: Where good alternatives are not within the competent authority's remit, it may be worthwhile negotiating with the authority whose remit they are to try to get them implemented.

The team also revisit the original plan statements, and decide to remove T1 and T2 from further consideration because they are clearly not in keeping with the new plan objective. They decide to consider the first sentence of T3 – 'In Standstill priority will be given to pedestrians and public transport' – as a variant to alternative h on full pedestrianization. They decide that the second half of T3 – 'Appropriate comprehensive local policies for service areas will be sought' – should not be a plan statement, as it essentially says 'we know that we should look at this in more detail but can't do it as part of this plan'.

Predict, evaluate and mitigate impacts

The transport planning team then appraises the remaining options using the topics from Table 4.1. They ask themselves:

- What will this option look like on the ground?
- What impact will this option have on each SEA topic?
- If the impact is negative, can this be avoided, reduced or compensated for?
- If the impact is positive, can it be enhanced?
- If the impact depends on how the option is implemented, how can we ensure that it is implemented well?

The resulting analysis is shown in Table 4.2. They also check whether the different options are compatible with each other: this is shown in Table 4.3.

Tip: Several rounds of appraisal may be necessary, either to test broad approaches and then more specific ones (eg reduce parking or not, then details about location of parking sites) or to get more specific information where an initial appraisal is uncertain (eg computer modelling of likely traffic flows with and without pedestrianization before deciding whether the impact of pedestrianization would be positive or negative).

Table 4.2 *Impact appraisal of some of the options for Tooton Rush's District Transport Plan*

Option	Impact of option on…								Comments/possible mitigation
	water	air & climate*	biodiversity, flora, fauna	human health*	social inclusiveness	cultural heritage, landscape	economic development	efficiency and access*	
b. Congestion charging in Standstill		++		+	+/–		–	+/–	Impact depends on whether you are rich or poor and have a car or not. Will have a direct cost to businesses in Standstill that depend on motorized vehicles
e. Reduce the number of parking spaces in towns		+		+	–		–		Could negatively affect people with mobility problems. Could also affect businesses, particularly retail businesses depending on short-term parking
f. Require businesses to develop travel plans		+		+	–		–	–	Many impacts depend on implementation, eg how travel plans are used, and whether they apply to all businesses (or only large companies, or new businesses)
h. Pedestrianization of town centres		++		+		–	–/+	+	Previous experience with pedestrianization suggests that retailers' earnings go down for the first 6–18 months, then rise to levels above those pre-pedestrianization. Possible impact on people with disabilities and delivery vehicles. Through-traffic would need different route around town centre

Option	Impact of option on...								Comments/possible mitigation
	water	air & climate*	biodiversity, flora, fauna	human health*	social inclusiveness	cultural heritage, landscape	economic development	efficiency and access*	
h1/T3. Pedestrian priority in town centres		+		+				+	Could slow down traffic. Extend priority to cyclists and emergency vehicles?
i. Park and Ride system for Standstill	–	+/–	–	+	–	–		+	P+Rs improve air quality, etc in urban areas but have negative impacts on edge of towns – on land take and wildlife during construction, and on air quality and quality of life for local residents during operation. They could also increase commuting
k. Cycle lanes parallel to roads		+	–	++	+			+	Improves conditions for cyclists and could encourage drivers to cycle. Impact on biodiversity depends on whether lane goes on previously developed land or not

Key: + positive impact; – negative impact; I depends on implementation; * identified as particularly important criterion in previous SEA stage

Table 4.3 *Compatibility appraisal of some of the options for Tooton Rush's District Transport Plan*

	b. Congestion charging	e. Reduce parking spaces	f. Travel plans	h. Pedestrian- ization	hI. Pedestrian priority	i. Park and Ride
e. Reduce parking spaces	✔					
f. Travel plans	✔	✔				
h. Pedestrianization	✔	✔	✔			
hI. Pedestrian priority	✔	✔	✔	choose either h or hI		
i. Park and Ride	potential to integrate	where does parking go?	don't encourage commuting	✔	✔	
k. Cycle lanes	✔	✔	✔	who has priority?	who has priority?	potential to integrate

Based on these analyses, and in discussion with local elected representatives, the planners decide that congestion charging, a Park and Ride system for Standstill, priority for pedestrians in town centres and cycle lanes merit further consideration. They brainstorm possible mitigation measures for the impacts caused by these measures (Table 4.4).

Tip: Positive impacts can be enhanced as well as negative impacts reduced. Mitigation measures can include details of design and construction.

The team then write their final plan statements to integrate the mitigation measures into them, minimize conflicts, and avoid problems with implementation. The final, chosen, mitigated plan statements are:

TA1. Two Park and Ride sites will be built on the edge of Standstill adjacent to major routes into Standstill. They will be located on previously developed land where possible, else on land with low biodiversity value. Recycled aggregates and permeable paving will be used in their construction. The sites will be landscaped with indigenous plantings and include bicycle storage and links to the network of cycle lanes. The sites will be operational by June 2007.

TA2. In Standstill, Rushmore and Walkerton priority will be given, in decreasing order, to wheelchair users, pedestrians and emergency vehicles; cyclists; and public transport.

Table 4.4 *Mitigation measures for impacts identified in Tables 4.2 and 4.3*

Identified impacts	Possible mitigation measure(s)
– Costs to businesses from congestion charging	• reduce tax rates for shopkeepers temporarily
– Impact on those who rely heavily on motorized vehicles	• provide electric buggies for people who are less mobile • allow cars and deliveries at certain times of day • reduce congestion and parking charges for Standstill residents • hypothecate income from congestion charging and parking for improvements to public transport*
+ Improvement in pedestrian environment, visual amenity	• provide spaces for outdoor cafes, benches, sculptures*
– Land take and wildlife implications of P+R and new cycle lanes	• ensure that P+R sites and cycle lanes are built on previously developed land where possible • add wildlife-friendly plantings and try to link with wildlife corridors
+ Decreased air pollution, improved health	• put up monitoring station with read-out to 'advertise' improvements and educate on air quality • ensure that P+R buses are low-emission vehicles or use clean fuels* • add cycle storage at P+R sites for Park-and-Cycle

Note: *These are outside the remit of the transport planning department and need discussion with other departments.

TA3. A pilot congestion charging scheme will be instituted in Standstill city centre (as defined in Map S) during June–December 2007. The revenues generated from the scheme will be used to improve public transport services. Residents and businesses based in the congestion charging zone will receive an 80 per cent discount. At the end of the pilot period a public referendum will be held to determine whether the scheme should be continued.

TA4. Off-road cycle lanes will be built parallel to roads marked in red on Map T. They will be built on previously developed land where possible. Indigenous plantings will be used to separate the cycle lanes from the roads unless this conflicts with safety considerations.

Document the process

Finally the team documents the SEA process and results in an SEA report which looks much like this section of this book. The SEA report is made available for public comment at the same time as the new DTP itself.

Summing up, the SEA helped to revise the objective of Tooton Rush's DTP, identify options, choose preferred options and refine these options. The new Tooton Rush DTP looks completely different from the old one. The objective has been changed, and only fragments of the original statements remain. The new DTP is more sustainable, more responsive to public concerns, and more in line with higher-level policy. Of course not all of this is attributable to the SEA: in fact, it is difficult to disentangle which changes are due to the SEA and which resulted from the plan-making process itself. Wanda Duright has inextricably integrated the two by starting the SEA early and involving her team fully in it.

What is crucial in SEA?

What is essential to SEA and what is icing? At what point is SEA so minimal that it is no longer really SEA? There is no one answer to this. In part, legal requirements will determine what has to be done. I would argue that any SEA must be good enough to fulfil the aim of SEA, namely to protect the environment and promote sustainability. This means, at minimum, that one needs to understand the environment well enough to be able to determine whether a strategic action would harm it; assess the impacts of a strategic action enough to identify whether it would harm the environment; and mitigate any negative environmental impacts. Colleagues have argued that documentation of the SEA process and consultation of the public are also essential to SEA.

Table 4.5 gives an indicative hierarchy of SEA approaches, including the value added of each approach and who could carry it out.

Quality assurance

The quality of the SEA will depend on its timing, on how well the decision-makers take its findings on board, on the resources put into the SEA process and many other factors. These are discussed more in Chapter 10. However, as an overview of the SEA process as a whole, Box 4.3 presents a checklist that SEA practitioners could use as a rough test of the quality of their SEA process.

The SEA Process as a Whole

Table 4.5 *Possible hierarchy of importance of SEA approaches*

SEA approach	Carried out by	Is it needed?	Value added of approach
Develop a vision for a sustainable future: 'visioning'		∞	Helps decision-makers to look at the long term and sustainability, not just short term and fire-fighting
Identify environmental/sustainability indicators		✓	Focuses on key environmental/sustainability issues; streamlines the subsequent baseline description and monitoring stages
Describe the environmental baseline		☐	Provides a base for impact prediction and monitoring; helps to identify environmental problems
Identify problem areas		✓	Focuses SEA on key issues
Analyse links with other strategic actions		☐	Makes transparent how the strategic action is affected by outside factors; suggests ideas for how any inappropriate constraints can be overcome
'Scope' the SEA: agree on assessment methods, environmental criteria, alternatives to consider, level of detail, etc of the SEA		☐	Ensures that the SEA covers key issues, helps to streamline the SEA, helps to prevent subsequent critique of the SEA
Identify statements that most/don't need assessment: 'screening'		∞	Focuses the SEA on key aspects of the strategic action
Identify (more) sustainable alternatives and compare alternatives		☐	Helps to ensure that the strategic action is as good as possible, including as sustainable as possible
Test the sustainability of the strategic action objectives, alternatives, statements		✓ ☐ ∞	The core of SEA

SEA approach	Carried out by	Is it needed?	Value added of approach
Involve the public and environmental experts in the SEA	(icons)	□ ♂	Ensures comprehensive understanding of the environmental/sustainability baseline, identification of problems, identification of alternatives, and consideration of mitigation measures
Ensure that the strategic action objectives and statements are compatible with each other	(icon)	♂	Ensures that the strategic action is internally coherent and that different elements of the strategic action do not pull against each other
Document the SEA findings	(icons)	✓ □	♂
Audit the SEA findings	(icons)	♂	Helps to ensure SEA quality

Note: Organized roughly chronologically in terms of when they would be used in the SEA process.

Key:

	SEA coordinator
	planners who wrote strategic action
	local residents
	environmental authorities
	consultant
✓	fundamental: don't miss this
□	in EC, legally required from July 2004
♂	best practice

Box 4.3 Quality assurance checklist for SEA

Objectives
- The strategic action's objective, area covered, timescale and objectives are given.
- The SEA objectives are given, linked to indicators and targets where appropriate.
- Environmental and sustainability visions and problems are adequately considered in developing the objectives, indicators and targets.

Scoping
- Appropriate environmental authorities are consulted when deciding on the scope and level of the information which must be included in the SEA report.
- The SEA focuses on significant issues and disregards less significant ones.
- Technical, procedural and other difficulties encountered (such as technical deficiencies or lack of know-how) are discussed; assumptions and uncertainties are made explicit.
- Reasons for eliminating issues from further consideration are documented.

Baseline information
- Relevant aspects of the current state of the environment and their likely evolution without the strategic action are described.
- Environmental characteristics of areas likely to be significantly affected are described in more detail.
- SEA objectives and indicators cover an appropriate range of environmental/sustainability topics, including on biodiversity, population, human health, fauna, flora, soil, water, air, climate factors, material assets, cultural heritage, landscape and their interrelationships.
- They integrate environmental, social and economic issues.
- They cover equity and resilience.
- The SEA objectives and baseline data collection are mutually reinforcing.
- The methods used to investigate the affected baseline are appropriate to the size and complexity of the assessment task.

Links to other strategic actions
- Links between the strategic action and related higher and local tiers of strategic actions are identified and explained.
- Where strategic actions conflict, the reasons are clearly documented and recommendations are made on how to reconcile the strategic actions so as to promote sustainability.

Alternatives/options
- Alternatives are considered that are appropriate to the scale (international, national, etc) and level (policy, plan, programme) of decision-making.
- Alternatives are considered that deal with the issues identified as a result of the baseline assessment and/or achieve sustainability visions.

- Alternatives include the 'do nothing', 'do minimum' and 'most environmentally beneficial' alternatives.
- Reasons for eliminating alternatives from further consideration are given.
- The environmental and sustainability effects of each alternative are identified and compared.

Identification and evaluation of key effects
- The likely significant impacts on the environment are identified and evaluated.
- Likely indirect, cumulative and secondary impacts are identified and evaluated.
- Appropriate impact prediction and evaluation techniques have been used.
- Impact evaluation is carried out in relation to relevant, accepted standards, regulations, and thresholds where appropriate.

Mitigation and monitoring of effects
- The measures envisaged to avoid, reduce, repair, compensate and/or enhance any significant impacts of implementing the strategic action are indicated.
- Links to project EIA are made explicit.
- Measures for monitoring of impacts are made explicit.
- Monitoring is linked to provision of future baseline data.

Consultation and decision-making
- The SEA is conducted as an integral part of the decision-making process, starting when the strategic action objectives were developed and continuing throughout the decision-making process.
- An appropriate range of 'environmental authorities' and public are consulted.
- The draft strategic action and SEA report are made available for comment to the public and all relevant bodies/countries consulted.[*]
- Environmental and other authorities and the public are given an early and effective opportunity within appropriate timeframes to express their opinion on the draft strategic action and SEA report before adoption of the strategic action.[*]
- The views of the public and relevant bodies/countries are summarized and responded to.[*]
- An explanation is given of how environmental/sustainability considerations are integrated into the strategic action, what changes (if any) were made to the strategic action as a result of the SEA, and the reasons for choosing the strategic action as adopted, in light of other reasonable alternatives.[*]

The SEA report:

- identifies the decision-maker and who carried out the SEA, and their competences;

- is clear and concise in its layout and presentation, is presented as an integrated whole, and uses maps and other illustrations where appropriate;
- uses simple, clear language and avoids technical jargon;
- describes the methodology used in the SEA, including who was consulted and how;
- focuses on the big issues;
- acknowledges external sources of information, including expert judgement and matters of opinion;
- contains a non-technical summary which includes an explanation of the overall approach to the SEA; the objectives of the strategic action; the main alternatives considered, and how the strategic action was changed by the SEA;
- is written without bias in an impartial and open manner.

Note: * This may not be able to be tested using only the SEA report.

Source: adapted from ODPM (2002)

Conclusions

The SEA process works best when it is fully integrated in the decision-making process. It can act as an educational tool, help to ensure that the plan is as robust and environment-friendly as possible, and help to make its implementation faster and smoother. SEA does not have to be a horrible, daunting process: some aspects are more crucial than others and must be done, whilst others are refinements on the basic approach. The checklist of Box 4.3 will help to ensure that the SEA is of a good quality.

Part II discusses the stages of SEA in greater detail: the SEA context; the baseline environment and problems; alternatives; prediction, evaluation and mitigation; and decision-making and documentation.

Part II

The SEA Process

Chapter 5

Setting the Context for SEA

This chapter considers the early, context-setting stages of the SEA process (see Figure 5.1):

A   Screening: Deciding whether a given strategic action requires SEA. In the early stages of a new SEA system, some kind of agreed screening 'rules' will need to be set up (normally at the national level) which specify what broad categories of strategic actions require SEA. Subsequently, at the level of the individual strategic action, a decision will need to be taken about whether that strategic action falls within the 'rules' and requires SEA or not.
B   How to link SEA and the strategic action, especially in terms of timing.
C   How SEA can fit with other existing assessment requirements. This again applies both when central SEA guidance and regulations are devised, and at the individual SEA level when it is carried out in the context of other assessment requirements.
D   Who should be involved in SEA.

The chapter also looks at how the individual strategic action relates to other strategic actions (E in Figure 5.1).

Deciding whether a strategic action requires SEA: 'screening'

The first question that anyone contemplating SEA asks is 'do I need to do it?'. The process of answering this question is the screening process. The faster and more definite the screening process is, the less uncertainty and wasted time (and apprehension) will result.

Different countries have different screening requirements. Section 102(2) of the US National Environmental Policy Act (NEPA) requires a 'detailed statement' to be prepared for all 'major Federal actions

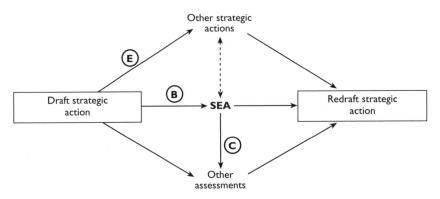

Figure 5.1 *Context of SEA: Links to decision-making and other assessment processes*

significantly affecting the quality of the human environment'. The term 'actions' covers both projects which become subject to EIA, and strategic actions which become subject to a form of SEA called 'programmatic EIA'. The flexibility inherent in this definition has led to great uncertainty and a truly impressive number of lawsuits about whether any given activity is major, Federal, an action, and with significant effects on the human environment. But it is this same flexibility and foresight – which requires assessment of 'actions' rather than just projects – that makes the NEPA an SEA as well as an EIA regulation, and which means that the USA's SEA system precedes all others by about 20 years.

In some other countries and organizations, SEA requirements are limited to a particular type of strategic action, for instance regional and sectoral development activities by the World Bank, proposals to Parliament in Denmark, policies and plans that cover resource consents in New Zealand (Sadler, 2003).

In the UK, at the time of writing (late 2003), there is still considerable uncertainty about exactly which strategic actions are covered by the complex 'and/or' screening requirements of the SEA Directive. Some types of plans and programmes have already been identified as definitely requiring SEA, notably Local Development Frameworks, Regional Spatial Strategies (RSS) and Local Transport Plans in England, and Unitary Development Plans, Regional Minerals Plans and the Spatial Plan in Wales. Formal decisions on other clusters of similar types of strategic actions – for instance Catchment Management Plans and Community Strategies – will be made before the Directive becomes operational in July 2004. In still other cases, decisions are likely to be made on a case-by-case basis for the foreseeable future. Table 5.1 shows the results of an unofficial screening process for some UK transport plans, carried out before formal screening decisions had been made. It gives a feel for how such screening could be carried out.

Table 5.1 *Example of screening of some UK transport plans and programmes under the SEA Directive*

	1. formally required by national, regional or local authority (SEA Directive Art. 2(a))	AND 2. likely to have significant environmental effects (Art. 3.1)	AND 3a. sets framework for development consent of projects requiring EIA (Art. 3.2(a), 4c)	OR 3b. could require appropriate assessment under Habitats Directive (Art. 3.2(b))	= requires SEA?
Europe					
Trans-European Transport Network	probably not	yes	yes	yes	probably not
UK/England					
Overarching policy: New Deal for Transport, Transport 2010, Transport Act 2000	no	yes	no	yes	no
Mode-specific strategies: Road Safety Strategy, National Cycling Strategy, Better Role for Bus Travel, New Deal for Railways	no	yes	no	possibly	no
Strategies that identify specific projects: New Deal for Trunk Roads, Future Development of Air Transport in the UK	no	yes	yes	yes	probably not
Office of Rail Regulator business plans	possibly	yes	no	possibly	no

	1. formally required by national, regional or local authority (SEA Directive Art. 2(a))	AND 2. likely to have significant environmental effects (Art. 3.1)	AND 3a. sets framework for development consent of projects requiring EIA (Art. 3.2(a), 4c)	OR 3b. could require appropriate assessment under Habitats Directive (Art. 3.2(b))	= requires SEA?
Regional/local					
Regional Transport Strategies, Local Transport Plans	yes	yes	yes	yes	yes
Multi-modal studies	yes	yes	yes	yes	yes
Private sector transport infrastructure plans/programmes: construction or expansion of railways, ports, inland waterways, airports, roads, etc	no	yes	yes	yes	probably not
Road user charging, workplace parking levy, congestion charging	no	yes	probably not	no	no
Site					
Major transport projects, eg Channel Tunnel Rail Link, Heathrow Terminal 5, Dibden Bay, Central Rail	no	yes	no	possibly	EIA not SEA

Note: This table was prepared in spring 2003 before official screening decisions had been made. It is meant to demonstrate the type of thinking required under the SEA Directive rather than final confirmed screening. The table is not comprehensive, and the cell contents are not definitive.

Source: Levett-Therivel (2002)

Even where SEA is not legally required for a given strategic action, authorities should consider carrying out SEA, especially where the strategic action influences lower-level ones that require SEA or EIA. Otherwise, where SEAs/EIAs for the lower-level strategic actions identify that the higher-level strategic action is not sustainable or environmentally sound, then the higher-level strategic action's validity may be in doubt. Where no SEA is deemed to be required, it may be useful to write a justification for this. Where an SEA has already been carried out on an earlier version of the strategic action, the new SEA should probably aim, on efficiency grounds, to update the original SEA rather than starting afresh.

Links between SEA and decision-making

Early in decision-making, it may be worthwhile mapping out the decision-making process and deciding how the SEA should best be integrated in it. This can identify those points where SEA information can usefully inform the decision-making process, ie 'decision windows' (ANSEA Team, 2002). Figure 5.2 shows such a flowchart for the Tooton Rush example of Chapter 4. Decision flowcharts for other case studies discussed in this book are shown in Chapter 10. Note that the main difference between these processes is how they deal with alternatives and more detailed statements.

In most cases, SEA should fit elegantly with the strategic decision-making process. In fact, there is potential for so completely integrating planning processes and SEA that the only added requirement for formal SEA would be the documentation of this process (Figure 5.3).

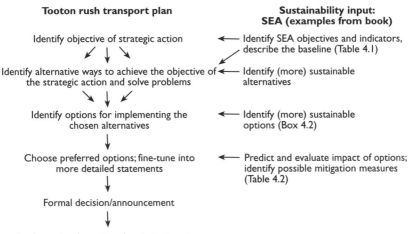

Figure 5.2 *Decision flowchart and SEA inputs for Tooton Rush*

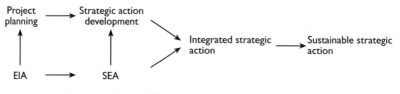

Source: adapted from Partidario (1992)

Figure 5.3 *Evolution towards sustainable strategic actions*

Fitting SEA with other existing assessment requirements

In many countries, SEA will be one of a range of assessments required for strategic actions. Others could include, for instance, assessment of the strategic action's compliance with other regulations, effect on health, on equity, on vulnerable groups (eg the elderly, minorities, farmers), on businesses, or on sustainability or the environment (existing SEA-type systems). In European Union countries, 'appropriate assessment' under the Habitats Directive is also needed (Box 5.1).

Where other assessment systems already exist, a decision will need to be made about whether the SEA and other systems can be integrated, or whether they should run side by side. Whether or not to integrate will depend on the degree of overlap of the different assessment systems in terms of what strategic actions they apply to (policy/plan/programme, what sectors); the impacts that they consider, for instance whether only a limited range (eg 'appropriate assessment' or health impact assessment), or the full range of sustainability considerations; whether they focus on a particular receptor group (eg 'rural proofing' which aims to ensure that rural communities are not adversely affected by emerging strategic actions); and the rigour of their requirements.

This decision could be made centrally, for instance through guidance on integrated assessments, or on a case-by-case basis. A range of approaches are possible:

- carry out separate SEA and other assessment(s);
- carry out SEA, plus an additional separate analysis of those aspects of the current assessment system(s) not covered by SEA;
- carry out the other assessment(s), plus an additional separate analysis of those aspects of SEA not covered by the current assessment system(s); or
- integrate SEA and the other assessment systems.

Table 5.2 summarizes some of their advantages and disadvantages.

Generally integration is preferable on grounds of coherence and efficiency, but it could reduce SEA's emphasis on the environment. Any

Box 5.1 'Appropriate assessment' under the European Union Habitats Directive

The Directive on Conservation of Natural Habitats and of Flora and Fauna 92/43/EEC (known as the Habitats Directive) is the key European legislation for protecting biodiversity. The Directive aims to 'contribute towards ensuring biodiversity through the conservation of natural habitats and of wild fauna and flora in the European territory of the Member States to which the Treaty applies' (Art. 2). It does this by identifying a pan-European network – Natura 2000 – of Special Protection Areas (SPAs) and Special Areas of Conservation (SACs); and by protecting these sites against development through 'appropriate assessment'.

Articles 6(3) and 6(4) of the Habitats Directive require an appropriate assessment to be prepared for any plan or project, alone or in combination with other plans or projects, that is likely to have a significant effect on a Natura 2000 site. If the appropriate assessment shows that the plan or project will affect the integrity of the site – its ecological functioning – the plan or project should not be permitted unless there are imperative reasons of overriding public interest and no alternative solutions are possible, in which case the Member State must take compensatory measures to ensure the overall coherence of the Natura 2000 network.

Article 6 of the Habitats Directive is normally implemented using the following steps (European Commission, 2000, 2001a):

- *Screening* – identify the likely impacts on a Natura 2000 site of a project or plan, either alone or in combination with other projects or plans, and consider whether these impacts are likely to be significant.
- *Appropriate assessment* – consider the impact on the integrity of the Natura 2000 site of the project or plan, either alone or in combination with other projects or plans, with respect to the site's structure and function and its conservation objectives. Additionally, where there are adverse impacts, assess the potential mitigation of those impacts.
- *Assessment of alternative solutions* – examine alternative ways of achieving the objectives of the project or plan that avoid adverse impacts on the integrity of the Natura 2000 site.
- *Assessment where adverse impacts remain* – assess compensatory measures where, in the light of an assessment of imperative reasons of overriding public interest, it is deemed that the project or plan should proceed.

Clearly there are large areas of overlap between SEA and appropriate assessment. Their aims and broad methodologies are similar. Appropriate assessment focuses particularly on the baseline environment and cumulative impacts; the SEA Directive on the integration of the assessment information into decision-making. Due to its wider remit (air, water, etc as well as biodiversity) the SEA Directive has the potential to integrate many parts of appropriate assessment.

Source: Southwest Ecological Surveys et al (2003)

Table 5.2 *Advantages and disadvantages of different approaches to fitting SEA with other assessment systems*

Option	Advantages	Disadvantages
Separate SEA + other assessment	• Easiest to write regulations and guidance for • Copes most easily with different areas of application (policy, plan, programme; different sectors)	• Confusing for implementing bodies • Inefficient
SEA + separate analysis of aspects of other assessment systems not covered by SEA	• Where SEA is legally required and other assessment systems are discretionary, then SEA provides a regulatory basis and should thus be the main basis for guidance • Deals with any problem of other assessment systems being outdated (which was the case, for instance, with the UK's approach to environmental appraisal)	• Somewhat confusing for implementing bodies • Sustainability is often best tackled in an integrated (environment – social – economic) manner rather than by treating them as separate issues
Other assessment systems + separate analysis of aspects of SEA not covered by those systems	• Would require the least change of practice by implementing bodies	• Where SEA is legally required and other assessment systems are discretionary, then SEA should be the main basis for guidance • Current guidance on other assessments may be outdated
Integrate SEA + other assessment systems	• Efficient; eliminates duplication • Easy to understand for implementing bodies • Can incorporate best practice from the different assessment systems • Sustainability is often best tackled in an integrated (environment – social – economic) manner rather than by treating them as separate issues	• Potentially the most difficult to write guidance for, not least because it requires approval by officials responsible for the other systems of assessment • Could dilute SEA's emphasis on the environment

integrated system will also require collaborative working between agencies that may well not have a tradition of cooperation.

Example: Developing English guidance on integrated SEA and sustainability appraisal for land use plans

This section considers, as an example of the above, the issues discussed as guidance on the SEA Directive was being developed in England. The original UK system of environmental appraisal (see Box 3.1) covered only local land use plans, considered environmental and a very limited range of social issues, did not focus on a particular receptor group, and required only agreement on environmental indicators, a check of the plan against higher-level policies, and a test of the plan against the environmental indicators. As it evolved into sustainability appraisal in the late 1990s, it began to consider the full range of sustainability issues but otherwise remained much the same. This system of sustainability appraisal was, at the time when the Directive was agreed, well-established, and carried out for the great majority of regional and local land use plans.

The new SEA Directive applies to a much wider range of plans and programmes (but not policies), focuses primarily on the environment, does not focus on a particular receptor group, and requires considerably more data and analysis than sustainability appraisal. It requires greater 'depth' of assessment, but only for the environmental aspects of SEA. This narrow-but-deep SEA Directive approach fit uncomfortably with the existing shallow-but-wide sustainability appraisal approach (see Figure 5.4). Integration of the two systems was generally favoured by the authorities that would need to carry out SEA and sustainability appraisal and by central government,[1] but there was considerable uncertainty about whether such integration should merely superimpose the two systems to get a T shape (d) in Figure 5.4, aim for a broad-and-wide approach (e) in Figure 5.4 with its resource implications, or whether integration would prove to be too horribly complicated so that two parallel systems would end up being the only viable solution. In particular, could the systems be integrated to keep the good aspects of sustainability appraisal – efficiency, links to sustainability – whilst also unambiguously fulfilling the legal requirements of the SEA Directive?

Box 5.2 (based on Box 3.2) shows the difference in *depth* between the SEA Directive and sustainability appraisal. It shows in grey which SEA Directive requirements were already commonly carried out as part of sustainability appraisal and good planning, and in white which were not. The key new requirements of the SEA Directive relate to the collection of baseline data, identification of problem areas, consideration of alternatives, provision of information on the decision, and monitoring. To a lesser extent impact prediction and mitigation

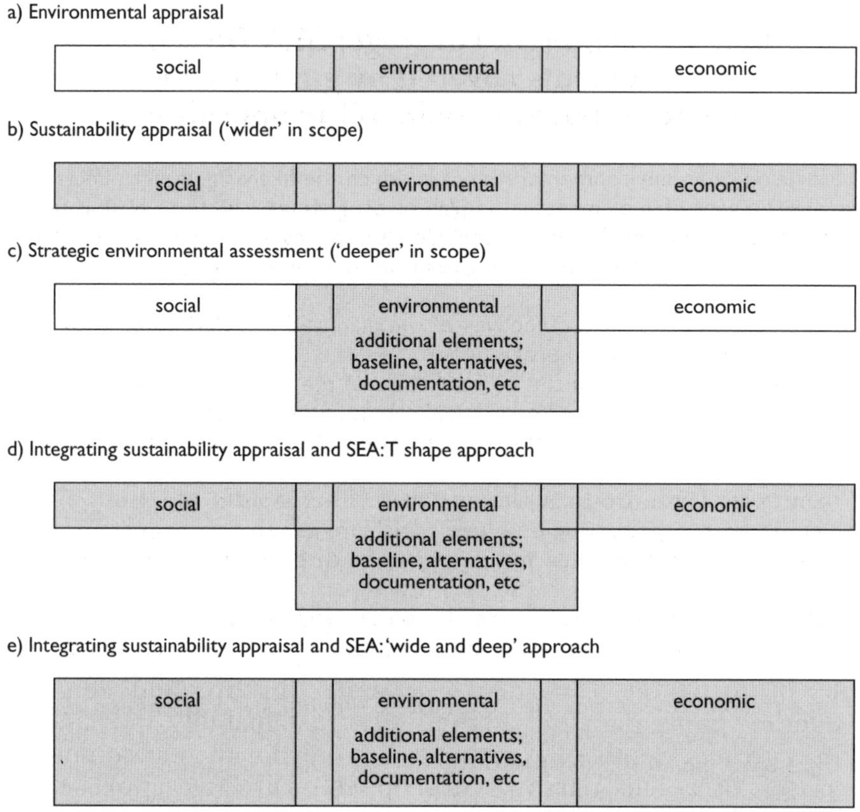

a) Environmental appraisal

social	environmental	economic

b) Sustainability appraisal ('wider' in scope)

social	environmental	economic

c) Strategic environmental assessment ('deeper' in scope)

social	environmental	economic
	additional elements; baseline, alternatives, documentation, etc	

d) Integrating sustainability appraisal and SEA: T shape approach

social	environmental	economic
	additional elements; baseline, alternatives, documentation, etc	

e) Integrating sustainability appraisal and SEA: 'wide and deep' approach

social	environmental	economic
	additional elements; baseline, alternatives, documentation, etc	

Source: adapted from TRL (2002)

Figure 5.4 *Evolution from environmental appraisal to SEA*

need to be carried out in greater depth to meet the Directive's requirements.

Looking at the *breadth* of the issues covered by the Directive and sustainability appraisal, Table 5.3 shows how the sustainability objectives of the UK guidance on sustainability appraisal (DTLR, 2001) fit with the environmental issues listed in the SEA Directive. The sustainability appraisal guidance includes much more on economic development than the SEA Directive, but little on human health and material assets, and nothing on cultural heritage. However, overall there is considerable overlap, suggesting that the Directive's requirements (broadly interpreted) already extend far into the social and economic spheres, and that only relatively minor tweaks would be needed for the Directive to take on board the 'wider' issues covered in existing UK guidance.

Box 5.2 'Depth' of coverage: SEA Directive requirements covered by guidance on environmental/sustainability appraisal

Preparation of an environmental report in which the likely significant effects on the environment of implementing the plan or programme (the term 'plan' is used hereafter to denote both), and reasonable alternatives are identified, described and evaluated. The information to be given is (Art. 5 and Annex 1):

a) the contents and main objectives of the plan, and its relationship with other relevant plans and programmes;
b) the relevant aspects of the current state of the environment and the likely evolution thereof without implementation of the plan;
c) the environmental characteristics of areas likely to be significantly affected;
d) any existing environmental problems which are relevant to the plan;
e) environmental protection objectives which are relevant to the plan, and the way those objectives and any environmental considerations have been taken into account during its preparation;
f) the likely significant effects of the plan on the environment;
g) proposed ways of mitigating any significant adverse environmental effects;
h) the reasons for selecting the alternatives dealt with, and a description of how the assessment was undertaken;
i) proposed monitoring measures; and
j) a non-technical summary of the above.

The report shall include the information that may reasonably be required taking into account current knowledge and methods of assessment, the contents and level of detail in the plan, its stage in the decision-making process and the extent to which certain matters are more appropriately assessed at different levels in that process in order to avoid duplication of the assessment (Art. 5.2).

The environmental reports should be of a sufficient standard to meet the requirements of the SEA Directive (Art. 12.2).

Consultation
- of environmental authorities when deciding on the scope and level of detail of the information which must be included in the environmental report (Art. 5.4);
- of environmental authorities and the public, which shall be given an early and effective opportunity within appropriate time frames to express their opinion on the draft plan and the accompanying environmental report before the plan's adoption (Art. 6.1, 6.2);
- of other EU Member States where the plan's implementation is considered likely to have significant effects on the environment of those States (Art. 7).

The environmental report and the results of the consultations must be taken into account in decision-making (Art. 8).

Provision of information on the decision
When the plan is adopted, the public and any EU Member State consulted under Art. 7 shall be informed and the following items made available to those so informed:

•   the plan as adopted;
•   a statement summarizing how environmental considerations have been integrated into the plan and how the environmental report of Art. 5, the opinions expressed pursuant to Art. 6 and the results of consultations entered into pursuant to Art. 7 have been taken into account in accordance with Art. 8, and the reasons for choosing the plan as adopted, in the light of the other reasonable alternatives dealt with; and
•   the measures decided concerning monitoring (Art. 9).

Monitoring of the significant environmental effects of the plan's implementation (Art. 10).

Note: Unshaded = generally not undertaken; shaded = generally undertaken.

In the end, given that the additional depth would be required in any case, and that the additional breadth would not be particularly difficult to achieve, the ODPM decided to promote a wide-and-deep approach as shown at e) in Figure 5.4. The English guidance on the SEA Directive (ODPM, 2003) thus promotes consideration of the full range of sustainability criteria, all with the rigour of the Directive.

Who should be involved in the SEA?

Three groups of people and organizations are likely to be involved in an SEA: the decision-maker and possibly their consultants; environmental or sustainability organizations; and the public. Inspectors, auditors and others interested in quality assurance of the SEA process may also be involved. Normally the SEA will be carried out by the decision-maker with involvement from the other groups.

Decision-maker or consultant?

Whereas project EIA is primarily carried out by consultants because of the specialist skills it requires, SEAs are often carried out by the decision-makers. Studies of UK environmental appraisal practice (Therivel 1995, 1996, 1998; Therivel and Minas, 2002) suggest that the most effective appraisals were carried out by mixed groups of

Table 5.3 *'Breadth' of coverage: Environmental/sustainability issues covered by the SEA Directive and guidance on sustainability appraisal*

'Environmental' issues listed in SEA Directive Annex I(f)	'Sustainability' objectives from the UK guidance on sustainability appraisal (DTLR, 2001)
Population	• Find a balance in the distribution of population, employment and housing • Reduce disparities in income, and access to jobs, housing and services between areas within the region and between segments of the population
Human health	
Biodiversity, flora, fauna	• Maintain and increase biodiversity
Soil	• Reduce consumption of undeveloped land • Use agricultural land more sustainably • Promote a move up through the waste management hierarchy • Reduce consumption of minerals from primary sources
Water	• Maintain and improve the quality of ground, river and sea waters • Ensure that water is efficiently used to meet needs whilst reducing environmental impact and resource depletion
Air, climatic factors	• Improve atmospheric integrity and air quality
Material assets	• Provide decent housing for every household requiring a home
Cultural heritage including architectural and archaeological heritage	
Landscape	• Maintain and enhance the quality and distinctiveness of the landscape • Make towns and cities more attractive places to live
(Not covered)	• Encourage and accommodate the maintenance of a steady rate of economic growth • Provide for good accessibility to and movement of goods by businesses within the region • Encourage and accommodate the expansion of selected economic sectors involved with advanced manufacturing and exports • Encourage stronger linkages between firms and the development of clusters and specialisms within an area • Build economic activity on local strengths • Ensure good accessibility to jobs, facilities and services

Table 5.4 *Advantages and disadvantages of different approaches to who should carry out the SEA*

	Advantages	Disadvantages
In-house	• Decision-makers are better placed to conduct an iterative process that extends throughout the development of the strategic action • Decision-makers get side-benefit of better understanding the strategic action and sustainability issues (Therivel and Minas, 2002)	• Decision-makers are unlikely to have SEA expertise • Resource/time problems • If undertaken by decision-makers who wrote the plan, not independent
Consultants	• Ensures expertise in sustainability issues and SEA • Provides independent, fresh outlook and ideas • Prevents accusations of bias	• Consultants are unlikely to know local circumstances and context • Financial cost to the decision-maker, especially if consultants are involved throughout the decision-making process (Smith and Sheate, 2001b) • Difficult to do as an integral process of the development of the strategic action

planners and consultants, followed by groups of planners, and then individual consultants or planners. Table 5.4 summarizes the advantages and disadvantages of different approaches to who undertakes the SEA.

Perhaps more useful than this simple categorization is the concept that the SEA team should have the right competences: independence, the authority to implement the SEA's recommendations, and experience. Independence, objectivity and credibility could be achieved through post-audit review (eg a citizens review panel) or through involvement with external agencies such as consultants or academics. Close integration between the SEA and the decision-making process – which is needed so that SEA recommendations can be taken on board easily and efficiently – is probably most easily done by involving the decision-makers in the SEA. Where external consultants are involved, then a close working partnership with the decision-makers should be stressed, and how the resulting formal recommendations are taken on board by the authority should be documented. Experience is needed in terms of full coverage of relevant social, economic, environmental, health and public participation issues; understanding of the decision-making process; and a knowledge of the local area.

Involving environmental/sustainability authorities

The SEA Directive and Protocol require that environmental authorities' views be sought on the scope of the SEA and on the draft SEA report. Environmental/sustainability authorities will normally be government agencies and non-governmental organizations (NGOs) with specialist data or expertise in environmental/sustainability issues. For instance, they could be a country's environment department, nature conservation bureau, pollution inspectorate, etc: in England they are generally the Environment Agency (air, water, soil), Countryside Agency (landscape, rural issues), English Nature (biodiversity, flora, fauna) and English Heritage (archaeological, historical and cultural issues). They could also include NGOs such as wildlife trusts and local government environmental departments.

The environmental/sustainability experts will be able to provide environmental data; help identify environmental problems; help decide the level of detail that the SEA should go into, methods it should use, and alternatives it should consider ('scoping'); identify other strategic actions that influence, or are influenced by, the strategic action in question; suggest sustainable alternatives; help to choose between alternatives; and suggest mitigation measures.

The most effective way to get this expert input is during the course of the SEA process, for instance by inviting the organizations to SEA steering group meetings or involving them actively in the analysis of alternatives.

Involving the public

Involving the public in decision-making and SEA takes advantage of local skills, knowledge and resources, leads to more socially and politically acceptable decisions, improves 'ownership' of decisions and makes the strategic action more likely to be implemented, can resolve conflict between stakeholder groups, and improves democracy by ensuring that community views are taken into account in decision-making. Public participation is a key principle of sustainable development. It is also in line with the Aarhus Convention, which aims to 'ensure that the public are given early and effective opportunities to participate in the preparation and review of [strategic actions]'.

Public involvement in the SEA process can help to ensure that the strategic action meets people's aspirations for the future and does not just respond to today's problems. The public can contribute to setting the SEA objectives; help to ensure that baseline data is comprehensive and that the full range of environmental/sustainability problems are understood; identify innovative, sustainable, and/or politically acceptable alternatives; choose between alternatives; identify mitigation measures; and ensure that the strategic action is implemented effectively.

On the other hand, public participation may not result in the most environmental or sustainable solution, or even come close to it. Participants may only become involved when they feel threatened, so NIMBY (not in my back yard) approaches can dominate. It may be difficult to identify and engage the public, in particular groups that have traditionally been disenfranchised, such as young people and minorities. Specialist skills are often needed to achieve effective participation and, if done poorly, the public's expectations can be raised unrealistically and participants can be left feeling frustrated. Certain public participation processes can be biased against participants who are not comfortable attending meetings, writing letters, speaking in public, etc, or whose language is not that used in the participation process. There may be 'consultation fatigue'.

I have to be honest here (and I get told off about this regularly, so do feel free to disagree): involving the public in SEA is not easy, and I am not certain that the benefits of such involvement outweigh its costs in all circumstances. SEAs and the strategic actions they relate to are often too strategic, too removed from people's everyday concerns to elicit 'participation' from more than an extremely limited and unrepresentative group of people. This is borne out by UK planners' experience with sustainability appraisal, where attempts to involve the public have generally received a 'negligible' or 'poor' response (Therivel and Minas, 2002).

Public participation techniques range from basic consultation – provision of information and the opportunity to comment – through to extended involvement as members of an SEA steering group or SEA team, with the ability to genuinely influence the SEA and planning processes. Table 5.5 summarizes some of the key techniques for public participation, along with their underlying philosophies. Further information on these techniques can be found in publications by, eg, the Audit Commission (1999), Bishop (2001), Institute of Environmental Management and Assessment (IEMA) (2002), New Economics Foundation (1998) and World Bank (1996). Gauthier et al (2000) critically discuss how the public is currently involved in SEA in several countries. Most countries' SEA systems – including the SEA Directive – include only a minimal form of public consultation in the form of an opportunity to comment on an SEA report.

An alternative to 'public' participation is to involve representatives of the wider public in the SEA. These could be elected representatives or politicians, or pressure groups that represent various public views (business organizations, environmental organizations, etc). In some

Table 5.5 *Public participation techniques and approaches*

Type	Public consultation	Public involvement
Common techniques	Public meetings Printed materials Newspaper articles/ads Information on websites Draft SEA reports for comment Questionnaires (eg Figure 7.3) Planning inquiries	Small meetings, focus groups Workshops, eg SEA assessment exercises Citizens' juries Future Search Planning for Real Quality of Life Assessment (see Appendix C) Visioning
Applied through	Individuals, separately	Groups, collaboratively
Kinds of value/style of input most encouraged	Private interest/adversarial	Public interest/consensus seeking
Prevailing tone	Argumentative	Deliberative
Underlying political philosophy	'Society' is basically the sum of the individuals in it	Society is more than just the sum of the individuals in it; society's preference is not just the sum of individual preferences

Source: adapted from CAG (2000)

SEA processes, steering groups made up of representatives of the public oversee the entire process or carry out the assessment themselves.

It may be useful to set up a public participation programme early in the SEA process which identifies the role of the public, representatives and/or stakeholders; how and when they will be involved; and expected outputs. Annex V of the SEA Protocol gives an indication of what this might contain.

Conclusions

Several decisions need to be made before any SEA can begin:

*   Is an SEA needed?
*   If so, at what stages of the decision-making process should which aspects of SEA be carried out?
*   Do other assessment processes apply to the strategic action?
*   If so, what is the best way to deal with any overlaps between the assessment systems?

- Who should be involved in the SEA, when and in what capacity?

Once these decisions have been made, the real work can start: describing the baseline, identifying problems, and analysing links to other strategic actions. These are discussed in Chapter 6.

Note

1   The majority of the 140 respondents to the ODPM's (2002) draft guidance on SEA supported integration of sustainability appraisal and SEA, but 10–20 per cent of respondents were concerned that such integration would reduce the 'weight' that this would give to environmental issues.

Describing the Environmental Baseline, Identifying Problems, Links to Other Strategic Actions

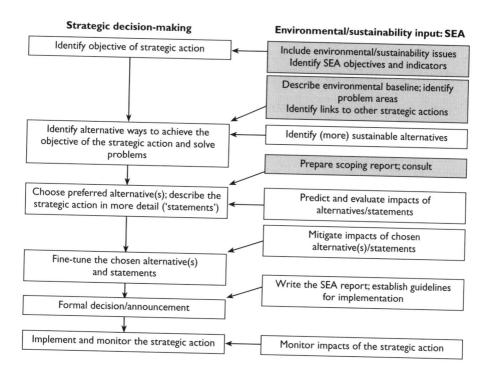

Strategic decision-making

Identify objective of strategic action

Identify alternative ways to achieve the objective of the strategic action and solve problems

Choose preferred alternative(s); describe the strategic action in more detail ('statements')

Fine-tune the chosen alternative(s) and statements

Formal decision/announcement

Implement and monitor the strategic action

Environmental/sustainability input: SEA

Include environmental/sustainability issues Identify SEA objectives and indicators

Describe environmental baseline; identify problem areas Identify links to other strategic actions

Identify (more) sustainable alternatives

Prepare scoping report; consult

Predict and evaluate impacts of alternatives/statements

Mitigate impacts of chosen alternative(s)/statements

Write the SEA report; establish guidelines for implementation

Monitor impacts of the strategic action

SEA stage	What to decide	What to record
Identify SEA objectives, indicators and targets	What environmental and sustainability objectives, targets and/or indicators to test the strategic action against	List of SEA objectives, indicators and targets where relevant
Describe environmental baseline, including future trends; identify environmental issues and problems	What environmental and sustainability issues and constraints to consider during decision-making	Data on the baseline environment; list of relevant environmental and sustainability issues and constraints
Identify links to other relevant strategic actions	What other strategic actions influence the strategic action in question and how	List of relevant strategic actions, their requirements, and any constraints or conflicts with the strategic action in question

The baseline environment needs to be identified in SEA in order to set a basis for the subsequent stages of SEA: impact prediction, evaluation and monitoring. Environmental problems need to be identified so that the evolving strategic action does not make the problems worse, and ideally helps to rectify them. Links to other strategic actions need to be identified to determine the constraints that they pose and possible ways to deal with these constraints.

This chapter discusses:

- the building blocks of the baseline environment description: indicators, objectives, targets;
- things to think about when establishing SEA objectives and indicators;
- how to collect and present baseline data;
- how to set targets (where appropriate);
- how to identify environmental problems; and
- links to other strategic actions.

Indicators, objectives, targets

There is no way that an SEA can describe the baseline environment in as much detail as a project environmental impact assessment would. Even if it was physically possible to do so, one would get so lost in the welter of detail that the information would become essentially meaningless. Instead, SEA uses overarching themes or objectives to represent larger clusters of environmental data, or more detailed indicators to act as representative examples of such data for monitoring purposes. *Themes* are broad categories of impacts, for instance air pollution or human health. *Objectives* specify a desired direction for change, for instance 'reduce air pollution' or 'improve human health'. Objectives often form a hierarchy which goes from a general statement (eg 'to improve human health') to more detailed *targets* (eg 'to reduce the number of traffic accidents by x'). *Indicators* are measures of variables over time, for instance NO_x levels at specified monitoring stations or traffic accidents in a given region.

In SEA, indicators are normally used to describe and monitor the baseline environment (Figure 6.1), and indicators or objectives are used to predict impacts. For instance the number of traffic accidents can be monitored annually, and quantitative predictions can be made of accidents resulting from different approaches to transport management or the location of future development.

Clearly, which themes/objectives/indicators are used in SEA will affect what baseline data are collected, what predictions are made and what monitoring systems are set up. Poorly chosen ones will lead to a biased or limited SEA process: for instance (to take an obvious example)

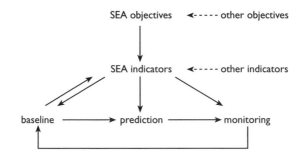

Figure 6.1 *Links between indicators and other aspects of SEA*

an SEA for an energy policy that does not consider CO_2 emissions would lead to very different conclusions about the acceptability of certain forms of power generation than one that does. As such, the first list of SEA themes/objectives/indicators should be treated as a draft and as part of a feedback cycle: as more baseline data are collected and problems identified, that should help to focus the objectives on issues of greatest concern, and in turn this should help to focus and restrict the collection of further baseline information.

Table 6.1 shows the indicative SEA objectives of the guidance on SEA for English land use plans (ODPM, 2003), arranged into environmental, social and economic categories. They are probably not a bad start for many SEAs, although they obviously need to be adapted to local circumstances and problems. For instance, a minerals plan might have more objectives, and more detailed indicators, on land and soil but fewer on social inclusiveness; an urban programme would not include information on countryside character.

Table 6.2 shows another list of objectives, this time with more detailed indicators. This list was used to test the effects of different UK policies on farming and food. Clearly it is more oriented to the agricultural sector, but, like the list in Table 6.1, it considers the whole range of sustainability issues, including equity (who wins and who loses from the policies).

The SEA system discussed in this book is 'baseline-led': a distinct environmental yardstick of discrete SEA themes, objectives and/or indicators is established, which is used to describe the baseline environment and identify problems, which in turn are expected to influence the strategic action objective. Box 6.1 clarifies the distinction between the strategic action objectives and SEA objectives. Instead in some SEA systems – notably in UK sustainability appraisal (Box 3.1) – the approach is 'objectives-led': sustainable objectives for the strategic action are developed first, then indicators which test whether various alternatives achieve the strategic action objectives (Smith and Sheate, 2001a). The 'objectives-led' approach assumes that if the strategic action objectives are sustainable and the strategic action is internally

Table 6.1 *Possible list of SEA objectives for land use plans*

SEA theme	Possible SEA objectives (adapt to regional/local circumstances: delete, add to, refine)
Environmental	
Water and soil	• limit water pollution to levels that do not damage natural systems
	• maintain water abstraction, run-off and recharge within carrying capacity (including future capacity)
	• reduce contamination, and safeguard soil quality and quantity
	• minimize waste, then re-use or recover it through recycling, composting or energy recovery
	• maintain and restore key ecological processes (eg hydrology, water quality, coastal processes)
Air	• limit air pollution to levels that do not damage natural systems
	• reduce the need to travel
Climatic factors	• reduce greenhouse gas emissions
	• reduce vulnerability to the effects of climate change, eg flooding, disruption to travel by extreme weather, etc
Biodiversity, fauna and flora	• avoid damage to designated wildlife sites and protected species
	• maintain biodiversity, avoiding irreversible losses
	• restore the full range of characteristic habitats and species to viable levels
	• ensure the sustainable management of key wildlife sites and the ecological processes on which they depend
	• provide opportunities for people to come into contact with and appreciate wildlife and wild places
Social	
Population and human health	• protect and enhance human health
	• reduce and prevent crime, reduce fear of crime
	• decrease noise and vibration
Social inclusiveness*	• *improve access to skills and knowledge*
	• *make opportunities for culture, leisure and recreation readily available to all*
	• *redress inequalities related to, for instance: age, gender, disability, race and faith, deprivation (including lack of access to car), regions and localities (including rural/urban)*
Cultural heritage and landscape	• preserve historic buildings, archaeological sites, and other culturally important features
	• create places, spaces and buildings that work well, wear well and look well
	• enhance countryside and townscape character

	• value and protect diversity and local distinctiveness
	• improve the quantity and quality of publicly accessible open space
Economic	
*Economic development**	• *give access to satisfying and rewarding work, reduce unemployment*
	• *increase investment in people, equipment, infrastructure and other assets*
	• *increase the efficiency of transport and economic activities*
Other	• enhance other issues not discussed above, or reduce their negative effects

Note: * These objectives go beyond the remit of the SEA Directive and broaden it out into sustainability assessment.

Source: adapted from ODPM (2002)

coherent, then the whole strategic action is sustainable: essentially it conflates the objectives of the SEA and the strategic action. The 'baseline-led' approach tries to solve today's problems; the 'objectives-led' approach tries to achieve tomorrow's vision. The two approaches can thus be seen as complementary rather than conflicting. However, they do involve different emphases and techniques which must be taken into account when deciding how to carry out SEA. Table 6.3 summarizes the advantages and disadvantages of the two approaches.

What you measure and what you care about should be mutually dependent: any data collection exercise involves a judgement (at least implicitly) about which issues matter. But these judgements, in turn, rest on (more or less complete and reliable) information about the environment/sustainability. This suggests that the difference between 'objectives-led' and 'baseline-led' may be more symbolic than actual. However 'baseline-led' approaches must acknowledge that the choice of what to measure is not a neutral, technical issue, but one that implies or presupposes judgements about what matters; and 'objectives-led' approaches must be careful to go beyond a mere test of internal compatibility.

Things to think about when establishing SEA objectives and indicators

Developing SEA objectives and indicators is a complex task because of the many things that they should do and mistakes they should avoid. Later in this section, the issue of whether SEA should focus on the environment or sustainability is discussed. A list is presented here of what SEA objectives and indicators should do.

Table 6.2 *Objectives and indicators used to test alternative UK policies for farming and food*

SEA objectives	SEA indicators
1. Produce safe, healthy food and non-food products; make a healthy, nutritious and enjoyable diet available and affordable to everyone	• food security, eg short chain between producer and consumer • food health and safety • food affordability • non-food products
2. Enable viable livelihoods to be made from sustainable land management	• number and security of jobs in rural areas • value-added processing near producers • tourism • international competitiveness of UK farming sector
3. Provide environmental improvements and other benefits	• access to countryside, recreation • landscape • public value placed on benefits provided by farming
4. Minimize the total public funding needed	• opportunity cost of rural policies, eg subsidies
5. Support the vitality of rural economies and the diversity of rural culture	• economic autonomy/control by farmers/rural residents • education and training of rural workforce • vitality of rural communities, age balance • ability to sustain services, access to services • quality and affordability of housing • deprivation • (diversity of) rural traditions/cultures, diversity
6. Operate within biophysical constraints and conform to other environmental limits	• energy balance – energy produced (biomass, windfarm etc) minus energy used • transport and traffic • energy used per food unit produced/transported/consumed • biodiversity • populations of rare species
7. Sustain the resource available for growing food	• water quality and quantity • soil quality and quantity • waste arisings and management • air pollution, odours, nuisance, acidification • genetic impacts

8. Achieve high standards of animal health and welfare	• animal health and welfare
9. Allow use of undeveloped land for development that genuinely meets human needs	• development on previously developed land
10. Be resilient to future changes	• eg to climate/flooding/drought, subsidies, petrol prices, availability of resources from abroad
11. Distributional impacts: who wins, who loses	• farming sub-sectors: pig and poultry, dairy, beef and sheep, arable, horticulture • farm sizes/types: family farm, agri-business, 'alternative lifestyle' • farm tenure: owner, tenant • other rural dwellers • recreational: walkers/cyclists/horse riders, drivers, hunters, fishermen, foreign tourists, others • consumers (choice, empowerment, quality, affordability) • other interests: landscape, environment, etc • taxpayers • international: fair access to/from international markets, fair trade on equal terms • animal welfare

Source: adapted from SDC (2001)

SEA objectives and indicators should *focus on outcomes*, not how the outcomes will be achieved ('inputs'); on ends rather than means; on the state of the environment rather than on responses to pressures on it. For instance, they should focus on improving biodiversity or improving access (what is really wanted), rather than, say, establishing wildlife areas or protecting rail corridors (different ways of getting to what is really wanted). The indicators of Tables 6.1 and 6.2 are outcome indicators; in contrast, many of those in Table 5.3 – particularly those for the economy – are input indicators.

The focus on outcomes is not universally popular. Authorities generally find it easier to monitor what they do ('input') than final outcomes. They also like to show that they are making an effort to do environmentally beneficial things even if other factors mean that the effort may not fully achieve the intended outcome. Box 6.2 discusses this in more detail. On the other hand it is the outcomes, not the good intentions, that really matter from an environmental perspective. Furthermore, the only real way to analyse cumulative impacts on the

---

Box 6.1 Relation of SEA objectives to other objectives

Three types of objectives can affect an SEA:

1   *Strategic action objectives* are those objectives adopted for the strategic action in question. They are generally separate from SEA objectives, although the development of SEA objectives may provide inspiration for making the strategic action objectives more environmentally friendly or sustainable. Unless a strategic action is purely conservationist, its objectives will also take account of economic and social considerations.
2   *External objectives* are those other existing objectives to which decision-makers must pay heed independently from the SEA process. They may be environmental, but they can also include economic or social objectives, for instance the need to build a given number of houses or provide a given amount of aggregates.
3   *SEA objectives* provide a methodological 'yardstick' against which the environmental and sustainability effects of the strategic action can be tested. SEA objectives will often overlap with strategic action objectives, although they may go beyond what is achievable solely through the strategic action; they will also often be 'inherited' from environmental protection objectives, although they may also include additional (often more locally focused) objectives.

Source: ODPM (2002)

---

environment is to consider the environmental outcome of multiple inputs.

SEA objectives and indicators should *say what they mean*, and not be able to be manipulated. For instance, in a laudable attempt to improve the quality of health care, the UK government set targets for reducing the average wait for operations. This has resulted, in addition to some genuine improvements, in some patients 'disappearing' from lists, and in others being made to wait longer before being referred to consultants, since the clock only starts ticking once a patient has been referred. Similarly, research has suggested that GDP (gross domestic product), which has traditionally been used as an unofficial political proxy for quality of life, is far from appropriate for this (see Box 6.3).

SEA objectives and indicators should *be of the appropriate scale*. In most situations it makes no sense to use national-level data as an indicator for local-level trends or vice versa. Some issues may be more important at one scale than another: at the national level, for instance, noise is likely to be less important than greenhouse gas emissions. As such, any indicative lists of objectives and criteria must be checked and adapted to the strategic action in question: local objectives may need to be added to reflect local-level circumstances; objectives that are irrelevant to the area may be deleted; and more detailed objectives may be added.

Table 6.3 *Advantages and disadvantages of the baseline-led v. objectives-led approach*

	Advantages	Disadvantages
Baseline-led	• rigorous: acts as an environmental/sustainability 'yardstick' • focuses on identifying environmental/sustainability problems • makes it easier to identify cumulative impacts	• acts as a 'test' rather than as a method of integrating sustainability in decision-making • likely to make SEAs very varied
Objectives-led	• aims to fully integrate sustainability considerations in decision-making • could reduce the baseline data needed by enabling data not relevant to the objectives to be ignored	• has the potential to be a mere test of internal compatibility rather than ensuring that the strategic action is sustainable • economic indicators may dominate; objectives don't necessarily relate to, or take on board, environmental constraints

The amount of data available at different scales may vary considerably. For instance, in the UK considerable environmental data are available at the national and county levels, less at the regional level (between national and county), and relatively little at the district and ward levels (under county). Different authorities may refer to slightly different boundaries: for instance local authority boundaries may not be the same as the river catchment boundaries used for water management plans. Any inconsistencies need to be clearly stated in the SEA report.

SEA objectives and indicators should *already be available* where possible. For the sake of consistency and efficiency, existing objectives and indicators – those used for other strategic actions and other assessment systems – should be used where possible, as long as they meet the other criteria. Existing monitoring systems and data should also be used to provide information for SEA where possible.

SEA objectives and indicators should *be needed* and should not duplicate or overlap with others. Obviously they should, at minimum, reflect legal requirements. Experience suggests that between 12 and 30 objectives are normally enough to cover the range of topics needed for SEA and to keep the process efficient and manageable.

SEA objectives and indicators should ideally *be compatible with each other*. In practice, there may well be tensions between objectives that cannot be resolved, for instance between economic development and

Box 6.2 Input v. outcome indicators: An example

In the UK, the transport sector accounts for most carbon dioxide emissions and almost half of nitrogen oxide emissions, and is the only sector in which carbon dioxide emissions are growing. More than 3000 deaths occur each year on UK roads. In 1998 the government set a target of reducing traffic growth, with an absolute reduction where environmental damage is greatest. It has also set a target of reducing CO_2 emissions by 12.5 per cent from 1990 to 2008/2012 (Department of Environment, Food and Rural Affairs (DEFRA), 2001; DETR, 1998; Department for Transport (DfT), 2002).

Since then local authorities have consistently established policies to try to reduce traffic-related air pollution and accidents, for instance by establishing land use policies on siting new housing near services and jobs, converting units over shops into housing, and promoting home-based working. Many local authorities have also converted their vehicle fleets to low-emission or alternative fuels (LPG, electric) to help reduce vehicle emissions. However, despite these very laudable actions, traffic levels in England increased by 19 per cent between 1990 and 2000 (DETR, 2001).

Figure 6.2 gives an indication of why the link between local authority input and environmental outcomes is so tenuous. Each outcome – reduced accidents and emissions – is affected by such a wide range of inputs, each with multiple possible pathways before it achieves the outcome, that a single input becomes meaningless. In particular, individuals' actions are notoriously difficult to influence and manage centrally.

environmental protection. A compatibility assessment (see Appendix C) can help to identify these tensions. Personally I feel that conflicting objectives should be modified to make them compatible, but others argue that the role of SEA is to make conflicts explicit, not to try to resolve them.

Should the SEA focus on the environment or sustainability?

The question of whether SEA should be limited to environmental issues or broadened out to include the full range of sustainability issues is a key early question in the establishment of objectives and indicators. Unfortunately it is also a particularly complex one. What sustainable development is and how to assess whether something is 'sustainable' are still contested questions; and sustainable development has come to prominence as a policy objective at the same time as SEA has evolved, so cognition of sustainability issues in SEA is patchy and inconsistent.

The SEA Directive and Protocol themselves are ambivalent about this issue. Both aim to provide for a high level of protection of the environment 'with a view to promoting sustainable development' (Directive) or 'to further sustainable development' (Protocol). In other words, they imply that:

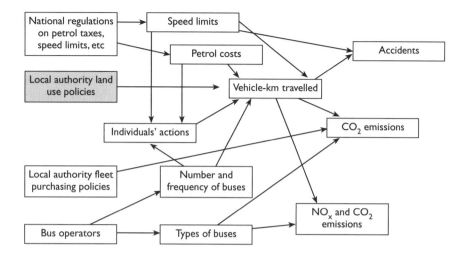

Figure 6.2 *Simple example of the tenuous links between local authority inputs and final environmental outcomes*

- environmental protection and sustainable development are both policy goals – but distinct ones;
- integrating the environment into strategic actions will promote sustainable development; and
- environmental assessment (not sustainability assessment) is a good way to do this.

But is this funny halfway position the best one? There are good arguments on both sides. The environmental ones are as follows.

First, many requirements for environmental assessment (including the SEA Directive and Protocol) were prompted by concerns that environmental consequences of decisions are being given insufficient weight compared to social ones, and particularly to the economic ones which arguably dominate policy. If the point of environmental assessment is to redress this balance, then expanding it to include social and economic elements would be both unnecessary and self-defeating.

Second, sustainability assessment increases the risk that, beneath the comforting rhetoric of integration and 'joining up', environmental concerns continue to be marginalized because economic interests continue to have the institutional power. By keeping environmental arguments separate, a clear environmental case can be made and environmental constraints clearly stated, so it will at least be clear if they are set aside.

Third, environmental assessment depends on evidence about the physical world, even if the evidence that should be collected and how it is interpreted are matters of judgement, and even if, in practice, there are gaps and uncertainties in the data that have to be filled by further

Box 6.3 Index of Sustainable Economic Welfare as an indicator of quality of life

Do you feel that quality of life has gone up or down since the 1950s? Many people feel that it has gone up, but not in all ways: we have more material possessions and greater possibilities for travel, and we have generally become more accepting of religious and cultural diversity. On the other hand, crime and stress are higher, traffic levels are worse, there are greater inequalities between rich and poor, and the world is a busier, more crowded place.

GDP has traditionally been used as an indicator of quality of life, and has risen steadily in most countries since the 1950s. But GDP is a blunt instrument which does not account for many of the issues raised above. It does not reflect the many situations where GDP grows but quality of life goes down, or where quality of life grows without a commensurate increase in GDP. Accidents are an example of the first: they are clearly bad for quality of life, but are excellent for GDP since they provide employment for, eg, health professionals, insurance agents and car mechanics. Growing your own vegetables and taking care of children at home (as opposed to sending them to a childminder) are examples of the latter: they do not increase GDP but do increase quality of life. Can a more sensitive indicator for quality of life be found than GDP?

Since the early 1970s, different researchers have attempted to describe quality of life as GDP with adjustments made for aspects such as those described above. The Index of Sustainable Economic Welfare (ISEW) was pioneered in the USA (Daly and Cobb, 1989; Cobb and Cobb, 1994) and subsequently developed for other countries (Jackson and Marks, 1994). The ISEW adjusts GDP to:

- take out spending to offset social and environmental costs (eg accidents, pollution);
- account for longer-term environmental damage and depreciation of natural capital (eg reduction of fish stocks);
- reflect inequalities in the distribution of income since the same amount of money is worth more to a poor person than to a rich one; and
- include a value for household labour.

Figure 6.3 shows the results for the UK. When these adjustments are taken into account over time, the results are much more in line with our intuitive feel for changes in quality of life. After a steady rise to the mid 1970s (albeit slower than the rise in GDP), the UK ISEW started levelling off and then falling. Recently, the ISEW has declined by about 1 per cent per year, compared to an increase in GDP of about 1 per cent per year. The key factors contributing to this decline were environmental degradation and income inequality.

The lesson for SEA is that one needs to be very careful which indicators one chooses. In this case, GDP is only one aspect of quality of life.

Source: based on Mayo et al (1997)

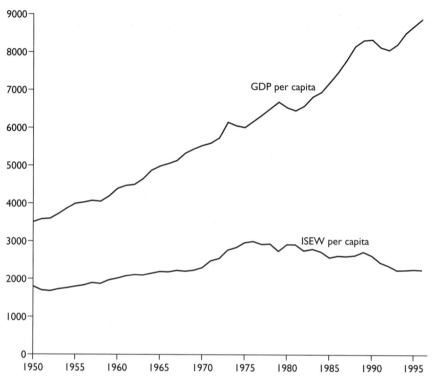

Source: Friends of the Earth and New Economics Foundation (2003)

Figure 6.3 *Index of Sustainable Economic Welfare for the UK*

judgement. Economic assessment can also use ostensibly 'objective' data, despite debate about how well economic indicators measure quality of life (see Box 6.3). However for the non-economic aspects of quality of life, the question of 'evidence' is elusive: measuring issues such as contentment, security and quality of social life is notoriously difficult. So sustainability assessment would be trying to compare apples and oranges, which might be better analysed separately.

The sustainability arguments refer back to the fundamental reasons why we value the environment. They go as follows.

Sustainable development is an anthropocentric concept – that is, it puts human interests first. The classic Brundtland definition, 'development which meets the needs of the present without compromising the ability of future generations to meet their own needs' (World Commission on Environment and Development (WCED), 1987), does not even mention the environment. According to this definition, sustainable development has things to say about the environment because, and only because, the way that humans are currently treating it in order to meet some of the 'needs of the present', notably through economic production and consumption, is interfering with other 'needs of the present' such as healthy and pleasant living conditions (especially for poorer people and countries), and jeopardizing the ability of future generations to meet basic needs such as water, food and land tolerably free from floods, droughts and other climatic disasters.

Another widely accepted definition of sustainable development is 'improving the quality of life within the carrying capacity of supporting ecosystems' (International Union for the Conservation of Nature (IUCN), 1991). This does make explicit reference to one aspect of the environment, but it is the instrumental one of avoiding breaches of carrying capacities because they could undermine the future quality of (human) life. This does not exclude concern for other aspects of the environment, but they would have to come under the 'quality of life' part of the definition, not the 'carrying capacities' one.

In contrast, the SEA Directive's and Protocol's phrase 'protection of the environment' implies a moral aim to protect the external world for its own sake – an ecocentric view. This begs the question of precisely what should be protected, which in turn begs the question of what constitutes 'damage'. Every time a human being eats, breathes or walks across a lawn they are altering the environment – so how do we decide which alterations the environment should be protected from? The environment has never been in a state of equilibrium: land masses form and reform, mountains are created and erode, species evolve and become extinct. So from an earth-centred perspective, it is hard to say why recent human impacts on the environment should be wrong when the same kinds of impacts have happened throughout time.

The environment matters because it affects human well-being. For example, climate change is important not because it is wrong or unnatural, but because the rapid and extreme climate change which human greenhouse gas emissions are causing is likely to lead to vast human suffering (eg loss of low land, changes in crop patterns). Likewise, maintenance of biodiversity does not matter because every species has a right to live forever: species are always emerging and dying out. It matters because humans benefit from the range of useful products, the resilience, and the delight of exquisite variety and natural beauty that diversity provides. In other words, the apparently ecocentric idea of 'protection of the environment' rapidly bring us back to anthropocentric judgements about what matters for human quality of life. There is no list of environmental imperatives that can be 'read off' purely from science without the intervention of any normative judgements about what matters to humankind.

If this is so (and many environmentalists and philosophers would hotly dispute it) there are interesting consequences for SEA. If the basis of even apparently 'environmental' objectives is human well-being, there is no profound difference in principle between assessing the effects of a strategic action on the environment, and assessing its effects on a wider range of outcomes that matter for human well-being. It follows that environmental assessment (and, using the same argument, economic assessment) should be understood simply as a subset of sustainability assessment. 'Protection of the environment' is not a separate policy goal from sustainable development, as the SEA Directive and Protocol imply, but must be understood as a contributor to or sub-goal of it.

Separating social, economic and environmental issues into assessment ghettoes can also make it harder to integrate environmental issues in decision-making, as they come to be seen as a special interest subject which constrains other aspirations. Such a separation also makes it harder to have transparent decisions and to identify win–win–win solutions that integrate all three.

Cross-cutting approaches

The fact that sustainability objectives often transcend the straightforward 'addition' of environmental plus social plus economic objectives may help to provide a solution to this dilemma. Some approaches to development – for instance increasing accessibility, providing for local needs locally, and redressing social inequalities – are genuinely better environmentally, socially and economically. The Local Government Management Board's (1994) sustainability themes, shown in Box 6.4, are an example of where all three are integrated. These themes have been used as a basis for many SEA objectives and indicators, including those in Table 6.1.

A key cross-cutting component of sustainability is *equity*, both intra-generational (between groups of people who are currently alive) and inter-generational (between today's generations and future ones). The concept of equity brings together environmental (future generations enjoying the same environmental benefits as current ones) and economic (improved access and skills, reduced dependence, etc) as well as social issues.

Equity implies that no group should be affected unfairly, particularly by cumulative impacts. Examples of inequity are unequal access to transport or hospital services, fuel poverty (where poor people pay a disproportionate part of their income on keeping warm) and water conflict. Many forms of development have a particularly strong effect on groups that are already disadvantaged. For instance in the UK:

Most of the negative effects of increased traffic and car use most heavily impact on those same groups that benefit least from the present transport system... As well as the disproportionate impact of traffic accidents on children and pensioners, higher numbers of lower socio-economic groups

---

Box 6.4 Local Government Management Board sustainability themes

1   Resources are used efficiently and waste is minimized by closing cycles.
2   Pollution is limited to levels which natural systems can cope with and without damage.
3   The diversity of nature is valued and protected.
4   Where possible, local needs are met locally.
5   Everyone has access to good food, water, shelter and fuel at reasonable cost.
6   Everyone has the opportunity to undertake satisfying work in a diverse economy.
7   The value of unpaid work is recognized, whilst payments for work are fair and fairly distributed.
8   Peoples' good health is protected by creating safe, clean, pleasant environments and health services which emphasize prevention of illness as well as proper care for the sick.
9   Access to facilities, services, goods and other people is not achieved at the expense of the environment or limited to those with cars.
10 People live without fear of personal violence from crime or persecution because of their personal beliefs, race, gender or sexuality.
11 Everyone has access to the skills, knowledge and information needed to enable them to play a full part in society.
12 All sections of the community are empowered to participate in decision-making. Opportunities for culture, leisure and recreation are readily available to all.
13 Places, spaces and objects combine meaning and beauty with utility. Settlements are 'human' in scale and form. Diversity and local distinctiveness are valued and protected.

Source: Local Government Management Board (LGMB) (1994)

---

are killed or injured on the road as a consequence of greater exposure to risk. Low income groups are more likely to live on or near main roads; they are more likely to walk or cycle, while the lack of gardens means children playing near busy main roads ... lower income households tend to bear a greater share of external accident risk, air pollution and noise costs (Lucas and Simpson, 2000).

An underlying objective of any strategic action should be to help redress – or at least not exacerbate – any existing imbalances in equity. SEA should thus ask who would win and lose under the strategic action, focusing on those groups who might be particularly disadvantaged. This depends on 1) the strategic action in question, and 2) which groups are already disadvantaged. For instance a policy on land use and transport may focus particularly on differential impacts on urban

v. rural dwellers, small v. larger businesses, or people who own v. do not own a car. An SEA for the closure of military bases could focus on whether the closures are in areas of deprivation or not. In some countries, indices of deprivation already exist, along with lists/maps showing areas of relative deprivation: this simplifies the identification of currently disadvantaged groups.

The bottom of Table 6.2 shows an example of how equity issues can be integrated in SEA. It includes criteria on who would win and lose under different UK policies on farming and food, including different farming sub-sectors, farm sizes and types; farmer owners v. tenant farmers; farmers in other countries; non-farmers; and animals. An analysis of 16 policies (SDC, 2001) suggested that the promotion of liberalization and globalization generally benefits larger agri-businesses; a move to local foods benefits those areas of the country that can diversify more easily; many agri-environment schemes are more likely to be taken up by, and benefit, owners rather than tenants of farms; and promotion of local foods would mean that consumers would probably pay more but animal welfare might be higher. Different regions may be affected differently: for instance farms in the east of England are generally large-scale arable agri-businesses, whereas those in the south-west are small-scale family-owned sheep farms; so the same policy might affect them quite differently. Box 6.5 gives another example of equity assessment.

Another cross-cutting aspect of sustainability is *resilience*, or lack of vulnerability. A strategic action should be able to withstand and counter problems such as changes in climate, petrol prices, subsidies and currency exchange rates; and disease, war and terrorism. Resilience is one way of operationalizing long-term thinking and the precautionary principle.

For instance, approaches to food and farming that enhance resilience are those that reduce:

- the need to travel – and thus dependence on petrol and the rapid spread of diseases – through more farmer's markets, shorter supply chains, fewer animal movements, more local abattoirs;
- the likelihood of, and vulnerability to, flood and droughts by paying farmers for flood control and carbon banks ('trees'), and the managed retreat of coastlines;
- the likelihood of disease through better food standards, less reliance on animal drugs and supplements (leading, over time, to increased resilience in the animal stocks), greater variety of crops, better maintenance of the soil resource and decreased application of herbicides, pesticides and fertilizers;
- the risk of farmers facing economic failure by promoting a wider variety of income streams for farmers so that any effects on one commodity are buffered by its relatively small market share,

---

Box 6.5 Example of equity assessment: Northern Ireland policy on the location of civil service jobs

Section 75 of the Northern Ireland Act 1998 requires that:

> A public authority shall ... have due regard to the need to promote equality of opportunity between:
> - persons of different religious belief, political opinion, racial group, age, marital status or sexual orientation;
> - men and women generally;
> - persons with a disability and persons without; and
> - persons with dependants and persons without.
>
> [It shall also] have regard to the desirability of promoting good relations between persons of different religious belief, political opinion or racial groups.

This requirement was applied to the Department of Finance and Personnel's (2002) evolving policy on the location of civil service jobs. The department's equality impact assessment, which was carried out in discussion with a wide range of local authorities, trade unions, commissions on fair employment and human rights and others, noted that the current location of civil service jobs is broadly neutral across the categories of Section 75. However, it identified a range of possible and perceived equality issues that could affect any change in location of jobs, including:

- lobbying for jobs tied to local economic benefits;
- the need to relocate some jobs to more 'religion-neutral' and accessible working environments;
- the need – in the past at least – to relocate jobs from the Greater Belfast Area to areas of Northern Ireland which have a higher representation of one section of the community compared to the other, primarily as a way of encouraging members of the Roman Catholic section of the community to apply for civil service jobs;
- the possibility of using new technologies and homeworking to benefit women and people with a disability; and
- the possibility of revitalizing towns, particularly Omagh and Strabane, if jobs were moved outside Belfast.

The policy will be developed to take these issues into consideration.

---

reducing subsidies, use of the same amount of subsidies for a wider range of schemes, promoting value added close to source (eg processing and packaging of crops), and greater genetic diversity; and
- the likelihood of political instability by promoting fair trade, reducing inequitable subsidy schemes, and reducing reliance on (and thus conflict over) non-renewable resources (SDC, 2001).

Collecting and documenting baseline data

Once the SEA objectives and indicators have been agreed, data on the baseline environment should be collected using the indicators as a framework. The baseline environment is the current environment and the likely future environment in the absence of the strategic action. Data sources on the baseline environment include websites and reports from governments at all levels (international to local), universities, non-government organizations, etc; old maps which can show trends in land use; surveys of local residents; and information known by experts but not formally recorded.

In many cases data about the baseline environment will be 'hard' quantitative data based on monitoring information. In other cases it will be 'soft' qualitative and/or perceived data. Box 6.6 shows part of a baseline analysis for Taunton, a town in the county of Somerset in South West England. It incorporates 'hard' data in the beginning; the 'soft' views of the Taunton Vision Commission (local stakeholders who met regularly to identify a future 'vision' for Taunton) in the middle; and targets at the end. The entire baseline was, in this case, compiled in six person-days, based on a review of relevant websites plus reports from the Vision Commission.

Tables 6.4 and 4.1 use a very different approach to document the baseline. Instead of a verbal description, they use a matrix that shows the current environmental state, comparative data from other authorities, any targets that exist for that topic, and trends in the data. This allows much data to be presented in a very condensed format, can help to constrain the amount of data collected, and clearly identifies data gaps that may need monitoring in the future. Experience suggests that, where the baseline data already exist and do not need to be collected anew, then it takes between four and 20 person-days to fill in such a table.

The disadvantage is that, in many cases, the right data will not be available. There are several possible problems.

There may not be *any* data about the objective, particularly if the objective refers to perceptual or social issues. For instance, little is known about the average number of years of healthy life lived by UK residents, or about whether people feel that they have enough access to open space. In such a case it might be possible to make assumptions based on other data, for instance on average years of life rather than healthy life, or average distance to open space rather than perceptions about adequacy of access to open space. But this opens up the possibility of slowly sliding into a situation where inappropriate indicators are used (like GDP has been used as an indicator for quality of life; see Box 6.3).

The data may not be at the right scale: they may be at the national rather than local level or vice versa. In such a situation it may be

Box 6.6 Part of a baseline analysis: Taunton's cultural heritage

Built heritage
Somerset has a rich built heritage, including 11,500 listed buildings. Around 60 such buildings are currently considered to be in a poor state of repair and 'at risk'. From analysis of archaeological and historic evidence, Somerset County Council has identified outstanding Heritage Settlements, to be given priority for designation and review of Conservation Areas, and for protection and enhancement of their character. In Taunton Deane district they include Bishops Lydeard, Milverton, North Curry, Taunton, Wellington and Wiveliscombe.

Facilities
Less than half of Somerset's villages have a general store/food shop.

Cultural amenities
The 'Taunton Vision' Commission has suggested that Taunton Deane district needs to develop an identity for itself, possibly through culture by redeveloping the Museum, Archives and Art Gallery. Others have suggested that the key to improving cultural provision lies in increasing the capacity of local auditoria, which are perceived as not being large enough to hold a large concert or operatic event. However, Taunton is also perceived as having a lack of bed space and parking which could hamper such proposals unless addressed as a priority... Any [proposal for improving cultural amenities] should ensure that it is an asset to the entire community, and not just the upper/middle classes. Other cultural amenities include the Somerset County Cricket Club which provides a significant boost to the local economy (£3 million per year) and has been on site since 1875, giving Taunton a positive sporting and cultural image.

Social cohesion
Taunton's public places and spaces are perceived to reflect white, middle class and older ideas of entertainment, culture, heritage, affordability, etc. There is a need to prioritize public policies which encourage social cohesion and inclusion. Taunton should encourage a wider range of businesses and industries, and develop services and facilities that reflect the diversity of experiences, beliefs and cultures from all ethnic backgrounds.

Somerset County Council's targets for cultural heritage
- All proposals for new built development requiring planning consent should include a completed 'sustainability checklist'.
- A 50 per cent reduction in the number of listed buildings on the 'at risk' register by 2015.
- Every village having access to a community centre/hall for social and educational uses, and, where possible, a village shop by 2015.

Source: Levett-Therivel (2003b)

reasonable to assume, say, that national trends also hold locally, although the underlying assumptions need to be checked carefully. Local data could also be aggregated into regional or national data, although this may not be possible where local-level data are not available in a consistent format (this is a strong argument for nationally agreed indicator lists).

The data may be out of date, or may include only individual 'snapshots' of data rather than several years' worth of trends. This is particularly problematic where the baseline changes rapidly, for instance in areas of rapid urban expansion. In such cases, field surveys or discussions with experts may be needed to check whether the data are worth including at all.

There may well be a welter of detailed but uncoordinated data which needs to be drawn together into an integrated whole. In such a case there is the possibility of bias: who decides which information to use and which to ignore? on what basis?

In all of these cases, it would be worth considering whether data should be collected specifically for the SEA, for instance through field surveys or interviews. Alternatively, particularly for strategic actions that are rewritten on a cyclical basis, it may be worthwhile establishing a monitoring system to collect missing data for the next SEA.

Finally, baseline data collection should be an iterative process, with the results of the baseline data collection helping to refine the SEA objectives, targets and indicators. In particular, any environmental problems identified during the baseline analysis may need more data.

Identifying the future environment in the absence of the strategic action

One cannot assume that the current baseline environment will continue into the future. Existing trends can continue or change. For instance, people may continue to live longer, or else obesity and heart disease may start to reverse the trend. New technologies can clear up existing problems or create new ones, for instance the widespread use of catalytic converters is improving air quality, the masts associated with mobile telephones are a new form of landscape impact, and many effects of genetically modified organisms are not yet understood. Other strategic actions may affect the baseline environment even without the plan: for instance the Water Framework Directive is likely to improve water quality, and congestion charging policies would probably reduce traffic levels even in the absence of any other strategic actions.

Unfortunately, few data sources predict future trends, with population, road traffic and greenhouse gas statistics being some of the few exceptions. On the other hand, it is often possible to predict the future state of the environment based on past trends and/or the judgement of knowledgeable planners. Relevant questions include:

Table 6.4 *Part of a baseline data matrix: Cotswold District Council*

Indicator	Quantified data (for CDC unless noted otherwise)	Comparators and targets	Trend
Development on brownfield sites	55% completions on brownfield land	Average for Glos, high for SW (50%), low nationally (60%); CDC target >50% new housing on brownfield	Above 50% for last 3 years; CDC planners expect this to continue to be good; they are not aware of major changes in policy or developer activities that could cause this to change
Vehicle-kilometres	0% growth 1996–2002	Bucking national trends of increasing traffic. CDC targets: allocated housing within 600 metres of food shop and primary school; developments of >100 houses within 600 metres or with public access to range of services; new major non-residential developments within 600 metres or 45–60 minutes public transport journey of potential users; prevent developments likely to increase traffic through Cirencester	0% growth 1996–2000. Likely to increase, based on national trends
Accidents	Glos CC: 393 in 2001		360 casualties average 1994–8, 353 in 1999, 386 in 2000. Overall accident record getting worse, but from a low base. Expected increases in vehicle–kilometres are likely to exacerbate this trend
Population	74,000 in 1991 18.3% below age 16; 23.1% over pensionable age; 40% of households have at least one pensioner	Glos 529,000 in 1991, 568,000 in 2001, projected 591,000 in 2011 19.5%, 19.9% and 34.9% in Glos. respectively	UK population census expects Glos to grow to approx. 587,000 by 2021. Out-migration of young people and existing high level of one-person households suggests that future households will increase more slowly
Unemployment	1.2% unemployment	Low compared with 2.1% Glos; 5.2% nationally CDC target: maintain supply of employment land, ensure no net loss of employment land/allocations	Labour supply set to grow by 7000 by 2011; but labour demand growing faster still according to economic projections

Note: Cotswold District Council (CDC) is a local authority in the county of Gloucestershire (Glos) in South West England (SW). Some of the indicators are input rather than outcome indicators.

- What is the current trend?
- Is this likely to change due to:
  - social/lifestyle patterns (eg breakdown of families, increased wealth)?
  - economic circumstances (eg recession)?
  - environmental circumstances (eg depletion of fish stocks, global warming)?
- Are we getting near capacity or a breaking point on any of these, and would that cause a sharp change?
- Will new technology, or the spread of existing technology affect the baseline?
- Will other strategic actions affect the baseline?

Table 6.4 shows, in the final column, an example of expectations for the future environmental state for Cotswold District Council, with an explanation of why these trends are assumed.

The *reversibility* (or not) of trends is also important. Examples of irreversible trends include loss of historic features or landscapes, species extinction, the build-up of persistent pollutants (eg some radioactive materials) and loss of productive land to hard development.

Setting targets (where appropriate)

Ideally, SEA indicators should be accompanied by targets and/or thresholds, so that one can get a feel for whether current and likely future environmental conditions are good or problematic. Targets and thresholds are particularly important when cumulative impacts are assessed (see Chapter 8).

A *threshold* is a level which should not be exceeded: a limit, a boundary. Going beyond a threshold should trigger some exceptional remedial action, such as traffic bans, increased insurance payments, children sent home from school or special conservation measures.

A target is a desirable level. *'Pragmatic' targets* are often set by policy makers on the basis of some judgement that they are realistically attainable or politically acceptable. They do not necessarily bear any relationship to environmental limits. For example, the pragmatic greenhouse gas reduction targets of about 5–20 per cent, negotiated at Kyoto, are only a small first step towards the much higher levels needed for climate security. The UK's 25 per cent recycling target for domestic waste was the most ambitious number that was judged plausible, but has no clear basis in science or economics. Pragmatic targets can help to secure public support and help to get things moving in the right direction without having to wait for agreement on more daunting or contentious targets.

'*Ideal*' *or* '*aspirational*' *targets*, instead, specify the desired state of affairs regardless of the practicalities of reaching them. The ideal levels of greenhouse gas reduction would be 60 per cent or higher. The ideal level of crime is zero. The ideal level of rare species and habitats might be population levels and extents that keep them well clear of any significant risk of extinction (Countryside Agency et al, 2002).

Again, a distinction needs to be drawn between input and outcome targets. There are many different ways to, for instance, reduce global CO_2 levels (the outcome): plant trees, walk instead of drive a car, use renewable energy, etc (the inputs). Setting and achieving input targets can help to achieve the outcome target, but may not necessarily do so, and it can also limit the efficiency with which the outcome target is achieved.

Some targets are *quantitative*, and specify a definite goal to be achieved. Table 6.5 shows some of these. However, authorities are often worried about setting quantitative outcome targets for fear that they will not be achieved. As such, targets are often *directional*: they specify the direction of change rather than any quantified end value. Examples are to 'increase' the proportion of the population that lives within 200 metres of a park, or 'reduce' traffic levels.

In many countries, targets are set by the national, regional and/or local government. These are generally pragmatic rather than ideal, and are often based on technical appraisal (eg 'safe' levels of pollution). Other legally mandated thresholds already exist in the form of pollution standards, safety regulations, and other legislation. Non- or quasi-governmental organizations may also have set targets, for instance Biodiversity Action Plans or Local Agenda 21 plans. These have political legitimacy and sometimes legislative force, so it is sensible to use them wherever possible and relevant. On the other hand, one can question the reasoning behind some targets, such as the rail target at Table 6.5.

Where experts have not set formal targets, local residents can help to determine them. Often a gut reaction to a simple question about 'is there enough of x' is all that is necessary. Satisfaction or dissatisfaction over (for example) access to open space, quality of shopping facilities, jobs for particular social groups, and transport to particular places at particular times all give a feel for thresholds and targets (Countryside Agency et al, 2002).

Target setting is always a matter of judgement and choice: targets are points on a continuum. Even where some level is determined 'scientifically', the choice to make it a policy target is political. For instance, greenhouse gas reduction targets depend on how much climate change is regarded as acceptable: this is a value judgement. But who makes these judgements and on what basis? how ambitious should they be? how can we prevent minimum standards being treated

Table 6.5 *Examples of UK targets*

Theme	UK target	Comments	Source
Energy use in buildings, renewable energy production	Reduce emission of greenhouse gases for the UK by 12.5% between 1990 and 2008/2012	Pragmatic, quantitative	DETR, 2001
	Reduce emissions of carbon dioxide worldwide by 60–70% to stabilize atmospheric concentrations of CO_2 at their current levels	Aspirational, quantitative	Hadley Centre, 2003
Accessibility/ transport	Reduce rate of road traffic growth, with an absolute reduction where environmental damage is greatest	Pragmatic, directional (weakened from original target of reducing road traffic)	DETR, 2001
	Increase the number of rail passenger miles in Great Britain by 15% between 1997/8 and 2001/2	Pragmatic, quantitative (dropped); unclear why this is a target, as increasing rail passengers does not necessarily lead to a reduction in road traffic	DETR, 2001
	Increase the proportion of travel by non-car modes	Pragmatic, directional	Bedfordshire, 1995
Biodiversity/ wildlife	Reverse the long-term decline in populations of woodland and farmland birds	Pragmatic, directional	DETR, 2001
	Prevent deterioration of Natura 2000 sites	Threshold, directional	EC Birds and Habitats Directives

as targets (for instance developers using the minimum levels of energy efficiency set out in building regulations as the standard they build to)? how should targets at different spatial scales be related (for example, how should national greenhouse gas emission targets be reflected in a local plan, or in a housing development)? These issues could easily take another book of this size to discuss. So I will stop here, at the moment of maximum confusion, and move on to the identification of environmental problems.

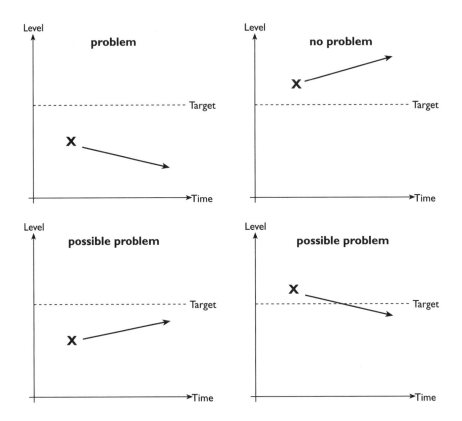

Source: adapted from Countryside Agency et al (2002)

Figure 6.4 *Problem identification through analysis of trends and targets*

Identifying environmental problems

The current and likely future environmental baseline could be anywhere in comparison with the targets/thresholds: better than the target (eg no development is taking place in flood risk areas), worse than the threshold (eg most development is in flood risk areas), or in between. Environmental problems arise where there is conflict between current conditions and ideal targets. Where things are already worse than target and expected to get worse, this is clearly a problem. Where things are fine and expected to stay fine, it is not. The rest are potential problems, and probably worth monitoring to ensure that they do not evolve into problems. Figure 6.4 illustrates this concept.

   This is the theory anyway. For many issues, however, information about trends and/or targets does not exist. Furthermore, the problems identified through a process such as that shown in Figure 6.4 may not correspond to those that the decision-makers or the public would identify: they may be too bitty, too constrained by which data are available, or too biased by the initial choice of indicators. In all cases, decision-makers should ask themselves – and possibly the public – what *they* think the key environmental problems are. This may confirm the findings of the baseline study, or may raise additional issues that should be investigated in the baseline analysis.

It may be useful to map those problems that have a spatial element, for instance contaminated land, floodplains, non-tranquil areas, areas prone to landslides, areas with poor public transport access, accident sites on roads, areas poorly provided with open space, or vacant buildings. This could help to identify areas that are particularly sensitive, that are already affected by multiple constraints, or that should be promoted for future development.

Managing for constraints

The current status and future trend of an environmental component relative to its target help to determine how that issue should be managed, and help to suggest mitigation measures. For instance the SEA baseline situation and trend analysis of Table 6.4 identified some problems faced by Cotswold District Council:

- Cotswold District has a very high proportion of older people and a very low proportion of young people. Should the plan actively promote the development of health care facilities and sheltered housing for older people, and affordable housing for health care workers?
- By 2011 it is expected that there will not be enough people to fill jobs in Cotswold District, in part because of the lack of affordable housing for care workers. The majority of the predicted unfilled jobs would be relatively low paid, eg care workers, health workers, emergency services. Should there be a policy for balancing out jobs and housing?
- Accidents – particularly road accidents – are a continuing problem, due in part to the high number of tourists on small rural roads. Should there be more emphasis on reducing (and enforcing) speed limits on roads in the district?

Cotswold District's planners had already considered these issues in their plan-making process prior to the SEA, but the SEA helped to formalize and document their analysis.

Tables 6.6 and 6.7 present a more formal structure for deciding how to manage environmental assets. Note that this is starting to suggest approaches for the mitigation of future impacts.

Table 6.6 *Managing non-replaceable environmental assets or benefits*

Importance of asset	Trend relative to target		
	Doing badly	On target	Doing well
High	Proactively promote improvements as a high priority in all relevant decision-making processes. Highest possible protection	Seek improvements. High protection. Loss only justified by overriding need	Can be affected if strong need and high compensation
Medium	Proactively promote improvements. High protection	Take opportunities for improvement	Not a priority
Low	Seek improvements. Loss must be justified by need	Not a priority	Not a priority

Source: adapted from Countryside Agency et al (2002)

Links to other strategic actions

Strategic actions are almost inevitably constrained by other strategic actions, and in turn constrain yet other strategic actions. As such, it is useful to ask two questions early in the SEA: 1) could other strategic actions have a significant impact or constraint on what this strategic action is trying to do (or alternatively does it support certain objectives of this strategic action)? and 2) does anything in this strategic action have a significant impact or constraint on other strategic actions?

Although these questions are not strictly 'SEA', they are necessary for SEA for several reasons. First, where the other strategic action is primarily environmental or sustainable, it can set targets or thresholds for the SEA. For instance national or international air quality standards can act as environmental tests for the strategic action in question.

Second, the other strategic action may limit what the strategic action in question can achieve, and hence its sustainability. For instance the UK's approach to farming and food production is strongly limited by the Common Agricultural Policy which (in the past at least) has promoted food production to the detriment of more integrated land management. Similarly, World Trade Organisation rules which do not allow countries to discriminate against imports on the basis of the process and production methods used (eg organic, high animal welfare) financially disadvantage and thus discourage those food producers who aim to achieve higher environmental or animal welfare standards. Alternatively, the other strategic action may support the

Table 6.7 *Managing replaceable environmental assets or benefits*

Importance of asset	Trend relative to target		
	Doing badly	On target	Doing well
High	Proactively promote enhancement as a high priority in all relevant decision-making processes. Loss must be substituted at greater than 1:1	Seek improvements. High protection. Loss must be substituted at 1:1 (and preferably higher)	Loss must be justified by need
Medium	Proactively promote enhancement. Loss should be substituted at greater than 1:1	Take opportunities for enhancement. Loss should be substituted at 1:1 (and preferably higher)	Loss should be justified by need
Low	Seek improvements. Loss should be substituted where practicable	Not a priority	Not a priority

Source: adapted from Countryside Agency et al (2002)

strategic action in question. For instance, policies that require local authorities or the military to procure locally grown food for school children, nursing home residents or soldiers would support national government policies on reducing the need to travel and promotion of locally produced foods.

Third, the strategic action in question can promote the sustainability of other strategic actions, or conversely close off sustainable options for those strategic actions. A farming policy that focuses on large-scale production and retailing will lead to pressures for the development of large supermarkets on sites outside town centres, and large distribution depots that rely heavily on an efficient system of road distribution. Historically these developments have made smaller local stores economically unviable, leading to their closure and people having to travel further to buy their food. These cumulative trends put pressures on the road network and support calls for the construction of new (unsustainable) roads. In this example, a strategic action about farming influences retail and transport policy.

How to document links between strategic actions

The traditional way of showing how a higher-tier strategic action affects a lower-tier one is through a table such as Table 6.8. The table shows

Table 6.8 *Part of a compatibility analysis which shows constraints of higher-level strategic actions on a lower-level strategic action*

Strategic action objectives and requirements		How the Hampshire Local Minerals Plan could take the strategic action's requirements on board
EU Habitats Directive and Birds Directive		
EC Directive 92/43/EEC ('Habitats Directive') aims to conserve fauna, flora and natural habitats of EU importance. It establishes a network of protected areas – Natura 2000 – throughout the Community designed to maintain the distribution and abundance of threatened species and habitats, both terrestrial and marine. The Directive complements the EU Directive on the Conservation of Wild Birds...		Ensure that the minerals planning authority is aware of the locations of SPAs and SACs and take these into account during any site selection/area of search work.
If as a result of an application there is 'likely to be a significant effect' on the designated features of the SAC (this could include impacts from activities not within the boundaries of the SAC and the cumulative effect of several separate applications) then the planning authority must obtain an 'appropriate assessment' of the application and its likely effect.		The Plan should also ensure that provision is made for undertaking 'appropriate assessments' where required due to the location of applications.
PPG 1 General Policies and Principles (Feb 1997)		
Para 1 – introduction	Promoting competitiveness whilst protecting the environment and amenity.	Ensure Plan will meet this objective: that an appropriate balance is struck between protecting the environment and ensuring the viability of the industry.
Para 5 – sustainable development	A sustainable planning framework should provide for the nation's need for minerals extraction, while respecting environmental objectives. Conserve the cultural heritage and natural resources taking particular care to safeguard designations of national and international importance.	Helps to set objectives for the MLP.
Para 21 – planning for industry and commerce	It is important that the locational demands of businesses are taken into account in the preparation of development plans.	Ensure MLP considers locational requirements to ensure mineral supply, including infrastructure issues.

Source: Land Use Consultants (2003)

part of a compatibility assessment carried out early in the development of the Hampshire Local Minerals Plan, which analysed how the Plan could be affected by national-level Planning Policy Guidance and Mineral Planning Guidance, the Regional Sustainable Development Framework for the South East, and the EU Habitats and Birds Directives.

Note that the table was prepared early in the decision-making process: the right-hand column is written so as to influence the objectives and structure of the plan. The exercise took about 2–2.5 days to complete using an existing in-house framework. If starting from scratch, and if including all relevant international, national, regional and local strategic actions, it would take far longer (Land Use Consultants, 2003).

Where the strategic action in question is at the same level as other strategic actions – for instance a local land use plan and local transport plan – then a different format is needed for the compatibility analysis. This is discussed at Appendix C.

Dealing with conflicting strategic actions

What happens if two strategic actions conflict? Examples of such conflict include:

- lower-level strategic actions needing, for practical purposes, to be prepared before higher-level ones, and thus constraining the higher-level strategic actions, for instance urgent flood defence works that need to be carried out before an integrated, larger-scale flood management plan can be devised;
- higher-level strategic actions constraining the ability of lower-level strategic actions to be sustainable, for instance national-level strategies on the provision of new housing or airports imposing development on local authorities that make their sustainability targets on land use or air quality impossible to achieve;
- strategic actions at one level being prepared before other plans at the *same* level and thus constraining the subsequent strategic actions;
- overlapping strategic actions that partly duplicate each other, for instance separate plans for flood control, water abstraction and conservation of wetland habitats in the same river catchment; and
- strategic actions constrained by activities in other sectors or the private sphere, for instance transport policy affected by bus company plans.

Box 6.7 gives a brief example of another type of problem, where several higher-level strategic actions conflict, and so set an unclear and potentially unsustainable context for the strategic action in question.

Box 6.7 Example of conflicting and unsustainable strategic actions

An analysis of strategic actions affecting the Newtown (not its real name) Unitary Development Plan (UDP) identified that:

1   the draft Regional Spatial Strategy (RSS), which sets the context for the UDP, proposes an average of 400 net new dwellings per year for Newtown;
2   the city's regeneration strategy, which is also supposed to set the context for the UDP, proposes about 1000 net new dwellings per year;
3   the Regional Sustainable Development Framework has an objective to maintain the total area of green belt; and
4   the Community Strategy aims for 75 per cent of new housing to be on brownfield sites.

The UDP cannot achieve all of them. 1 and 2 are in obvious conflict, as are 1/2 and 3. The first two are probably unsustainable on environmental grounds, and the third possibly on social grounds.

Source: CAG Consultants (2003)

The timing of strategic actions – which precedes the other – is often a problem, particularly where neither strategic action has clear precedence. Indeed an absence of clear hierarchy could lead to an unintended paralysis and inability to change. For instance, assume that a region's economic strategy and its spatial strategy are at the same level. Assume that the economic strategy is written first and includes an unsustainable objective, say increasing GDP by 2 per cent per year. The spatial strategy has to accept this because the economic strategy was written first. The spatial strategy gets adopted complete with the unwanted objective and associated implementation measures. When the time comes to review the economic strategy, even if the economic strategy wanted to abandon the unsustainable objective, it would not be able to do so because it is now in the spatial strategy that has now 'got there first' (Levett-Therivel, 2003a).

In cases of conflicting strategic actions, the general assumption is that higher-level strategic actions 'win' over lower-level ones, but this is not always the case. For instance the higher-level strategic action could be due for replacement, clearly unsustainable, or not have been subject to SEA. In such cases the higher-level (or earlier) strategic actions could be treated not as constraints but as options or scenarios, and queried as being unsustainable. For instance in the example above, the evolving spatial strategy could treat potentially unsustainable targets set by the economic strategy as one of several possible scenarios. But often the best that an SEA can do is to document, not resolve, conflicts.

All of these are not strictly SEA issues, but rather problems already present in decision-making processes which SEA makes more visible and urgent. There are several possible ways forward. Organizations can aim to rationalize their decision-making processes to try to minimize these problems. Integrated Spatial Strategies could help to bring together disparate strategic actions (Royal Commission on Environmental Pollution, 2002). Governments could clarify, in cases of uncertainty, which plan has precedence. SEA may itself help ease some of the problems by encouraging the convergence of strategic actions onto common sustainability objectives.

When to stop collecting information: 'Scoping'

It is perfectly possible to keep collecting baseline data and analysing related strategic actions indefinitely, until the poor researcher becomes a cobweb-ridden skeleton or the plan has gone through multiple cycles of implementation and revision. What is 'enough' baseline data? What are 'enough' related strategic actions? At what point do the costs of collecting the information outweigh the information's benefits?

Early in SEA a decision needs to be taken about the coverage and level of detail of the SEA study. This is the scoping stage. In the SEA Directive, Article 5.2 gives some guidance on scoping, noting that the level of detail should relate to the

> *current knowledge and methods of assessment, the contents and level of detail in the plan or programme, its stage in the decision-making process and the extent to which certain matters are more appropriately assessed at different levels in that process in order to avoid duplication of the assessment* (Article 5.2).

However, this gives little practical assistance to the potential skeleton.

A possible way forward might be to focus on why the information is needed. One needs baseline data in SEA to 1) allow environmental problems to be identified and addressed, 2) provide a baseline against which future monitoring can be carried out, and 3) provide a basis for impact prediction. Any data that do not do this are superfluous, and enough data are needed to allow this to be done. Where, for instance, locational constraints could affect whether *any* project is acceptable, then data on these constraints would be needed; where location is clearly not a constraint, then such data are not necessary.

One needs to analyse links with other strategic actions so as to know what constraints are posed on, and by, the strategic action. The importance of another strategic action for the SEA could thus be tested by using criteria such as whether it is a statutory requirement, whether it has geographical links to the strategic action in question, whether there is stakeholder concern over the issue covered in that strategic action, and how up to date the strategic action is.

Discussions with environmental authorities, required by the SEA Directive (Article 5.4), are likely to be very useful in the scoping process. The reasons for deciding to *not* consider specific issues in the baseline, or specific strategic actions, should be documented.

Conclusions

This is the time for a self-check, based on the quality assurance criteria of Box 4.3:

- Have relevant aspects of the current state of the environment and their likely evolution without the strategic action been described?
- Have environmental characteristics of areas likely to be significantly affected been described in more detail?
- Do the SEA objectives and indicators cover an appropriate range of environmental/sustainability topics?
- Do they integrate environmental, social and economic issues?
- Do they cover equity and resilience?
- Are the SEA objectives and baseline data collection mutually reinforcing?
- Were the methods used to investigate the affected baseline appropriate to the size and complexity of the assessment task?
- Have links between the strategic action and related higher- and lower-tier strategic actions been considered?
- Where strategic actions conflict, have the reasons been clearly documented and have recommendations been made on how to reconcile the strategic actions so as to promote sustainability?
- Were appropriate environmental authorities consulted when deciding on the scope and level of the information which must be included in the SEA report?
- Have reasons for eliminating issues from further consideration been documented?

The following chapter considers strategic action alternatives, and how the SEA can help to ensure that environmental/sustainability issues are considered in such alternatives.

Chapter 7

Identifying Alternatives

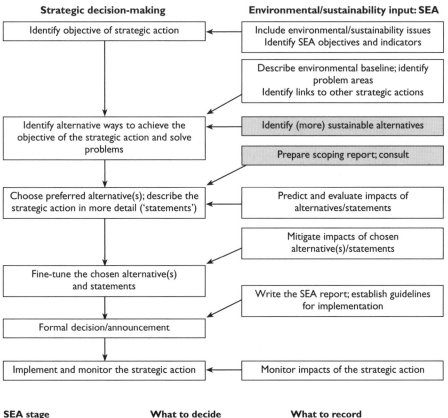

Strategic decision-making	Environmental/sustainability input: SEA

SEA stage
Identify (more) sustainable
alternatives for dealing with
the problems and implementing
the strategic action objective

What to decide
What alternatives or options
to consider

What to record
List of alternatives or options

The way that alternatives are typically considered in decision-making
goes something like this. 'We have congestion in central Standstill, so
we will need a bypass from South Standstill to North Standstill. Should

we choose route A, B or C?' Or 'having carried out traffic studies, we district planners recommend a Park and Ride system at Robust Road as a way of solving the congestion problem, but Politician Meddlemuch lives near there, so we'd better put it at Sensitive Street instead'.

There are several things to observe here. First, without SEA, alternatives are usually proposed in response to problems rather than as ways of achieving a future vision: they are reactive rather than proactive. Second, the alternatives considered are often detailed, project-level alternatives rather than strategic ones ('can we avoid congestion in the first place?'). Third, the choice of alternatives is often determined politically.

The role of SEA is to help identify more long-term, sustainable alternatives; identify and assess the environmental impacts of different alternatives to help inform and support the choice of alternatives and hopefully make that choice more sustainable; and help to document how the preferred alternative(s) was chosen as a way of leading to more transparent, inclusive decision-making. In other words, SEA aims to make the decision-making process more proactive, more strategic, more sustainable and less political. SEA can also provide reassurance that, within the constraints facing decision-makers, they have not missed some other markedly better alternative.

This chapter discusses:

- types of alternatives;
- how to identify alternatives; and
- how to decide which alternatives are not worth pursuing.

Chapter 8 then discusses how alternatives can be compared, and how to document the process of identifying, appraising and choosing alternatives.

Types of alternatives

Figure 7.1 proposes a basic hierarchy of alternatives. This hierarchy was initially inspired by the waste hierarchy (reduce, reuse, recycle/recover, dispose), and also by a basic rule used when people install wind turbines or photovoltaics: minimize electricity demand first, and only then install renewables to provide for the reduced demand because demand reduction is cheaper and more environment-friendly than production. The same basic hierarchical thinking holds true for a wide range of other sectors and issues. It goes as follows.

First check whether anything new is really needed: *is it possible to obviate demand?* For instance, before a new reservoir is proposed, is it possible to reduce the demand for water to a level where no new water source is needed? Before a new power station is proposed, can

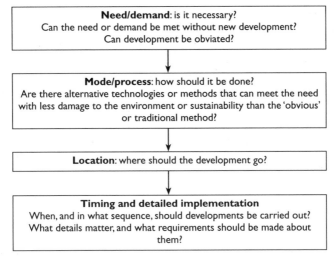

Source: ODPM (2002)

Figure 7.1 *'Hierarchy' of alternatives*

electricity use be reduced? Can we avoid the need for more roads, airports, science parks, golf courses, superstores, incinerators, houses, offshore wind turbines, dams, factories, call centres, landfill sites, mobile phone masts, pylons, trams and on and on altogether?

Taken to extremes, this approach could lead to a rather grey and bleak dystopia in which change is frowned upon, opportunities for progress are limited, and people wear their clothes until they are in shreds because they don't really *have* to have new clothes. On the other hand, a look at the second column in Table 7.1 suggests that, in moderation, it could lead to a lively, community-oriented future where people cycle and walk more, cooperate more in the provision of childcare and the growing of food, rediscover the pleasure of more local holidays, and support local stores serving locally grown foods rather than driving to the newest regional superstore which is in mad competition with the other new regional superstores.

In the context of worldwide trends towards globalization, consumerism and individualism, restraints on individuals' choices will not happen automatically through citizen action. It can only be achieved through a concerted, planned effort. Box 7.1 discusses this further. SEA is an obvious stage in the decision-making process in which to consider this issue.

Once alternatives for reducing demands have been explored and future needs agreed on, *different ways of providing for these needs*[1] can be identified. Water can be provided by groundwater abstraction, rainwater collection, systems of canals, importing and melting icebergs, desalination, and many other means as well as different sizes of new

Table 7.1 *Examples of alternatives/options*

Topic	Obviation	Mode/type	Location	Implementation/timing
Transport/ accessibility	Reduce the need to travel by: • locating amenities/services nearer their users, or housing the users nearer the amenities they need • helping people meet more needs at home (eg homeworking, information technology)	Encourage walking and cycling Support good public transport, matched to journey desires (eg provides sites for modal interchange, protect rail corridors)	Locate amenities/ services together, so people can accomplish several errands in one trip – eg multifunctional town centres	Have walking/cycling infrastructure and public transport services in place before development comes into use If extra traffic capacity is
	Develop community-scale infrastructure and services to reduce the need to transport goods, eg small-scale incinerators, reservoirs, wind turbines		Locate bike stands and bus stops more conveniently than car parking	unavoidable, design at minimum necessary capacity, avoid discouraging other modes (eg design in traffic calming, safe routes for pedestrians and cyclists), minimize noise, land take and visual intrusion
Economic development	Meet needs or provide occupation *without* more business development, eg community/cooperative schemes for childcare, home maintenance, food growing, play schemes (needing to *spend less* is as good for wealth as *earning more*)	Locally owned and managed; producing goods/services to meet local needs	Near customers and/or raw materials (eg market gardens around settlements)	Develop businesses in tandem with housing to reduce the need to commute long distance
		Repairers to avoid the need to buy new things		Develop at a pace and form that takes up 'slack' in staff and buildings as it occurs – neither displacing old but still viable businesses nor leaving a gap of unemployment/decay

Rural economic development, farm conversion and diversification	Save *having* to convert/diversify by adapting agriculture to new opportunities, eg organic, locally distinctive, locally processed and marketed, high value added	Promote activities that require extensive land and not quick or frequent access to urban amenities: eg wildlife, study/retreat	Given!	Develop in a manner that supports other agricultural/rural uses and the local community
Shopping/retail development	Provide services in a different way, eg wear clothes for longer, make things more durable, allotments that allow people to grow their own food, local non-monetary exchange schemes Meet demands through: • changes to existing businesses, eg village shops also providing banking/postal services • better use of existing property, eg subdivision, shop within a shop, use store rooms • new technologies, eg e-commerce (possibly using existing retailers/delivery rounds)	Buildings adaptable for multiple uses. Promote farm shops and other shops that provide local goods locally	Retail and service centres that allow multiple errands in single trips, near public transport, near users	Ensure that provision is in place and operative before housing is occupied, to avoid anti-sustainable transport habits becoming established
Tourism	Improve standard of where people live; encourage them to enjoy what they have on their doorsteps and need to travel less Provide local recreation/leisure facilities, green areas, etc	Activities aimed at local/short distance/ non-mechanized visitors Convenient reliable access by foot, cycle, public transport (eg coordinated services, integrated ticketing of transport and attractions)	Near users/ public transport	Engage local people in decision and implementation

Topic	Obviation	Mode/type	Location	Implementation/timing
Housing generally	Match supply to needs: • encourage adaptation of buildings to maximize the potential for comfortable occupation (eg loft and garage conversions, subdivision of large houses) • high standard sheltered accommodation for older people as an alternative to staying in unnecessarily large houses Make best use of existing building stock: • encourage living above shops • conversion of redundant non-domestic buildings, loft conversions, flexible subletting of surplus space Give tax relief for housing developers and buyers in less desirable areas	Make best use of land: • encourage infill, development of small sites, rebuilding at higher densities • promote dense and land-efficient built forms, eg terraces, low rise flats, communal open spaces • maximize density • use existing infrastructure in new construction	Minimize new infrastructure demands (eg by avoiding locations remote from amenities) Focus new housing on brownfield sites and away from floodplains	Match timing of housing development to needs and to public service provision Encourage self-build or community-build housing as a way of reducing costs and promoting participation
Affordable housing	Avoid economic overheating or wealthy in-migration that could price young and local people out of housing Reduce loss of affordable housing, eg disincentives to second homes	Social landlords, shared ownership/ cooperative schemes, shared facilities/ communal living Flexible/modular	Site and configure housing to maximize opportunities for people to stay near family, community ties and work	Match to demographic profile of customers

...housing where residents can buy a 'starter pack' and add onto this as circumstances permit

| Waste | Reduce generation of waste through waste management plan, limitations on packaging, tax on landfill | Use waste as a resource: recycling, composting, match producers of specialist waste (eg Pulverised Fuel Ash) with organizations that can use those wastes, waste to energy schemes | Locate waste management sites near source of waste and/or users of waste as resource | Provide recycling facilities at housing and employment sites |
| | | Ensure that waste can be used as a resource, eg by requiring products to be recyclable, providing facilities for storing recyclable products (eg architectural salvage yards, sites for storage of recycled aggregates) | Use waste as infill (eg of disused mineral working sites) where appropriate | Use materials efficiently in construction. Use recycled materials in construction |

Topic	Obviation	Mode/type	Location	Implementation/timing
Energy	Reduce demand for energy in housing by promoting low-energy lighting and appliances, very efficient boilers, high insulation standards, conservatories and lobbies, large south-facing and small north-facing windows, etc Reduce the need to travel	Promote renewable energy, energy from waste, combined heat and power Promote use of alternative energy vehicles	Community- and individual-owned renewable energy installations to minimize transmission loss	Use best available energy efficiency technologies in building construction and operation Site housing to optimize solar gain Use materials with low embodied energy (eg recycled materials, cob and straw rather than aluminium and concrete)
Water	Reduce demand for water through: • water metering • increased cost of water, greater increases with increasing consumption • in industry, more efficient (or different) processes	Reduce leakage in water pipes, rainwater collection systems, effluent recycling, use canals to move water from wetter to drier areas, etc	Consider several smaller facilities rather than one larger one	Install water-saving devices eg low-flow showers, low-flush toilets Landscaping using plants that do not require much watering

Source: adapted from ODPM (2002)

Box 7.1 Public v. private decisions, and the myth that 'choice' is always good

'Over the last quarter century the "long wave" pendulum of political values has swung to an extreme of individualism, market based solutions, and hostility to and distrust of anything that smacks of central planning and state intervention. This has happened before. But the discrediting and ignominious collapse of the planned economies of eastern Europe has left the discourse of individualism, choice and liberty so pervasive, and the image of collectivism, social choice and mutuality so tarnished, that we are in danger of forgetting that there is actually a debate to be had or a pendulum that can swing.

This matters because … individualism is not increasing wellbeing at all reliably for the wealthy; is disadvantaging the poor; and is making environmental problems insoluble. [We need] to renew the possibility of taking collective solutions seriously. Private choices are always conditioned by the quality of the public goods and wider networks within which any consumer must operate. The use of "choice" as shorthand for personal sovereignty and empowerment as private consumer conceals this. When this happens, what is presented as "choice", and may even be experienced as choice locally, is in fact coercion. In a complex society the choices other people make can be coercive just as much as the choices governments make – but without even the possibility of intelligent direction towards desirable goals…

Individual choice in markets or quasi-markets does not necessarily lead to the best, good or even tolerable outcomes. Individual choices have cumulatively led to an overall situation that no sane person would have chosen in transport. Parental choice is a major obstacle to providing acceptable standards for all in school education. In food and agriculture, a superabundance of trivial choice masks the absence of more important ones. The shift from state provision to market choice in financial services (especially pensions) has proved oppressive and bewildering, led to exploitation of many vulnerable people and deprived even the most prudent of security.

Increasing some choices precludes others. It is not good enough just to say that a policy "increases choice": policy makers must consider whether the choices being increased are useful and important ones, and consider the choices thereby being precluded or prevented. Choice should be treated as a means to enable people to get what they want, not an end in itself. Often, the choices that really matter must be taken collectively not by individuals. Government should act to make the right choice sets available… Standards should replace choice as the primary basis for appraising public services. Choice should not be allowed to undermine standards…

All these points lead towards the conclusion that in many areas we need more active government intervention [such as consideration of these issues through SEA]: to move the "choice sets" available to people towards less consumer choice, more social choice, less consumption but more quality of life benefits. This has logic; it makes policy problems soluble; it seems people are increasingly ready for it; it is – and can be presented as – a positive development of progressive ideas. It is also the only plausible and politically remotely practicable approach to address [today's] environmental problems.'

Source: Levett et al (2002)

reservoirs. Power can be produced from coal, gas, wind, wood, sewage, old tyres, dung, photovoltaics and many other sources.

Once the type and rough scale of development has been agreed, one can decide *where development should be located and how big it should be*. It is at this point that one thinks about different routes for a bypass, or locations for a Park and Ride site, reservoir, or power station. The issues of location and scale are interrelated: the possible locations will influence the size of development that is possible, and the size of the proposed development will constrain where it can be sited. For instance, there will be more possible sites for household-level wood chip burners than for an industrial-scale biofuel combined-heat-and-power plant.

Finally, at the most detailed level are alternatives about *how the development should be phased, designed and managed*: should all the wind turbines/houses/business units be put up at once? should the chicken manure power station be partly underground? should the reservoir include a wildlife area?

Clearly the levels of the hierarchy interrelate. Development may actively be needed in some areas, for instance in derelict former coal mining areas, so that demand reduction would not be appropriate in these cases. Some modes or types of development are more appropriate in some locations than in others: wind turbines where there is wind, chicken manure power stations where there are chickens. In some areas certain types of developments are inappropriate, so that location constrains the mode and type of development. For instance visually intrusive development would normally not be allowed in areas of particular landscape sensitivity, and no reservoirs would be built where the hydrogeology is inappropriate. In some cases this means that strategic-level decisions about major projects require detailed, local-level information to be collected before a decision can be made.

Generally the more strategic alternatives (demand reduction, mode/type) are more applicable at the policy and national levels, and the more detailed alternatives (location, implementation) at the programme/project and local/site levels. Swedish planning guidance, for instance, suggests that issues of 'why' and 'if' are strategic, whilst 'where' and 'how' are more project-specific, and that the former should set the context for the latter (Figure 7.2).

Alternatives, options, scenarios

So far the discussion has been about 'alternatives' generally. But there are two broad types of alternatives.

Some *alternatives* are discrete, self-contained packages: decision-makers need to choose one option from this limited set ('we could do X or Y or Z'). For instance, politicians may need to decide whether or not

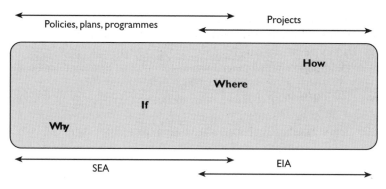

Source: Swedish National Board of Housing et al (2000)

Figure 7.2 *Different focuses of different levels of decision-making*

to promote nuclear power, or planners may need to select one approach to siting new housing, as shown in Box 7.2.

Other alternatives are mix-and-match combinations of individual components of the strategic action ('we could do A and/or B and/or C'). I call these *options*. For instance Box 7.3 shows some of the many different options for supporting the vitality of town centres in rural areas.

Alternatives or options could be devised to deal with various *scenarios* – factors that are outside of the control of the strategic action. For instance, one might want to consider alternative provision of employment land under scenarios of high v. low future economic growth; alternative waste management strategies under scenarios of

---

Box 7.2 Example of discrete alternatives: Oxfordshire County Council spatial strategy

In deciding where to locate 35,500 new homes and associated infrastructure between 1996 and 2011, Oxfordshire County Council's planners considered four broad alternatives:

1   put most of the new development in the 'country towns' of Banbury, Bicester, Didcot and Witney;
2   build one large new settlement at a disused Royal Air Force base;
3   develop the small towns on the railway corridors heading into Oxford;
4   disperse the development throughout Oxfordshire's small towns.

The benefits and costs of each of these alternatives were summarized in a leaflet that was made available for public consultation (Figure 7.3). Option 1 was finally chosen, although a variant was considered which focused on two, not four, of the country towns.

---

1. Country towns: continuation of existing strategy

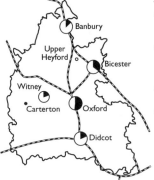

This could achieve:

• growth of jobs and services with population in Banbury, Bicester, Didcot and Witney
• scope for better long distance and public transport links and public transport within the country towns
• a boost to town centres in the country towns, especially Didcot
• continued protection for the green belt and countryside elsewhere in the county

But could also mean:

• potential loss of good quality farmland or landscape around Banbury, Bicester, Didcot and Witney
• growth of commuting to Oxford

2. New settlement at RAF Upper Heyford

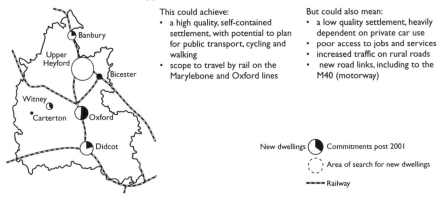

This could achieve:

• a high quality, self-contained settlement, with potential to plan for public transport, cycling and walking
• scope to travel by rail on the Marylebone and Oxford lines

But could also mean:

• a low quality settlement, heavily dependent on private car use
• poor access to jobs and services
• increased traffic on rural roads
• new road links, including to the M40 (motorway)

New dwellings ● Commitments post 2001

⌒ Area of search for new dwellings

━━ Railway

Figure 7.3 *Examples of discrete alternatives: Oxfordshire County Council spatial strategy*

high v. low waste generation (Verheem, 1996); or options for developing housing in the medium term depending on the type and form of housing built in the short term.

Identifying alternatives/options

Identification of alternatives and/or options involves two initial questions: what are we trying to achieve with the alternatives? how do we generate them?

Alternatives can aim to respond to specific problems, for instance issues raised in public meetings, environmental problems identified in the baseline environmental analysis, or widely known and agreed-upon constraints. The issue of traffic in Epping Forest (Box 7.4) is an example of this. The test of the alternative in such a case is 'does it help to solve the problem?'.

3. Rail corridors

This could achieve:
- good access to jobs and services in central Oxfordshire by public transport
- scope for developing better long distance public transport links and viable public transport corridors

But could also mean:
- potential loss of good quality farmland and threats to small settlements, high quality landscape, and green belt
- highway problems on minor roads likely
- major investment in public transport links in Oxford in order to achieve benefits

4. Dispersal to smaller towns

This could achieve:
- potential local balance between jobs and houses
- support and possible expansion of some local shops and services

But could also mean:
- potential loss of good quality farmland and high quality landscape
- possible coalescence of some towns and villages
- heavy reliance on private car use, and would be impossible to serve by public transport effectively
- increased traffic on rural roads

Source: Oxfordshire County Council (1995)

Figure 7.3 *Examples of discrete alternatives: Oxfordshire County Council spatial strategy (continued)*

Alternatives can also aim to achieve a future vision. For instance, Local Agenda 21 targets, community strategies or visions, and land use plan objectives are all statements of future intent, and alternatives can be suggested for how these can be achieved. The test of the alternative is 'does it meet the vision/objective?'.

Ideally, alternatives should not only do the former, as this is a sign of reactive, not proactive planning. The 'hierarchy of alternatives' can suggest the appropriate level of alternatives to consider.

There are many different ways to identify alternatives:

- expert judgement/brainstorming, as in the Oxfordshire and Vale of White Horse examples (Boxes 7.2 and 7.3);
- public consultation, as in the Epping Forest example (Box 7.4);

Box 7.3 Example of options: Promoting town centre vitality in the Vale of White Horse

The Vale of White Horse District Council is a predominantly rural authority located to the south of Oxford. An SEA of the emerging local plan for the Vale identified that the viability and vitality of town centres in the district was decreasing. The SEA suggested several possible options for how this could be improved:

- restriction of out-of-town retail development;
- relaxation of restrictions on changes in commercial land use;
- promotion of combined services, eg post office and store, pub and community centre;
- pedestrianization or environmental enhancement of the town centres to provide a focal point;
- reduction in rates (taxes) on shops in town centres;
- compulsory marketing of shops before building use can change; and/or
- provision of space in town centres for an open market.

Many combinations of these options can be considered: they are not 'either this or that' type alternatives like those in the Oxfordshire example.

Source: adapted from Speight et al (2003)

- a formal process of identifying Best Practicable Environmental Option: this is already often done as a matter of course in the UK when waste management strategies are developed, and the SEA process can piggy-back nicely on this process; or
- the analysis of links to other strategic actions can identify the constraints that they impose, and use these as alternatives (Box 7.5).

There may be a hierarchy of decisions, starting with a consideration of broad alternatives to a particular topic, and then focusing on different options for implementing the preferred alternative. The Tooton Rush example in Chapter 4 was an example of this; a decision to focus on reducing the need to travel preceded an analysis of options for how to achieve this.

Where a potentially huge number of alternatives could be considered, a more limited list of alternatives is often chosen which portray different themes or approaches. For instance, alternatives could emphasize renewable energy v. fossil fuels, or siting of new power stations in areas of electricity demand v. in areas of least impact. These may later be adapted, with different aspects of different alternatives brought together in a final, preferred alternative.

Box 7.4 Example of options that aim to deal with a specific problem: Traffic management in Epping Forest

A Quality of Life Assessment (see Appendix C) was carried out for the Epping Forest, a forest of more than 2500 hectares that provides a green corridor into London. As part of this study, four focus groups were run with local residents, 16 experts were interviewed, three expert workshops were held, and previous surveys of forest users were analysed.

Traffic was the topic of greatest contention and concern raised by the study. The roads going through the forest were felt to spoil the forest's naturalness, and pose a danger to wildlife and recreational users, but they allow people to access the forest and are an integral part of the wider highway system. Options suggested by local residents for reducing the impacts of traffic through Epping Forest spanned the range from demand reduction to detailed implementation:

- ensure that no large new development is permitted near or in the forest, to help prevent further increases in traffic;
- remove/close some roads;
- provide more cycle lanes;
- provide a large car park at the edge of the forest and use minibuses to carry people into the forest;
- improve bus services through/into the forest;
- add more junctions on the nearby motorway to siphon traffic from the forest roads onto the motorway;
- ensure any new roads are put in tunnels;
- reduce speed limits;
- traffic calming/humps for particular danger spots, particularly in villages;
- narrow sections of the roads, use traffic islands;
- enforcement of speed limits using speed cameras;
- provide lights or bridges along roads to enable walkers to cross the road more safely, but it is important not to lose the naturalness of the forest;
- make the forest roads a different colour so that visitors know they are in the forest;
- road surfaces should be of the sound-deadening/'whisper' type.

Note: Many of these options are not within the remit of the Corporation of London, who own the forest. The problem of remit is discussed later.

Source: Levett-Therivel and Land Use Consultants (2003)

The 'no action' alternative – the continuation of existing trends or the existing strategic action – can be considered. This is equivalent to asking whether the new strategic action is needed at all. Carrying out an SEA of the *existing* strategic action (if there is one) early in the development of the *new* strategic action is often an effective way of identifying the need for new approaches to a problem.

Box 7.5 Example of options suggested by links to other strategic actions: Providing housing in Newtown

Newtown (not its real name) has a declining population due to both regional population loss and a flight from the city (and especially its riverside social rented stock) to owner occupation in surrounding areas. The result is a high level of vacant properties in the inner city and many areas of unpopular housing. This has important implications for sustainability. Many inner city households live in unpopular areas with poor quality environments. The housing market in most other parts of Newtown is buoyant and these areas are becoming unaffordable to many. A growing mismatch also exists between the falling residential population and the large number of jobs in the city, leading to an increase in average distance travelled by commuters into the city for work and education. This will be further exacerbated by proposals to attract jobs into the inner city on major regeneration sites. Previously developed land in Newtown has not been consistently becoming available for housing, thus increasing demand for greenfield sites in neighbouring areas.

The City Council is reviewing its Unitary Development Plan, with a view to alleviating these problems. However the resulting new development plan will have to conform broadly with several high-level strategic actions, notably the city's regeneration strategy to 2020, the Regional Spatial Strategy (RSS), and the Regional Sustainable Development Framework. Regional housing and economic strategies will also be relevant. Box 6.7 highlights the key thrusts of these documents.

An analysis of the aspirations of these higher-level strategies identified three dimensions related to the provision of new housing (being one part of the wider exercise to stem population loss from the city):

1 the number of new houses needed to create sustainable neighbourhoods and attract households back to the city;
2 the density of housing, which has a bearing on house type and design and is a key determinant of what prospective occupiers might find attractive or not in comparison with outside the city;
3 the locations of housing: in simplistic terms, previously developed land v. greenfield.

Eight possible alternatives representing various combinations of these dimensions were identified:

1 Do the minimum: Little or no net new development – new build as replacement for demolition, only modest increases in dwellings through conversion of existing buildings, reduction in vacant properties and land, and more intensive use of buildings. De-allocate all existing greenfield allocations and no windfall developments, beyond those already with permission.
2 No change: Maintain existing densities and greenfield allocations and allow development on windfall sites. Modest net increase in housing stock.

> 3   Meet the slightly more ambitious RSS target (400 net new dwellings per year) through option 1, plus density increase on cleared sites and development on previously developed land not used as open space or earmarked for new open space. De-allocate all existing greenfield allocations.
> 4   Meet the RSS target through option 1, plus lower density increase than option 2, by retaining existing greenfield allocations.
> 5   Meet the RSS target through option 1, plus lower density increase than option 3, and increasing density on existing greenfield allocations, with up to 25 per cent of development on greenfield sites.
> 6   Meet the regeneration strategy target (about 1000 net new dwellings per year) by the same means as option 3, but with much higher densities.
> 7   Meet the regeneration strategy target by the same means as option 4, but with higher densities.
> 8   Meet the regeneration strategy target by the same means as option 5, with new greenfield allocations.
>
> *Note:* Clearly there could be many other targets between 400 and 1000 net new dwellings per year.
>
> *Source:* based on CAG Consultants (2003)

Similarly, considering the 'best for the environment' alternative can help to show how far the proposed alternative is from the ideal state, and can help to identify ways of making it more environmentally sustainable.

Should one consider alternatives to strategic actions that are environmentally benign anyway, such as those for renewable energy or nature conservation? Arguably, even an environmentally positive plan could be made more positive. For example, many renewable energy projects have unavoidable environmental downsides. These may be far less damaging than fossil or nuclear energy alternatives, but obviating the need for energy production in the first place might avoid even these lesser forms of damage. Such analysis would also provide evidence and reassurance that the (benign) strategic action is as benign as possible.

Deciding which alternatives/options are not worth pursuing: More scoping

Clearly not all alternatives apply in all cases. For instance, demand reduction measures are often outside the control of a given authority; some alternatives may not be legal or practical to consider; alternatives may not be appropriate to a particular stage of decision-making; and development may be more sustainable than no development – for example, attracting residents back into inner Newtown (see Box 7.5) by major housing development is likely to be more sustainable than not developing in Newtown, which would mean that new housing would need to be provided elsewhere, where there is less brownfield land, fewer possibilities to take advantage of existing infrastructure, etc. Some alternatives will be technically or financially impossible (though this reason for eliminating alternatives needs to be used very carefully: there may be good reasons to choose a strategy which forces the development of a new technology or brings about economies of scale for something that is not currently feasible).

Generally more alternatives are available at a strategic policy level than at a more detailed programme level; and at a national or regional than at a sub-local level where decisions made at a 'higher' level will have foreclosed many options. But, as mentioned earlier, not all higher-level decisions are sustainable, up to date and ambitious, and options that are not in accordance with such decisions should certainly be considered. It is not only at the regional (or higher) level where original sustainability thinking can take place. Box 7.6 gives a (long, but I think worthwhile) example of this.

In sum, alternatives and options to eliminate from further consideration are those that are:

- patently infeasible or ridiculous (eg the moon as an alternative site for food production);
- illegal; or
- clearly unsustainable (eg not providing homes in areas of high homelessness).

Alternatives that should *not* be immediately eliminated from further consideration are those that:

- conflict with higher-level strategic actions;
- have been rejected previously, because they may have been rejected for reasons that are no longer valid (eg new technologies were too expensive then but are not now);
- conflict with the draft strategic action objectives, because these may not be sustainable: the SEA findings should help to determine the final strategic action objectives; and
- are not within the remit of the decision-maker. It might be worthwhile pursuing these alternatives further through those authorities that do have them as their remit.

Reasons for eliminating alternatives should be documented in the SEA report. Table 7.2 shows how this can be done.

The remaining alternatives or options need to be phrased in a way that is consistent with what the final strategic action will look like: into formal statements. This is not an SEA activity, but is a precursor to the SEA impact assessment and evaluation stage discussed in Chapter 8.

Box 7.6 Dealing with constraints imposed by other strategic actions: Example of Swale Borough Local Plan

Swale is on the coast of North Kent, on historic communication routes between London and Dover. Swale's current local plan was adopted in 2000, runs to 2006, and is currently being reviewed. At the strategic level, Swale's room to manoeuvre is severely limited. The following quotes, kindly provided by Swale Borough Council from an early unpublished draft of the strategy chapter of the new Plan, show why.

*New **Regional Planning Guidance for the South East** was issued by Government in 2001. It confirmed the regeneration of the Thames Gateway as a regional and national priority[B] ... For those parts of Swale falling in the Thames Gateway, the objective is to:*
- *Improve economic performance and foster employment growth as the basis for regeneration.[B]*
- *Improve the opportunities for local employment, land at Ridham and northeast Sittingbourne, associated with a northern distributor road, is identified.[D]*
- *Maximise the economic opportunities of the area including its deep-water port facilities at Sheerness and the Borough's good accessibility to the motorway and trunk road network.[D]*
- *Use areas of previously developed and damaged land to regenerate the towns, to minimise the loss of the countryside, whilst protecting natural habitats and land resources of national or international significance.[A]*

*The **North Kent Area Investment Framework** is part of a process in which the Thames Gateway Kent Partnership has developed a Vision and priorities for investment in the area over the next 20 years. It identifies and targets the resources needed to implement regional objectives. For Swale, the provision of infrastructure is highlighted as being of crucial strategic importance.[E]*

*The **Kent and Medway Structure Plan** ... identifies quantities of employment and housing land to be provided by this Local Plan, whilst at the same time providing broad policies for the protection and enhancement of the environment. The Local Plan must be in general conformity with the Structure Plan and its principles... The current principles of relevance to this Local Plan include:*
- *Protecting the countryside by maximising the opportunities for the re-use of previously developed land, whilst concentrating development in and around existing towns*
- *Capitalising on the role of the Thames Gateway by increasing economic opportunity, reducing economic disparities and promoting targeted economic development, including: support for high value-added activities and skills development; business clusters; and knowledge based industries.[C]*

> • *Supporting the regeneration and renaissance of larger urban areas, whilst sustaining and improving the economic diversification and vitality of market towns and rural communities.*[A]

The constraints posed on the Swale Local Plan by the higher-level strategic actions fall into several different categories. Several, marked [A], are statements of broad principles governing development. At the local plan level they close off rather than open up options, for two reasons. First, they are derived explicitly from policies and/or guidance at higher spatial scales, and are therefore not open to change at local plan level. Second, in the way they are stated, they are so clearly good for a range of environmental and sustainability objectives that alternatives, such as 'opposing the regeneration and renaissance of larger urban areas' or 'undermining the economic diversification and vitality of market towns and rural communities' would plainly be absurd. However, the very generality of these statements means that the devil is in the detail.

How effective these principles are in promoting sustainable development, and whether they have undesirable side effects or clashes with each other, will depend on how they are implemented. For example 'Protecting the countryside by maximizing the opportunities for the re-use of previously developed land, whilst concentrating development in and around existing towns' is unexceptionable at the level of a broad principle. However, if it is applied through a strict and simplistic requirement to redevelop previously developed land within existing urban envelopes, the results could include 'town cramming' and loss of important habitats and amenity open space. SEA should ensure that the detailed plan statements apply such principles in ways that help achieve their implicit objectives. Issues to watch for later should be highlighted during assessment of options, but this is not a matter for the options identification stage itself.

In some other policy statements, those concerned with economic performance (marked [B]), this issue is even more pressing. The statements themselves are as hard to argue with as group A, and it would be possible in principle to implement them in ways that are entirely supportive of environmental/sustainability objectives, for example by developing businesses based on renewable resources, promoting low-input organic agriculture, and encouraging self-build low-energy housing. It therefore appears possible here to identify a meaningful choice between two distinct options: to pursue the overall economic development aims through a conventional economic development route or through green business opportunities. But just how practicable is this second option? There are good reasons why most economic development strategies give green businesses at best a marginal role: they are usually precarious 'niche' players, requiring careful and patient nurturing and providing only modest returns in conventional GDP terms, whereas anti-sustainable businesses (out-of-town business parks, distribution centres, etc) can deliver large benefits in jobs, income and wealth creation as conventionally measured. A strategic *objective* of developing 'green businesses' to the greatest extent possible would be good for the environment or sustainability, but an *option* of relying on them would be inconsistent with the aims at [B].

In any case, several of the other principles imposed from above call explicitly for a conventional economic development approach. [C] commits the Thames

Gateway to pursuing the same highly mobile, internationally competitive 'knowledge industries' that virtually every economic development strategy in the country wants (and which are therefore notoriously able to demand greenfield business park sites as their condition for going to one location rather than another). [D] explicitly promotes mobile businesses by improving and exploiting motorway connections, thus making clear what 'provision of infrastructure' [E] means.

A 'green development' or 'low development' option would thus be inconsistent with the whole thrust of the principles from higher levels which the Swale plan is meant to apply, and with the approach to infrastructure development already committed. However, the likely implications of this conventional economic development path are inconsistent with one of the plan's own three proposed sustainability principles: 'Enabling communities to be self-sufficient, as far as practicable, to reduce impacts elsewhere'. It is also likely to be problematic for a second one, 'Providing a robust, adaptable and enhanced environment' and may not be the best way to achieve even the third, 'Satisfying human needs – social, economic and aesthetic'.

Another constraint for Swale is that of existing planning permissions which have not yet been taken up. For instance, Swale includes a small market town with planning permission for a large business park. Planning permission has now been refused for the proposal and the council is considering an alternative approach for the town. However, there is an outstanding appeal, so until it is known whether the business park – long outstanding – will ever get off the ground, there will be continuing uncertainties over any alternative, and possibly more sustainable, future strategy for the market town.

This all suggests that there is very little scope for the Swale local plan to identify strategic-level options which do not either contradict higher-level strategic actions or prejudge details of implementation that cannot realistically be determined until later in the planning process. However, this is not completely the case.

First, the plan's objective of 'Conserving and promoting the rich heritage of Kent's natural and built environment' implies options in terms of which environmental resource to give priority to. For example, there are several towns in the borough, so development could be concentrated at one, or another, or scattered between them.

Second, the higher-level strategic actions which constrain the Swale local plan were all prepared some years ago and without the kind of systematic generation and consideration of options which SEA requires. In future they will be. As a result, regional and sub-regional economic development paths giving more emphasis to resilience, meeting local needs and local recirculation of income; and regional transport strategies based on reducing the need to travel and on increasing walking, cycling and public transport should at least be given more serious consideration.

Third, the planning system emphasizes 'top down' cascading of decisions through the various spatial levels of the planning hierarchy. However, information also needs to flow in the opposite direction, up the spatial hierarchy, so that regional and national policies can take account of implementational realities. This is particularly important where individually apparently sensible and desirable aims turn out to be mutually inconsistent in practice. The higher-level decision-makers therefore need to understand the reasons for the incompatibility and what could be done to resolve it, for example by reframing objectives or policies, or changing other contextual factors. For example, the apparent inconsistency between Swale's principle of 'Enabling communities to be self-sufficient, as far as practicable' and the trade- and mobility-intensive economic development path mandated for Swale by higher-level strategic actions is not just a practical problem for Swale, but also an issue which should be reported back up the hierarchy and addressed in the next reviews of the sub-regional and regional-level plans.

SEA can help achieve this by showing where policies which are good for some assessment criteria are unavoidably bad for others. But it can also help at the strategic options stage if strategies derived from higher-level plans are treated as options to be appraised against more sustainable options in the SEA. For example, the package of road-based economic development implied for Swale could be treated as one option, and compared to an alternative based on more local economic closure and self-sufficiency, reduction in the need to travel and improvements in rail rather than road transport.

Source: adapted from Levett-Therivel (2003c)

Where an (old, to be revised) strategic action already exists, this is the stage at which one would bring together the emerging alternatives/options and the statements from the existing strategic action (Figure 7.4). Where the alternative is already covered by an existing statement, then one would assess the existing statement.

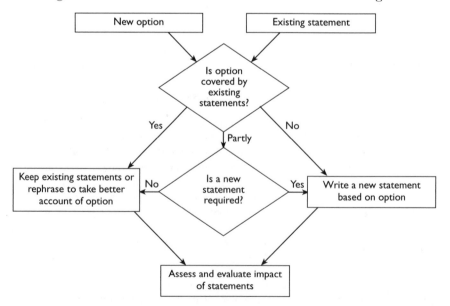

Figure 7.4 *Developing options into statements*

Table 7.2 *Documenting reasons for eliminating options from further consideration*

Option	Can option be addressed by the Local Plan?	Other reasons for eliminating option from further consideration
Restriction of out-of-town retail development	yes	
Relaxation of restrictions for change in commercial land use	yes	If this leads to loss of key services, then it will increase the need to travel by private car
Combined services	no: discuss with economic development department	
Pedestrianization or environmental enhancement of town centres	yes	
Reduce rates for shops	no: Inland Revenue (responsible for rates) has strict national-level guidelines. Not worth pursuing	
Compulsory marketing before building use change	yes	
Provision of space for open market	yes	

Note: This table is based on Box 7.3.

Source: adapted from Speight et al (2003)

Where the alternative is not covered, then one would phrase the alternative as a new statement and assess that. Where the alternative is partly covered by one or more existing statements, then one needs to ask whether the existing statements already cover the issue adequately or whether a new statement is needed, and proceed accordingly.

Conclusions

This is the time for a self-check, based on the quality assurance criteria of Box 4.3:

• Have alternatives been considered that are appropriate to the scale (international, national, etc) and level (policy, plan, programme) of decision-making?

- Have alternatives been considered that deal with the issues identified as a result of the baseline assessment and/or achieve sustainability visions?
- Do the alternatives include the 'do nothing', 'do minimum' and 'most environmentally beneficial' alternatives?
- Have reasons been given for why alternatives have been eliminated from further consideration?

The next chapter considers how the impacts of the emerging strategic action alternatives and statements can be identified, evaluated and mitigated.

Note

1   A distinction can be made between demands and needs. Demands are what people want; needs are what they need. Demands are almost always greater than needs. The literature on consumption (eg Ekins, 1986; Firat and Dholakia, 1998) is full of long discussions about when a demand becomes a need and vice versa, particularly given how, in many countries, consumption has become a vital method of self-expression. I don't intend to go into that here. My only point is that one should try to reduce demand before catering for the remaining demand, which I call 'need'.

Chapter 8

Predicting, Evaluating and Mitigating Impacts

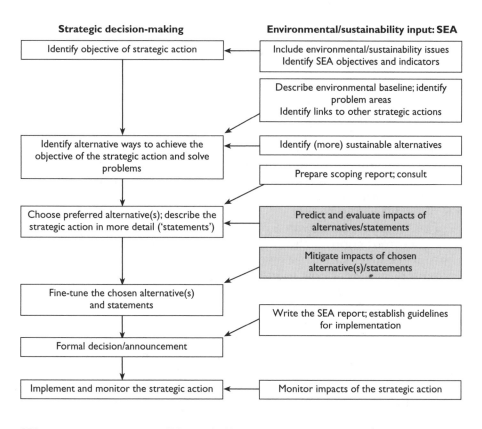

Strategic decision-making	Environmental/sustainability input: SEA
Identify objective of strategic action	Include environmental/sustainability issues Identify SEA objectives and indicators
	Describe environmental baseline; identify problem areas Identify links to other strategic actions
Identify alternative ways to achieve the objective of the strategic action and solve problems	Identify (more) sustainable alternatives
	Prepare scoping report; consult
Choose preferred alternative(s); describe the strategic action in more detail ('statements')	Predict and evaluate impacts of alternatives/statements
	Mitigate impacts of chosen alternative(s)/statements
Fine-tune the chosen alternative(s) and statements	
	Write the SEA report; establish guidelines for implementation
Formal decision/announcement	
Implement and monitor the strategic action	Monitor impacts of the strategic action

SEA stage

Predict and evaluate impact of alternatives/statements; compare alternatives; mitigate impacts of chosen alternative(s)/statements

What to decide

What are the effects of the alternatives/options and statements on the environmental/ sustainability objectives and indicators; what are the preferred alternatives; what mitigation measures to include

What to record

Summary of effects of alternatives/ options and statements on the environment and sustainability; list of preferred alternatives; explanation of why these are preferred; mitigation measures proposed

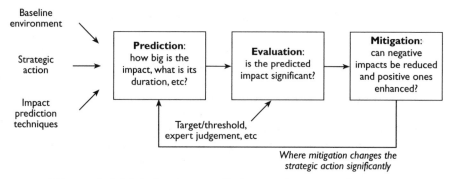

Figure 8.1 *Links between prediction, evaluation and mitigation*

Prediction, evaluation and mitigation of the impacts of a strategic action are the core of the SEA process. They are often the most time- and resource-intensive stages of the process. They frequently need to be carried out at several stages of decision-making, for instance evaluation of several alternatives for a broad plan strategy, choice of a preferred strategy, evaluation and mitigation of more detailed ways of implementing the preferred strategy, and evaluation of the refined/mitigated plan.

Prediction involves determining the scale, duration, likelihood, etc of the impact. Evaluation involves determining whether the predicted impact is significant or not: this requires an element of judgement. Mitigation involves trying to ameliorate any significant negative impacts or enhance positive impacts. The three stages are closely interlinked (see Figure 8.1).

This chapter begins with a discussion of principles and approaches to impact prediction, including how to deal with cumulative impacts and uncertainty, and what level of detail is needed. The section on evaluation considers how to identify significant impacts and compare alternatives. It includes a checklist of issues to consider when deciding on what SEA techniques might be appropriate, and a discussion of how different SEA techniques might be used sequentially to focus on particular impacts. The mitigation section explains what the different types of mitigation measures are, and discusses how environmental, social and economic issues can be integrated. Specific techniques for impact prediction and evaluation, for instance Geographical Information Systems (GIS), modelling and network analyses are discussed at Appendix C.

Prediction and evaluation principles

Impact prediction and evaluation have the potential to be horribly onerous and resource-intensive. Yet their only purpose is to identify key environmental issues to be taken into account in decision-making. As such, a first principle is that *impact prediction and evaluation should be 'fit for purpose': they should only be detailed enough to allow effective identification of key environmental issues.* For most impacts of most strategic actions, simple qualitative prediction methods will be perfectly adequate. There is no need to carry out detailed, quantitative predictions simply because they look more robust: they often aren't. This is discussed in more detail later in the chapter.

Second, the role of SEA is to inform decisions, not make them. As such, *SEA should not get drawn into any 'balancing' or judgements* about whether benefits for some criteria justify harm on others. SEA should clearly identify and report each significant positive and negative impact on each criterion individually. It is then up to the decision-makers to make and justify any decision to accept harm on some criteria for the sake of benefits on others. On the other hand, SEA should suggest ways to avoid or reconcile conflicts, for instance how environmental resources can be protected without worsening social inequities.

Finally, many environmental problems faced today result from the accumulation of multiple small, often indirect effects rather than a few large obvious ones. Examples include loss of tranquillity, changes in the landscape, loss of heathland and wetland, depletion of fish stocks and global warming. These effects are very hard to deal with on a project-by-project basis through EIA: EIA comes too late, is too detailed and is too focused on the short term. As such, despite the difficulties of doing so, *SEA should make a special effort to consider cumulative, indirect and long-term impacts.*

The following sections discuss how these principles can be put into practice.

Prediction

The aim of impact prediction is to identify various aspects of a strategic action's likely future impacts. These are then considered in the evaluation stage to form a judgement about the impact's significance. The impact of a strategic action is the difference in environmental/sustainability conditions with and without the strategic action. Typical stages in prediction are thus:

1   Predict what the strategic action/alternatives would 'look' like, for instance:
    • what activities would probably occur?
    • where would those activities probably occur?
    • when would they probably occur?
2   Determine, for each environmental/sustainability objective or indicator, the geographic area over which the predictions are being

made, and the timescale for the prediction. This can vary from indicator to indicator. For instance noise might be local, with predictions made over ten years; climate change is international, and predictions could be for more than 100 years.

3   Predict the likely changes to the environmental/sustainability baseline caused by the strategic action/alternatives. This is the difference between the baseline (including future changes) with and without the strategic action: direct impacts, indirect (including induced) impacts, and cumulative (including synergistic) impacts. These terms are discussed later in this chapter.

4   Analyse them in terms of:
   • whether they are positive or negative,
   • their magnitude (large or small impact),
   • their spatial distribution,
   • their duration (long or short term),
   • whether they are reversible or irreversible, and
   • their likelihood of occurring.

What will the strategic action 'look' like?

For SEA it is not necessary to determine in detail what a strategic action would look like on the ground. However, strategic actions, being the political tool that they are, often try to reconcile opposing views or say unpalatable things by making magnificently vague, 'motherhood and apple pie' type of statements. At times, in fact, they seem to say the exact opposite of what they mean. Table 8.1 gives some real-life examples of this and possible reasons why the mis-wording might have emerged.

Before the strategic action's impacts can be predicted, a clear agreement needs to be reached between the strategic action's author and the SEA team about what the strategic action really means. The easiest way is to ask what types of development it is likely to engender. Take an example from the draft Tooton Rush transport strategy: Wanda and Mohammed are assessing statement X which Chen has written.

W: 'Let's get on with the assessment. Statement X says that "The council will discourage the use of unsuitable minor roads". What will this look like on the ground?'

M: 'Well, obviously it means that there will be traffic management, like traffic humps and those things that cars need to weave around, on small roads in towns where there are lots of children.'

Table 8.1 *Examples of what statements in strategic actions do and don't mean*

Statement	'The conversion of historic agricultural buildings to an alternative use, particularly a use which would make a positive contribution to the local economy, will be permitted unless the proposal: a) would be significantly detrimental to the form, details, character or setting of the building; b)…. Conversions should ideally provide a source of employment. Conversion to workshops, meeting halls, indoor sports, storage or camping barns is likely to be more acceptable than conversion to residential uses.'	'The county council will work closely with the district councils to develop comprehensive policies for car parking'
What one might expect the statement at face value to look like on the ground	Sensitive conversion of historic agricultural buildings to workshops, meeting halls, etc	Policies for short-term and long-term parking, Park and Ride, etc
What the statement actually means	All of the recent conversions of historic agricultural buildings have been to housing. We want to slow this down a bit, say to 90% housing and 10% other uses.	Please, district councils, develop comprehensive parking policies.
Why the statement might have been written that way	Government guidance states that plans should make positive not negative statements ('you can build under these conditions …', not 'you cannot build …') so we cannot ban conversions to residential use. We are unlikely to see many proposals for conversion to non-residential uses but we'll give it a good try anyway with this strongly-worded statement.	County councils have no power to develop comprehensive parking policies but we need such policies to help achieve our transport targets. District councils control parking. Let's hope that they get the hint.

W: 'I think that it means that lorries will be channelled onto bigger roads, because they're the unsuitable use of minor roads.'

M: 'You're talking about a rural context and I'm thinking about the urban context. We need to figure out what is an "unsuitable" minor road: unsuitable for what?'

W: 'We need to ask Chen what he means.'

M: 'But we also need to ask what he means by "discourage". Does he mean financial disincentives like congestion charging, or bans for certain types of vehicles at certain times like your lorry restrictions, or small-scale building works like traffic humps? The impact of each of those will be different.'

In this case, before an adequate assessment can even start, Wanda, Mohammed and Chen need to agree on what is meant by 'discourage', 'unsuitable' and 'minor'. They would not need to know exactly *which* roads are unsuitable and minor, or exactly *how* traffic would be 'discouraged', but enough detail would be needed to allow reasonable predictions to be made. Chen may have a very clear idea in his head about what he wants his statement to say, but the statement is not clear enough for the SEA team, much less for anyone who needs to implement the statement. Alternatively, Chen may have included the statement because Politician Meddlemuch wants it and because it sounds unproblematic, without really thinking about its precise wording.

A side benefit of SEA in this case is that it helps to improve the clarity of the strategic action, which in turn makes it more likely that it will be well implemented: 'In urban areas, the council will discourage through-traffic on minor roads (those not marked in red on Map X) by the use of traffic calming such as speed humps.'

Approaches to impact prediction

SEA normally deals with large areas and large numbers of potential projects/actions, so there will be uncertainty about the strategic action's likely effects. Given these factors, and that SEA aims to help decision-making rather than achieving perfection, the SEA predictions can 'look' quite different from those in EIA. Here are some examples, all for the same impact:

Levels of pollutant Z in Tooton Rush...
a) will get worse over the next 15 years
b) ↓, or red (out of red, amber, green), or ☹
c) would be worse under Scenario A than under Scenario B
d) will exceed national Z standards within the next 15 years
e) will increase from 165 to 203 parts per million between 2005 and 2020
f) will increase by 23% between 2005 and 2020
g) would increase by 23% by 2020 under Scenario A, and by 16% under Scenario B
h) will exceed national Z standards by 6% by 2020

Table 8.2 *Advantages and disadvantages of approaches to impact prediction*

Option	Advantages	Disadvantages
Qualitative (a–d)[*]	• fast, low resource/staff requirements • decision-makers can 'own' results • arguably no more uncertain than the sum of the uncertainties that result from all of the assumptions used to make quantitative predictions	• vague, subjective, non-rigorous results • not easily replicable or comparable with other predictions • more obviously open to bias • can't be tested against outcomes • not a good basis for cumulative impact assessment
Quantitative (e–h)[*]	• detailed, rigorous, 'scientific', 'objective' • can be used as a basis for cumulative impact assessment • more likely to stand up to audit or inquiry	• resource intensive • assessment process inevitably moves from decision-makers to scientists/technocrats • risks spurious precision/certainty: pseudo-scientific • often requires large number of assumptions (especially at policy level), each with inherent uncertainties, so that the end result may be no more certain than qualitative predictions
Target-based (d and h)[*]	• clear links to monitoring and cumulative impact assessment • in keeping with planning approaches that include targets	• targets/thresholds may not exist for some issues, and may not reflect SEA objectives • targets may not be achievable solely through the strategic action

Note: [*] Letters refer to examples listed on page 138.

Clearly the latter, more quantitative and detailed predictions look similar to those in project EIA, but in SEA the former, 'directional' (getting better, getting worse) ones are much more likely to be seen. Table 8.2 summarizes the advantages and disadvantages of different approaches to impact prediction.

Quantitative predictions will always look more robust than qualitative ones. This means that, unless the assessment of strategic actions' impacts is done in a demonstrably robust (if not quantified) manner, it will be easier to 'prove' the benefits of projects (whose benefits are normally quantifiable) than those of the strategies that would avoid the need for the projects in the first place. Projects are often justified on the grounds of, for instance, improved travel times or provision of jobs: these benefits are immediate and quantifiable, even though, in the long term, they may cause problems. For instance roads often get filled up quickly because new roads generate new traffic (an induced impact), and call centres are often moved around to take advantage of cheap labour, leaving large numbers of unemployed people behind. Instead it is much harder to 'prove' the benefits of siting new houses so as to reduce the need to travel, or of policies that reduce reliance on multinational companies by, say promoting cooperatives or non-monetary exchange schemes.

Table 8.3 shows part of a typical SEA impact prediction matrix. It tests Objective B from Box 2.1 against the SEA indicators of Table 6.2. In the comments column, it describes whether Objective B would support the indicator or not. In the middle column, it interprets this in terms of significance: whether the impact is very significant (large circle) or not (small), and positive (white circle) or negative (black). Information about long- v. short-term, etc impacts is given in the comments column, but not in a systematic manner. The same basic format can be used to assess impacts on equity (Table 8.4); here, instead of positive/negative impacts, the focus is on who wins and who loses.

Table 8.5 shows part of a more complex impact prediction matrix prepared for the UK National Forest, a new forest of about 500 square kilometres in one of the least wooded areas of England. It shows extent, scale, probability and positive/negative aspects – all components of prediction – plus their policy importance (a component of significance) and scope for further mitigation. More explanation on the scores was given in the main text of the SEA report.

But matrices are only a way of presenting and summarizing information. Behind each matrix is a set of predictions made by using techniques such as network analysis, modelling, GIS, or (more commonly) expert judgement. These techniques are discussed further, with examples, in Appendix C.

Prediction techniques from project EIA can sometimes be extended to SEA. Topics such as waste and traffic management are already routinely modelled: Verheem (1996) gives examples of how this has been done in the Netherlands.

The impact of a strategic action will often depend on how it is implemented. For instance new housing could improve conditions for wildlife if it replaces a field of monoculture (say wheat or corn) with wildlife-friendly gardens. Alternatively, it could replace an area that is rich in wildlife with lots of paving and minimal plantings, and so have a negative effect. The role of the SEA is to highlight this, and to suggest how things can be improved – mitigated – at the implementation stage, for example: 'all existing hedges, woodlands, ponds and ditches will be maintained and enhanced where possible, wildlife corridors will be

Table 8.3 *Part of a simple impact prediction matrix:*
Policy on farming and food

SEA indicator	+/–, significance	Comments
1 Produce safe, healthy food and non-food products; make a healthy, nutritious and enjoyable diet available and affordable to everyone		
Food security, including short chain between producer and consumer	◯	Emphasizes short links, simpler food chain, less vulnerability, organic food, reduced use of antibiotics, etc. Could lead to short-term blips in production of specific foodstuffs, but would lead to improved long-term food security
Food health and safety	◐	Strong links to a healthy, lower-meat diet: promotes availability and affordability of fruit and vegetables. Reduces chemical residues
and		unnecessary antibiotics. Notes that 'healthy' does not mean 'sterile'
Food affordability	●○	Food is likely to become more expensive at the shop in the short run. The cost of an unhealthy diet – obesity, poor health, etc, which have the greatest impact on the poor – and of pollution are likely to go down in the long run
Non-food products		Not mentioned
2 Enable viable livelihoods to be made from sustainable land management		
Number/security of jobs in rural areas	◯	Proposes more labour-intensive farming systems, particularly more jobs in fruit/vegetable production
Value-added processing near producers	◯	Big emphasis on catering using local foods, and on re-opening local abattoirs
Tourism		Not mentioned
International competitiveness of UK farming sector	●	Argues that this is a foolish goal

Note: Table refers to the impact of Objective B from Box 2.1 on the first two SEA objectives of Table 6.2.

Key:

◯ large impact   ◔ medium impact   ○ small impact
● negative impact   ○ positive impact   ▸▸ neutral impact

Source: adapted from SDC (2001)

provided where possible, and communal areas will be planted with indigenous plants'.

Table 8.4 *Part of a simple equity impact prediction matrix: Policy on farming and food*

Interest groups	Winner/loser, importance	Comments
Farming sub-sectors: pig and poultry, dairy, beef and sheep, arable, horticulture	○ ●	Explicit move of investment/support to fruit and vegetables and away from livestock
Farm sizes/types: family farm, agri-business, alternative lifestyle	○ ●	Implicitly better for small family farms rather than agri-businesses
Farm tenure: owner, tenant	▶▶	Not mentioned
Other rural dwellers		
Recreational: walkers/cyclists/ horse riders, drivers, hunters, fishermen, foreign tourists, others		
Consumers (choice, empowerment, quality, affordability)	○ ●	Better quality, safety and choice through labelling, improved animal welfare etc. Affordability of food would get worse overall, though policy promotes idea of credit system to help out worse off
Other interests: landscape, environment, etc	▶▶	Not mentioned
Taxpayers	○	Avoids costly externalities (crises), more jobs
International: fair access to/from international markets, fair trade on equal terms	○	Strong emphasis on *fair* trade – meaning equal environmental/health/animal welfare standards, end to hypocrisy of dumping of subsidized northern overproduction on poor countries while obstructing their value-added exports
Animal welfare	○	More natural, extensive systems; less transport of live animals

Note: Table refers to the impact of Objective B from Box 2.1 on the last set of SEA objectives of Table 6.2.

Predicting indirect and cumulative impacts

The SEA should also identify overall trends in impacts. For instance, does the environment consistently lose out to social concerns? Are

Table 8.5 *Part of a more detailed impact prediction matrix:*
UK National Forest

Environmental effect	Policy importance of issue	Extent of effect	Scale of effect	Probability of effect occurring (at any scale/extent)	Scope for further mitigation or enhance-ment
Positive					
Employment creation	Regional	Extensive, beyond forest	++	Certain	Good
Employment effect on timber support industries	District	Extensive, beyond forest	+	Likely	None
Negative					
Employment effect of pest increases	District	Localized effects, but across the whole forest	0	Remote	None

Source: Land Use Consultants (1994)

economic targets always phrased very precisely while social ones are much vaguer? What are the cumulative and indirect impacts of the strategic action?

Indirect (or secondary) impacts are impacts that are not a direct result of the strategic actions, but occur away from the original impact and/or as a result of a complex pathway. Examples of indirect impacts are development that changes a water table and thus affects the ecology of a nearby wetland; construction of one project that enables and attracts other development, for instance a new motorway whose junctions start attracting retail or distribution developments; and construction of a road that generates additional traffic. The last two are examples of 'induced impacts', where one strategic action leads to other actions or developments, which generate further impacts of their own.

Cumulative impacts are impacts that result from incremental changes caused by the strategic action together with other past, present or reasonably foreseeable actions (Hyder, 1999). Examples of cumulative impacts include several developments with insignificant impacts individually but which together have a cumulative effect (eg traffic caused by several small projects together leading to significant congestion); or the combined effect of individual impacts of the strategic action (eg noise, dust and visual) on a particular receptor. Cumulative impacts can be:

- Additive, namely the simple sum of all the impacts (eg job opportunities in an area of high unemployment);
- Neutralizing, where impacts counteract each other, reducing the overall impact (eg impact on birds of one gravel extraction development is neutralized by a new wildlife habitat created through reclamation of another, nearby gravel extraction site); or
- Synergistic, where impacts interact to produce an impact greater than the sum of the individual impacts (eg closure of the only two footpaths that lead from a housing development to a much wider range of walking trails). Synergistic impacts often happen as habitats, resources or human communities get close to capacity. For instance wildlife habitats can become progressively fragmented with limited negative impact until they are so broken up that they hardly support a given population of wildlife and hardly act as a wildlife corridor any more; and then a final fragmentation tips them over the edge, the population dies, and they cannot be repopulated from other nearby wildlife sites.

Impact interactions are the reactions between impacts, whether between the impacts of one strategic action or between the impacts of other strategic actions or projects in the area. For instance SO_2 emissions from power stations can interact with NO_x from vehicles to affect the growth and health of plants (Morris and Therivel, 2000). Figure 8.2 summarizes these points.

Indirect and cumulative impacts, and impact interactions have traditionally been poorly considered in project EIA (Glasson et al, 1999; McCold and Holman, 1995; Piper, 2002), in part because project developers find it difficult, and are reluctant, to identify and be constrained by the actions of other developers. Some very good guidance on cumulative impact assessment has been published in recent years (eg Canadian Environmental Assessment Agency, 1999; Council on Environmental Quality, 1997; Hyder, 1999). This has focused primarily on projects rather than strategic actions, but the basic steps (see Box 8.1) hold true for all levels of decision-making. Appropriate assessment under the Habitats Directive (Articles 6.3 and 6.4) also provides a good model for analysing cumulative impacts.

The aspects of cumulative impact assessment that go beyond typical SEA are the consideration of past and likely future strategic actions and activities, identification of pathways between these actions and environmental components, and prediction of cumulative, etc effects. Past trends can be identified through records of official plans and environmental assessments; insurance, tax and other records; old maps and photos; and discussions with long-term residents of the area. Pathways between actions and environmental components are typically identified through expert judgement, network analysis, and sometimes deductions made based on monitoring data. Indirect and cumulative

Indirect and induced impacts

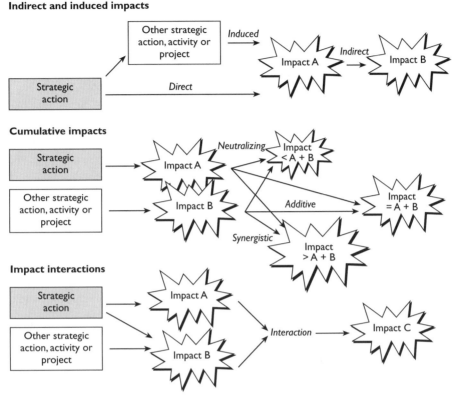

Source: Hyder (1999)

Figure 8.2 *Indirect and cumulative impacts, and impact interactions*

impacts, and impact interactions can be predicted using mathematical models, GIS and other mapping techniques, matrices, and the usual expert judgement.

Table 8.6 shows a very simple way of starting to think about cumulative impacts. In this example, each of the statements has, on average, an insignificant environmental impact (looking 'across'). However, looking 'down' (see arrow) through the various statements, it is clear the human health will be significantly affected by the cumulative impact of all the statements.

Targets are especially important for cumulative impact assessment because they provide a way of evaluating such impacts. Monitoring is also important because it helps to identify impacts that may otherwise be missed: the hole in the ozone layer, depletion of fish stocks, and accumulation of DDT in animals' fatty tissue are all examples of cumulative impacts that were identified after they had happened.

Box 8.1 Cumulative impact assessment process

Scoping:
• identify geographical and temporal boundaries;
• identify main cumulative issues;
• identify relevant management initiatives and policies.

Identify other activities:
• identify activities resulting from the strategic action;
• identify future trends, eg population growth;
• identify past trends;
• identify likely future strategic actions and activities;
• explain how these have been identified.

Identify sensitive/important environmental/sustainability components:
• identify sensitive/important resource, ecosystems, human communities;
• identify the current level of stress that they face, their sensitivity (response to change) and recoverability (capacity to withstand stress).

Predict and evaluate the impacts of the proposed strategic action plus past and likely future activities on the sensitive/important components:
• identify pathways between the strategic actions/activities and the sensitive/important components;
• predict direct, indirect and cumulative impacts, and interaction of impacts in terms of magnitude, likelihood, duration, frequency, sensitivity, recoverability, etc;
• assess the significance of these impacts, eg against thresholds.

Mitigate significant impacts

Monitor

Document the results of the process

Note: Shaded areas signify stages that are additional to a typical SEA process.

Sources: Alberta Energy and Utilities Board et al (2002); Canadian Environmental Assessment Agency (1999); Council on Environmental Quality (1997); Hyder (1999)

Dealing with uncertainty

SEA predictions are often affected by high levels of uncertainty, for instance about how the strategic action will be translated into actions on the ground, the likely future state of the environment, future technologies, and the effects of other strategic actions. The aim of SEA is to reduce uncertainty where it makes sense to, and otherwise to record it and cope with it. SEA should certainly not aim, as a general principle, to replicate the level of certainty of project EIA! In many

Table 8.6 *Impact prediction matrix used to identify and assess cumulative effects*

Option/statement	SEA objective			
	Biodiversity	Human health	Health-related behaviour	...
A1.				
A2.				
A3.				
A4.				
cumulative impacts of A1 + A2 + A3 + A4				

Key: Darker shading = more negative impact.

cases, a 'good enough' result for decision-making can be achieved despite uncertainties, so that uncertainties do not need to be dealt with specifically. For instance, future social conditions may clearly be better than current conditions; one alternative may be clearly better than another one; the economic benefits of a strategic action may clearly outweigh its environmental costs.

Techniques for *reducing uncertainty* include scenarios (including worst case scenarios), sensitivity analysis, clarifying assumptions, identifying risks and preparing contingency plans and monitoring. Scenarios and sensitivity analyses are discussed in Appendix C. Table 8.7 gives brief examples of the others.

Where strategic actions are vague and require assumptions to assess, these assumptions should be clearly stated, and measures should be put in place to try to ensure that the (positive) assumptions come about in practice. In such a case, SEA can encourage the strategy authors to be clear about what they have in mind, and to consider taking specific steps to encourage the 'right' implementation.

The most common techniques for recording uncertainty are to state that the uncertainty exists (in the way the probability of an effect occurring is stated in Table 8.5), or model it, for instance as ranges. Box 8.2 gives an example of the latter approach. For instance, uncertainty about the number of events per year is shown as an assumption that between 5 and 10 events per year would take place.

Box 8.2 shows that, with only five assumptions but quite wide ranges for each assumption, the result – the statement's impact on air quality – is so uncertain as to be little better than a statement that 'air pollution would get worse' – and the latter certainly is cheaper and

Table 8.7 *Examples of techniques for reducing uncertainty*

Technique	Brief example
Clarifying assumptions	'Policy H1 on location of housing assumes that housing will be built at 30–50 dwellings per hectare, and that their design will be consistent with Policy D1'
Preparing contingency plans	'In the case of a discharge, the oil terminal has access to six oil spill response contractors and the following on-site equipment: four boats of 4–5 metres; 500 metres of containment boom; two floating suction skimmers; and three oil/water separators. The terminal also has a Spill Prevention, Control, and Countermeasure Plan'
Monitoring	'Little is currently known about the general state of wildlife in the region. Bird populations have been monitored and are used here as an indicator for wildlife generally. As part of the implementation of programme X we will monitor populations of otters, water voles and bats in the area, to ensure that they are not adversely affected by the programme'

Note: See also Appendix C.

easier to derive than the former. On the other hand, the example does give us some further information:

1 Under the assumptions made, *any* cultural and sporting events will increase emissions of pollutant x, so that if x is already near its threshold and/or trends in x are already going in the wrong direction, then it is time to worry.
2 It raises ideas about mitigation. There are ways of minimizing the production of x, for instance by holding events close to centres of population, providing good public transport to the events, and using low-emission vehicles.
3 It indicates what kind of monitoring might be useful so that future predictions can be more accurate. For instance, if more was known about the number of journeys generated by such events, then the ranges of uncertainty could become narrower and future predictions more precise.

This example reinforces the concept that, in SEA, quantified predictions should only be made where the uncertainties inherent in such predictions do not completely swamp out the predictions themselves, and the additional work is justified by leading to a better strategic action.

Box 8.2 Example of modelling uncertainty using ranges: Air pollution caused by cultural and sporting events resulting from an economic strategy

A Regional Economic Strategy includes a statement which 'supports greater cultural and sporting activity to enhance the perceptions of the region'. If we tried to quantify the effect of this statement on air quality, we would need to make assumptions about:

- the number and type of activities that might take place (say 5–10 major sporting plus 5–10 major cultural events/year)
- the number and length of journeys associated with each event (say 200–1000 journeys per event, each 5–20 kilometres long)
- the type of journey (say 80–100% by car, 0–20% by bus)
- the amount of car sharing and ridership on buses (say 1–2 people per car, 5–10 per bus)
- the emissions of air pollution x per type of vehicle per kilometre (say 5–10 microgrammes of pollutant x per kilometre for cars, 20–30 for buses).

Multiplying together all of these ranges gives a prediction of 24,000–4 million microgrammes of x per year. The end result of multiplying together the different types of uncertainty leads to a range whose high end is more than 100 times greater than the low end. Clearly this has few benefits over a prediction of 'air pollution would get worse'!

However, even qualitative assessments should always be supported by evidence (for instance, reference to focus groups, visioning events or SEA team discussions that led to that conclusion) and details of how that evidence has been assessed. 'Qualitative' should not mean 'guessed': any data limitations should be documented, assumptions clearly stated and uncertainties documented.

Level of detail needed; keeping the process manageable

SEA predictions are a balancing act between getting into enough detail so that one is relatively certain that the predictions are correct, and keeping a firm focus on key impacts – on the wood rather than the trees. The former is done through quantification, consideration of cumulative impacts, consideration of uncertainty, etc: everything that has been discussed until now. The latter is done through scoping of the environmental components and the components of the strategic action.

Discussions with the environmental authorities and possibly the public as part of the scoping process (Chapter 6) should have broadly identified the requisite level of detail needed, and particularly what environmental components the SEA should focus on. Those

---

Box 8.3 Questions for screening of components/statements of the strategic action

1a Is the statement likely to have significant negative environmental, social or economic impacts?

1b Is it politically contentious?

If the answer to *either* question is yes (or 'don't know'), then the statement needs to be assessed in depth.

2a Is the statement *unlikely* to have significant negative environmental, social or economic impacts?

2b Is the statement as good as possible, ie is it not possible to enhance it?

If the answer to *both* questions is a clear yes, then the statement requires only enough analysis to confirm that its effects are minor (or to move it to one of the other categories).

The remaining statements require an intermediate level of assessment.

3a Are the effects of the statement very similar to those of any other statements?

If yes, then consider clustering the statements together for the assessment stage.

Source: ODPM (2002)

---

environmental components that are very *un*likely to be significantly affected by a strategic action do not need to be predicted: for instance the impact of an urban transport plan on soil quality, or of a minerals plan on social equity will not normally need to be assessed. Similarly, where the strategic action proposes little change, the SEA should focus on those aspects that *would* change.

At this stage, as the strategic action's final shape begins to emerge, one could also carry out a screening process on the different components/statements of the strategic action. This would determine what statements are:

- likely to have significant effects: the SEA should particularly focus on these;
- unlikely to have significant effects: the focus should not be on these; or
- in between: these should have an intermediate level of assessment.

The screening could be carried out by the SEA team or by consultants. The questions in Box 8.3 may help in this process. In case of doubt, the precautionary principle should be applied: the statement should be put in the 'worse' category.

> # Box 8.4 Example of different strategic levels for impact prediction: Part of a Regional Economic Strategy
>
> A   Improve the strategic communications infrastructure to support business needs
>   A.1   Improve the region's transport network
>   A.1.1   Ensure that new developments reduce the need to travel by car
>   A.1.2   Increase the availability of public transport
>   A.1.3   Establish multi-modal hubs
>   A.1.4   Lobby for and implement the region's most important and strategic transport projects, for example:
>   a)   Standstill to London rail line
>   b)   An international airport for the region
>   c)   Improvements to the strategic Standstill to Flimsby road corridor
>   A.2   Improve the coverage and usage of broadband communication technologies
>   A.2.1   Increase access to secure and reliable broadband networks
>   A.2.2   Promote digital technology demonstration projects
>   A.2.3   Harness public procurement to drive the delivery of a broadband network

For instance, statement A.2.2 in Box 8.4 ('Promote digital technology demonstration projects') is economically beneficial, socially neutral, and presumably politically acceptable. As long as the projects were unlikely to have significant environmental impacts – which one would determine after finding out what they might look like on the ground – they would not require detailed assessment. In contrast, statement A.1.4 ('Lobby for and implement the region's most important and strategic transport projects') is likely to have significant environmental impacts, might be socially divisive, and, in the real-life case, has been very politically contentious. Clearly more effort should be spent assessing and trying to mitigate the impacts of A.1.4 than A.2.2.

One question that I am often asked is what level of the strategic action should be assessed. For instance, given the strategy of Box 8.4 to assess, should one assess the broad principle of improved communications (A), the main types of communications infrastructure (A.1 and A.2), or the more detailed statements down to project level (A.1.4c)? Each requires different assumptions, types of analyses and mitigation measures; and each will have very different impacts. For instance, A.1 will have a very different effect on land take than A.2, and together their impacts will differ from those of A; A.1.4 is at a completely different level of the alternatives hierarchy from A.1.1; and the individual projects (rail, airport, road) of A.1.4 will have completely different impacts from each other and from A.1.4 as a whole. This is shown in Table 8.8.

The results of Table 8.8 suggest that SEA should be applied to all of the levels of a strategic action that allow the SEA to clearly distinguish between positive and negative impacts, and certainly to the most detailed level. Level A is probably too vague to profit from assessment in this example, but all of the lower levels should probably be assessed: certainly considering only A without considering it as the sum-total of its sub-sections could lead to huge, and quite possibly incorrect, assumptions being made. In the case of A.1.4c, this would imply a virtual EIA level of analysis. But if regional strategic decision-makers promote detailed projects, should they not take responsibility for properly assessing the impacts of such projects?

One problem that has been highlighted by past SEAs is high-level strategic actions that also propose quite specific projects, often 'in the national interest'. In many cases, these are major infrastructure projects such as airports or reservoirs. They pose a problem in SEA because of the varying levels of analyses needed: strategic and broad-brush for most of the strategic action, but detailed – almost to the EIA level – for the specific projects. However, this is merely symbolic of a deeper malaise in decision-making:

> *[Strategic decision-making is often] based on the assumption [of] a logical cascade or hierarchy: first you decide you need a project, then where to put it, then the details of how to do it. But in fact the 'higher' or 'earlier' decisions depend on the 'lower' or 'later' ones. The choice where to put a project (and what type of project, and its size) should be influenced by assessment of the different impacts it would have in different places. Even more important, the choice whether to have an infrastructure project [at all] should be influenced by whether there is any location where its impacts would be acceptable...*

> *This would seem perfectly reasonable where the national (or broader) benefits of a project were large, and the local disbenefits small, [but major infrastructure projects] are projects where both kinds of interest are substantial and important. Moreover ... many of the most important downsides will often be local in their effects and/or specific to the location where the project takes place... In view of this, deciding whether the project should go ahead after considering only the broader issues would be like conducting a trial where the verdict is decided after hearing only the prosecution case, leaving the defence able only to argue for a more lenient sentence after a 'guilty' verdict had already been passed* (National Trust, 2002).

Table 8.8 *Partial assessment of different scales of Strategy A from Box 8.4*

Level of strategic action	Environmental components				Comments
	Air pollution	Land take	Jobs	Equity (people with and without access to cars)	
A	?	?	++	?	Strong focus on business needs. Unclear what the infrastructure will look like at this level and thus its impacts
A.1, A.1.4	–	–	+	?	'Transport network' and 'important strategic transport projects' suggest land take and air pollution, though the precise mode (train, road, etc) is unclear so equity cannot be judged at this level. Links to business needs are no longer so clear
A.1.4c	0/–/– –	–	+	–	Road improvements mean that air pollution may decrease in the short term but will probably increase in the longer term. Would have negative effect on those without cars as it further promotes car-based travel

This suggests that a fair amount of data and analysis – equivalent much more to an EIA than an SEA – are needed before any strategic action can propose the development of specific projects. Arguably, if a strategic action wants to include reference to projects, it should be tested to the level of detail of a project. This may mean that, in the future, the more 'strategic' strategic actions refrain from inappropriately specifying specific projects; instead, they could set out the objectives that future development projects should achieve – speed up travel time in the wider Standstill area, minimize accidents, etc – rather than specifying the projects themselves.

Evaluation

The aim of impact evaluation is to translate the predicted impacts into statements of importance or significance. This gives information to the decision-maker about the significance of individual impacts, and who wins and loses because of these impacts. Impact evaluation brings together:

- characteristics of the strategic action: how influential it is for other strategic actions, subsequent projects, and environmental protection objectives (more influential = more significant);
- the effects of the strategic action (larger, longer, permanent, negative = more significant); and
- the value and sensitivity of the receiving environment (more valuable and vulnerable = more significant).

Annex II of the SEA Directive and Annex III of the SEA Protocol give more details on relevant characteristics of the strategic action (though these are oriented to the specific plans and programmes that the Directive and Protocol apply to, and are therefore not universal). Figure 8.3 shows how impact magnitude and the value/sensitivity of the baseline environment interact.

Much information about the value and sensitivity of the environment will come from the analysis of the baseline environment and relevant other strategic actions (Chapter 6). Value and sensitivity can be determined in several ways:

- Designations (eg national parks, historic monuments): these indicate areas that are valued because they are rare or particularly important. The level of their designation – international, national, local – gives an indication of their importance. These areas may be particularly good for one environmental aspect such as bird populations, but not at all good for others, like landscape.
- Other measures of value or vulnerability, for instance areas that are heavily used by people, or that are habitats for locally rare species, or buildings/people who are particularly sensitive to disturbance (eg hospitals, groups of people already subject to cumulative impacts).
- Standards and regulations (eg air quality standards, standards for insulation in housing): these set thresholds for environmental components such as air or water. The closer that the environmental component is to its threshold or capacity, the more significant it is.
- The public or stakeholders can be asked what environmental/ sustainability aspects they consider to be the most important. This would ensure that those people likely to be most affected by a strategic action have a chance to influence it, and to propose

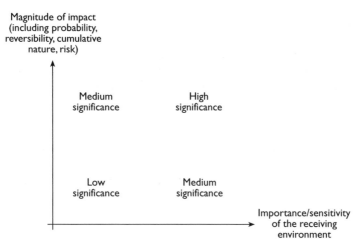

Source: Glasson et al (1999)

Figure 8.3 *Identifying impact significance*

mitigation measures. However, these views would need to be complemented by those of experts to ensure a well-rounded analysis: otherwise local interests could outweigh national ones, and cute, furry but common animals (like bunnies) could be given more priority than less lovely but more endangered species (like liverworts).

The evaluation should consider not only what impacts are significant but who will win and lose under the strategic action (Table 8.4). The whole point is to not make existing inequalities and other cumulative impacts worse.

Making trade-offs and comparing alternatives

The role of the SEA is to highlight the sustainability ramifications of strategic actions, not to make decisions. SEA should aim to clearly identify which aspects of sustainability would benefit and which would be worse off – and which individuals would win or lose – under a given scenario.

To the extent that SEA can help to steer decisions, however, there are some obvious rules of thumb to follow:

- avoid irreversible impacts;
- give greater weight to longer-term impacts;
- avoid impacts that would exceed environmental thresholds or limits;

- avoid impacts on particularly sensitive areas; and
- avoid impacts that affect ecosystems, resources or communities that have already been cumulatively affected.

Essentially, try to avoid significant negative impacts and optimize positive ones.

But even these rules of thumb depend on many factors. For instance, a Quality of Life Assessment study of Ashford, a city in South East England (Halcrow Group, 2002) revealed that water consumption was already a very high percentage of available rainfall; that increases in per capita water consumption and in planned housing numbers would take this to a dangerous level; that there were no further water supply opportunities in the sub-region that did not have serious environmental downsides; and that climate change was likely to further increase demand and reduce supply. Furthermore, the same factors affect the whole of the South and East of England, so Ashford could not bring in water from nearby. All these factors suggested that the availability of fresh water is a serious environmental constraint on further housing construction in Ashford. But this did not yield a single capacity figure which could be treated as a firm limit beyond which development could not go. Water companies argued that, at a price, they could raise existing reservoirs, pump water in, if necessary from far away, and develop new technologies. Many of these options were environmentally problematic as well as costly, but again it was impossible to identify a specific level of extra demand beyond which they became completely impracticable. Therefore, arguments that the South of England should not expand its housing stock because of water resources could easily be brushed aside: why this level and no more? why this extra expense and no more? etc.

Alternatives are normally compared using the indicators/objectives developed earlier. The comparison is typically done in a matrix format, with the alternatives along one axis and the indicators along the other. The table could contain straight – cardinal – statements (either qualitative or quantitative) of impacts, or it could compare alternatives against each other, against baseline conditions, or against the 'no action' alternative. Table 8.9 shows some ways of documenting the comparison of alternatives. This could then be used as a basis for discussions with stakeholders or the planning team.

In some cases, one alternative will clearly be better than all the others, but in many cases the decision will be more complex. For instance the choice of one alternative (eg location of housing) could also affect the choice of another alternative (eg on transport infrastructure), or one environmental component may be more important to the local community or decision-makers than another. In Table 8.10, Objective B is clearly more sustainable than Objective A if all criteria are given an equal weighting. However, if international

Table 8.9 *Examples of comparisons of alternatives: CO_2 emissions of four alternatives*

	Alternative			
	A	B	C	D
Cardinal/'straight'				
• Category	medium	high	low	high
• Quantified (eg tonnes per year)	3.0	3.3	2.7	3.6
Ordinal/comparative				
• Compared to the preferred option	preferred option	higher than the preferred option	lower than the preferred option	much higher than the preferred option
• Compared to the no action alternative	10% lower than the no action alternative	no action alternative	10% higher than the no action alternative	20% higher than the no action alternative
• Ranking	2	3	1	4

competitiveness is seen as particularly crucial (as is the case in UK agricultural policy at the moment), then Objective A may be preferable. These kinds of issues can be taken on board by using multi-criteria analysis or other weighting techniques (Appendix C).

The preferred alternative may not come from the original list of alternatives, but instead may include components of several of the original alternatives, or be a completely new option altogether.

The final choice will probably be a political decision, encompassing many issues in addition to the environment/sustainability, for instance higher-level edicts and security concerns. The reasons for choosing the preferred alternatives and suggested changes to the alternatives should be documented. Where a preferred alternative conflicts with another existing strategic action, this should also be documented and fed back into an early review of the conflicting strategic action. A final question to ask before the preferred alternative is finalized is, as for individual development projects: 'is this alternative good enough to welcome rather than bad enough to refuse?'.

Choosing prediction and evaluation techniques

Many SEA prediction and evaluation techniques have been mentioned so far, from the ubiquitous expert judgement, to life cycle analysis and multi-criteria analysis. Table 8.11 summarizes how some of these techniques can be used: they are discussed more in Appendix C.

Table 8.10 *Comparison of alternatives: Objectives for food and farming*

Criterion	Objective A	Objective B
1 Produce safe, healthy food and non-food products; make a healthy, nutritious and enjoyable diet available and affordable to everyone		
Food security, including short chain between producer and consumer	○	○
Food health and safety	○	○
Food affordability	○●	●○
Non-food products	▶▶	
2 Enable viable livelihoods to be made from sustainable land management		
Number/security of jobs in rural areas	○●	○
Value-added processing near producers	▶▶	○
Tourism	▶▶	▶▶
International competitiveness of UK farming sector	○●	●
3 Provide environmental improvements and other benefits		
Access to countryside, recreation	▶▶	▶▶
Landscape	▶▶	
Public value placed on benefits provided by farming	▶▶	
4 Minimize the total public funding needed		
Opportunity cost of rural policies, eg subsidies	?	○
5 Support the vitality of rural economies and the diversity of rural culture		
Vitality of rural economies	▶▶	○
Economic autonomy/control by farmers/rural residents	▶▶	
Education and training of rural workforce	○	○
Vitality of rural communities, age balance	▶▶	▶▶
Ability to sustain services, access to services		
Quality and affordability of housing		
Deprivation		
(Diversity of) rural traditions/cultures, diversity		
6 Operate within biophysical constraints and conform to other environmental limits		
Energy balance – energy produced (biomass, wind farm etc) minus energy used	▶▶	○
Transport	○	
Energy used/food unit produced/transported/consumed	▶▶	○
Biodiversity		
Populations of rare species		
7 Sustain the resource available for growing food		
Water quality and quantity	▶▶	○
Soil quality and quantity		▶▶
Waste		
Air pollution, odours, nuisance, acidification		○
Genetic impacts		○

Criterion	Objective A	Objective B
8 Achieve high standards of animal health and welfare		
Animal health and welfare	o	O
9 Allow use of undeveloped land for development that genuinely meets human needs		
Hard development	▸▸	▸▸
10 Be resilient to future changes		
For example, climate/flooding/drought, subsidies, petrol prices, availability of resources from abroad	o	O

Note: Table based on Box 2.1 and Table 8.3.

Source: SDC (2001)

There is no one set of SEA techniques that is best under all circumstances. Doing SEA is like planning a dinner party, with different tools and approaches providing possible menus, lighting and table decoration: one chooses the menu and lighting that one thinks will make the guests happiest. This section considers how one might choose which SEA techniques to use to ensure that the environment/ sustainability are best integrated in decision-making.

A rough distinction can be made between SEA techniques that are 'streamlined' and those that are 'comprehensive'. Table 8.12 summarizes the differences between these techniques.

In EIA, the more detailed and scientifically robust the impact prediction and evaluation technique is, the better it is. The 'comprehensive' techniques would thus be preferred. The same does not hold true in SEA for several reasons.

First, for the SEA to inform and influence decision-making, techniques are needed that convey environmental information effectively. Simple educational and psychological approaches, and techniques that foster good governance are thus often more appropriate than technical ones:

> *serious theoretical and methodological difficulties, including those related to the selection and framing of 'problems' and 'options', the treatment of deep uncertainties and the impossibility of aggregating in analysis the divergent social interests and value judgements which govern the prioritisation of the different dimensions of 'sustainability'... render futile any attempt to develop an 'analytical fix' for the problems of appraisal. In this light, systematic public participation is ... not just an issue of political efficacy and legitimacy, but also ... a fundamental matter of analytical rigour* (Stirling, 1999).

Table 8.11 *Possible applications of SEA prediction and evaluation techniques*

Type of technique	Technique	SEA stage				
		Describe baseline	Identify impacts	Predict impacts	Evaluate impacts	Ensure coherence
Qualitative, participatory	Expert judgement	✓	✓	✓	✓	✓
	Public participation (see Chapter 5)	✓	✓		✓	
	Quality of Life Assessment	✓			✓	
Mapping and simple spatial analysis	Overlay maps	✓		✓		
	Land unit partitioning analysis			✓		
	Geographical Information Systems	✓		✓	✓	
Impact prediction	Network analysis		✓	✓		
	Modelling			✓		
	Scenario/sensitivity analysis			✓		
Impact evaluation	Cost-benefit analysis				✓	
	Multi-criteria analysis				✓	
	Life cycle analysis				✓	
	Vulnerability analysis			✓	✓	
	Carrying capacity, ecological footprints				✓	
	Risk assessment			✓	✓	
Sound planning	Compatibility assessment					✓

> *quantitative assessment works fairly well when comparing similar alternatives, but if there are differences in principle, or a possibility of shifts in paradigm, measurement becomes nearly useless* (Jansson, 1999).

Second, it is vital that the SEA process keeps pace with the decision-making process, which is often very rapid. This means that techniques that take much time, require much data, require data that are comprehensive and not just partial snippets of information, and rely on the skills of busy specialists are often inappropriate. Some SEA approaches focus on identifying 'decision windows': moments in the decision-making process that are critical to the environmental outcome of the decision (ANSEA Team, 2002). Others – notably those of Brown (1997, 1998) but also other 'rapid assessment' techniques (eg Lucht and Jaubert, 2001; Münster, 2002) – aim to respond quickly once a 'decision window' opens up.

Table 8.12 *Streamlined v. comprehensive SEA techniques*

	Streamlined	Comprehensive
Examples of techniques	expert judgement public participation impact matrix overlay maps	forecasting, modelling sensitivity analysis life cycle assessment GIS
Carried out by	decision-maker	consultants
Relation to decision-making	integral	independent
Based on	policy appraisal	project EIA
Cost/resources needed	low	high
Scientific validity/rigour	low	high
Accessibility/ownership	high	low
Effectiveness in improving the strategic action	?	?

Third, strategic actions are inherently fluid and nebulous. Applying sledgehammer prediction techniques to the equivalent of cloud formations is inappropriate:

> *The level of abstraction for [SEA] should be balanced with the strategic level of information analysis, especially if details will be further elaborated in a tiered system of SEA/EIA... [T]he causes of the tendency towards unnecessary detail [in SEA] are that the environmental experts are not used to dealing with such a degree of uncertainty and that the public is too impatient to wait for more detailed impact predictions in later stages of decision-making* (DHV, 1994).

Fourth, even more than in EIA, many SEA impacts are by nature unquantifiable and/or not spatially fixed, so that techniques such as GIS or cost-benefit analysis would provide only partial and potentially biased information.

In other words, there are good reasons why expert judgement is the most commonly-used SEA technique. It is quick, cheap, needs little equipment, can cope with qualitative as well as quantitative data, and can take on board political sensitivities. However, in many cases, more robust and replicable techniques will be needed, particularly where the decision is contentious, or where environmental impacts are complex: cumulative, reversible, dependent on implementation, etc.

Factors to consider when deciding which SEA techniques are appropriate

Factors that determine which SEA techniques are appropriate include:

- What decision needs to be taken: the scale (international, national, regional, local) and strategic-ness (policy, plan, programme) of the strategic action. Qualitative approaches are often more applicable for policy-level and large-scale strategic actions, whilst quantitative techniques may be more relevant at the programme level and small scale.
- The type of decision: some techniques are particularly good at identifying mitigation measures, or helping to choose between sites, or making broad policy decisions.
- Who the SEA audience is/who would use the outputs: the more 'scientific' techniques may be appropriate for a specialist audience but not for public participation and vice versa.
- The context in which the SEA is being carried out: if the decision is, say, a political and contentious choice between a few distinct alternatives, then more 'scientific', data-based techniques that avoid the possibility of bias will be appropriate. Such techniques may be particularly required in situations of legal challenge, where the SEA results need to be able to stand up to intensive scrutiny. Where, instead, innovative solutions to a problem are being sought by a like-minded group of people, then quite different techniques will be best.
- The time available: more data-hungry and specialist-intensive techniques are fine where there is reasonable time in which to carry out the SEA. But quick-and-dirty techniques may be the only ones that can keep up with a rapid decision-making process.
- The resources, staff and equipment available: some techniques require computer facilities, new data or specialist expert input which may simply not be available in the time available for the SEA. On the other hand, this is not a permanent excuse ('sorry, we don't have the resources so we'll never be able to do it'): this may be a good time to identify what future SEAs might require and to start putting the resources and staff in place for that.
- What kind of data the technique requires as input: some techniques require little or nothing in the way of data, others require a great deal of data and cannot work until it is all comprehensively in place.
- Tradition and mindset: in some countries or situations, some techniques are simply more acceptable than others. In particular, streamlined techniques that are perceived as perfectly appropriate by some could be seen as woefully flabby by others, whereas comprehensive techniques may seem terrifying and a waste of

resources by those who are comfortable in the hurly-burly of streamlined techniques.

Whatever technique is used, though, please do *not* add up the assessment results (eg 27 'pluses' and 15 'minuses' equal 12 net 'pluses'): different criteria will have different importance in different contexts, and any summing up will only graft a spurious veneer of 'scientific-ness' onto something that is essentially a subjective process aimed at improving the strategic action.

Sequencing of SEA techniques

It may be appropriate to start with cheap, rapid SEA techniques to identify key issues and then, as more information is gleaned, to use more comprehensive techniques to focus on those issues that are most significant. The following example, based on a real-life case study, illustrates this.

Remember Wanda Duright, Tooton Rush District Council's transport planner? She has found that the council's land use plan is affecting the ability of her transport plan to be environment-friendly. In particular, the land use plan's current approach to locating freight distribution centres is leading to unnecessary lorry movements on small roads. The impressively charismatic and persuasive Wanda has convinced the head of land use planning, Goodlan Dyusz, not only to carry out an SEA of the evolving new land use plan but also to include a new draft statement in his plan that restricts lorry use:

> *L. Development that is likely to generate increased lorry movements which would cause an unacceptable adverse impact on the highway, residential amenity, safety or the local environment will not be permitted unless the impact can be adequately mitigated. Proposals for developments with significant freight requirements should be located along appropriate transport routes.*

So now Mr Dyusz is sitting down with his planning team to assess Statement L. The team starts by asking what the statement is likely to 'look' like on the ground. They agree that the first sentence will probably apply mostly to the town centres of Standstill, Rushmore and Walkerton, and would probably lead to a reduction in developments that generate a large number of lorry movements in those towns. They feel that the second sentence is unclear both about what 'significant' freight requirements are and about what an appropriate transport route would be. They agree that a definition is needed of the former and a map of the latter.

They then carry out a first rough impact prediction of Statement L using their 'expert judgement' (with much joking about how un-expert

Table 8.13 *Impact assessment matrix for Statement L (minimizing impact of lorries)*

Criterion (* = particularly important issue for Tooton Rush)	+/−	Reasons for +/−	Possible mitigation/ enhancement/way to deal with uncertainty
Land	−	Generally promotes restraint on development, but moves development with many freight movements to sites near major transport corridors, probably to previously undeveloped land. In the long term this could lead to strip development along transport corridors (probably roads) and to few developments that generate many lorry movements in towns	Identify possible sites for locating development likely to generate significant freight movements
Air pollution	+	Moves sources of noise and air pollution away from receptors	
*Biodiversity	?	Reduces road traffic hence road kill, etc, but builds on undeveloped sites with implications for wildlife habitats. Unclear whether overall effect is + or −	Investigate whether + or − effect by using network analysis
*Need to travel	++	Locates development in more accessible locations, hence reduces need to travel and impacts of traffic	
Vitality and viability of town centres	+	Pushes some potential development out of town centres, but probably outweighed cumulatively in the long term by the benefits of having fewer lorries in town centres	Relax Statement L in towns with high vacancy rates?
*Employment	?	Puts off businesses generating many lorry movements, so possibly fewer new jobs will come into the area. But businesses generating many lorry movements are also likely to provide fewer jobs per floor space and poorly paid jobs	Investigate if + or − by using network analysis
Energy and water efficiency; waste	+	Likely to reduce road trips and thus energy efficiency and accidents	
Accidents	+		

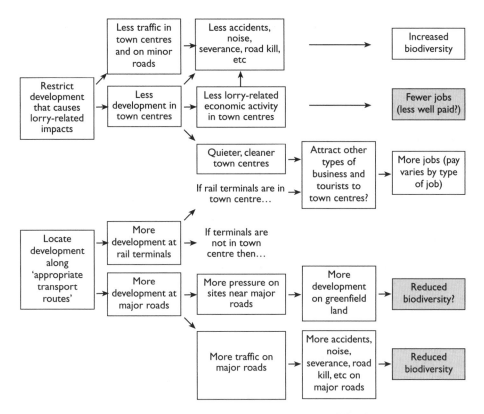

Figure 8.4 *Simple network diagram of employment and biodiversity impacts of Statement L (minimizing impact of lorries)*

they really are), and summarize the results in Table 8.13. The main possible problems that they identify are the statement's effects on employment and biodiversity: both are important issues for the council, but Table 8.13 suggests that Statement L's effects could be either positive or negative depending on the assumptions made.

Mr Dyusz's team try to untangle the impact of Statement L on biodiversity and employment by drawing a simple network analysis, shown in Figure 8.4. Figure 8.4 clarifies which (indirect) aspects of the statement are likely to have positive and negative impacts, and suggests some mitigation measures and further studies:

1 encourage businesses that generate many well-paying jobs in towns;
2 carry out a more detailed study of where rail terminals are, whether they can accommodate more freight transport, how more freight use of these terminals would affect nearby residents and businesses, and whether new freight terminals are needed; and

3   identify locations for future transport-dependent development so
    as to avoid sites with high biodiversity.

Mr Dyusz's team also prepare an overlay/constraints map to help
identify areas that would be inappropriate for development generating
many new lorry movements. The national rail authority confirms that
no funding exists for new rail lines for at least five years, so new rail
developments are unlikely. They show, on one map:

- designated areas (eg district parks) and other areas of biodiversity,
  heritage, etc value;
- areas within 200 metres of settlements of more than 30 people (to
  avoid areas where many people would be adversely affected by new
  lorry movements);
- major roads and rail terminals at capacity and with no plans for
  expansion (to avoid transport infrastructure that cannot cope with
  more freight movements); and
- areas further than 200 metres from access to major roads and rail
  terminals (to avoid inappropriate transport routes).

Those areas on the map that are not inappropriate could then be
considered at a more detailed level.

The map shows, in fact, that there are virtually no areas in Tooton
Rush that are not constrained. There is only one rail terminal but it is
in the middle of Standstill and thus in a settlement of more than 30
people. The concept of 'access to' roads turns out to be an important
limitation, as most of the main roads in Tooton Rush have restricted
access using junctions: simply using the criterion 'x metres from major
roads' (ie distance as the crow flies rather than road distance) in this
case would not have given accurate information. The planners now
need to consider whether to keep the second sentence of Statement L,
or to write something quite different instead.

In this example, the analysis by expert judgement identified a
range of positive impacts and some environmental mitigation
measures. It also identified the need for further analysis using network
analysis and a constraints map. The network analysis identified the
need for further studies, which in turn may suggest environmental
mitigation measures. The constraints map suggested further changes
and mitigation measures. This is summarized in Figure 8.5. Both the
network diagram and the map also help to visually represent some of
the more complex assessment processes: this could be particularly
helpful for people who have not been involved in the SEA in
understanding the thinking behind the SEA.

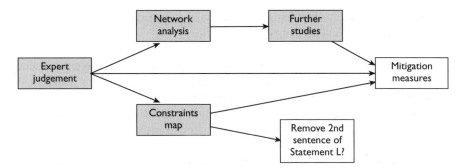

Figure 8.5 *Sequencing of SEA techniques in the example of Statement L*

Mitigation

The impact prediction and evaluation stage will have identified the strategic action's significant positive and negative impacts. The impact mitigation stage aims to minimize any negative impacts, optimize any positive ones, enhance sustainability in other ways if possible, and ensure that these mitigation measures do not themselves have negative impacts. The end result should be a list of agreed measures to change the strategic action, change other strategic actions where relevant, and/or set a context for future projects.

A major advantage of SEA over project EIA is that it allows consideration of a wider range of mitigation measures, particularly measures to prevent impacts at an earlier, more appropriate stage of decision-making. It allows sensitive areas to be avoided and environmentally beneficial developments to be promoted, rather than individual development proposals being considered on an ad hoc, reactive basis. It also allows for a wider range of specific environmental/sustainability measures to be taken, for instance the creation of new wildlife corridors or community facilities.

SEA mitigation measures do not look like those in EIA (which normally focus on location and design). Typical SEA mitigation measures could include:

- changes to the wording of the strategic action (or components/statements in it);
- the removal of components/statements that are not sustainable or do not promote the SEA objectives;
- the addition of new components/statements;
- the development of new options, possibly a combination of the best aspects of existing options;
- requirements to substitute or offset for certain types of impacts, for instance through projects which replace any benefits lost through

other projects (eg a new park near an area of open space that is being built on);

- requirements and terms of reference for EIA of certain types of projects, or sub-components of EIA such as landscape or traffic assessments (this can increase certainty for developers and speed up scoping of EIA);
- an explanation of why EIA (or lower-level SEA) might not be needed, or why some environmental or sustainability concerns do not need to be addressed in EIA (or lower-level SEA); and
- mitigation measures that should be taken on board in subsequent plans, programmes and projects.

The last three of these are examples of SEA 'tiering', where decisions made at a higher level can help to streamline decisions at lower levels. This is also where links between SEA and EIA emerge.

Mitigation measures can be fiscal, such as subsidies for converting intensively farmed agricultural land to woodland, congestion charging or tolls to help reduce traffic, reduced taxes for supermarkets that sell locally produced foods, or revenues hypothecated to various environmental projects. They can be regulatory, such as energy efficiency standards, regulations prohibiting development in certain areas, or laws only allowing vehicles that use 'green' fuels to use bus lanes. They can be educational, for instance energy awareness campaigns or walk-to-school schemes. They can be technical, for instance requirements for wastewater treatment by reedbeds, flood protection through sustainable urban drainage systems, or recycled materials to be used in construction. They can be procedural, for instance requiring public consultation before certain types of developments are designed, or a Best Practicable Environmental Option study before certain other projects are agreed. They can also be spatial, for instance requiring large new housing developments to be within 200 metres of a bus stop, or requiring certain quantities of open space to be provided for every 100 new houses.

Mitigation measures can roughly be divided into those that avoid impacts altogether, those that reduce the magnitude and/or severity of impacts, those that 'repair' impacts after they have occurred, those that compensate for impacts (try to balance out negative impacts with other positive ones, but not necessarily in a like-for-like manner), and those that enhance already positive impacts. The detailed classifications are less important than the fact that the different types of measures treat the impact differently. Broadly, avoidance of impacts is preferable to reduction, which in turn is preferable to reparation and compensation.

The final choice of mitigation measures will be influenced by several factors. First, those measures that are within the remit of the competent authority will be easier to agree and implement than those that are not. Second, timescales may be a constraining factor. Strategic actions can take many years to prepare or revise (although they can also be agreed and implemented extremely quickly): by the time the strategic action is adopted, circumstances may have radically altered. For example bus services may have stopped or the arrival of a motorway could have reduced traffic on nearby roads. This also means that it can take a very long time for other, complementary strategic actions to be implemented. Third, many mitigation measures often require public subsidy, but there is no certainty that sufficient public funds will be available (CAG, 2000). The final choice of mitigation measures will thus depend on a range of issues, and the 'perfect' mitigation package may well be unattainable.

Identifying mitigation measures

First and foremost, identifying mitigation measures involves a *mentality* and *timing* rather than a particular set of tools. Decision-makers must be willing to change their strategic action in response to the SEA, and the SEA must be carried out early enough to allow mitigation measures to be incorporated in the strategic action. Article 9 of the SEA Directive requires decision-makers to explain how environmental considerations have been taken into account in decision-making: identification and documentation of mitigation measures is a key component of this.

Identifying mitigation measures also means asking the right questions. Here is how this could be done, assuming a rapid, qualitative assessment (basically assuming that a format such as Table 8.13 will be used).

Get a good SEA team together, one with a wide range of interests and knowledge, ideally including the person who wrote the strategic action, the person(s) who will implement it, and someone with a good understanding of environmental/sustainability issues. Ensure that the recording form – the table in this case – includes somewhere to note down comments and assumptions, and somewhere to make recommendations for changes to the strategic action. Check the checklist in Box 8.5.

Before the assessment starts, the SEA team should repeat several times firmly 'the point of this assessment process is *not* to fill in the table, but to ensure that the strategic action is as good as possible. The table is only a tool for doing this'. For each component/statement of the strategic action the SEA team should then carry out the process outlined in Box 8.6. Box 8.7 gives examples of real-life mitigation measures that have arisen from this type of process.

Integrating social, economic and environmental impacts

Mitigation measures often aim to reconcile or integrate multiple objectives. But

---

Box 8.5 Checklist of items to prepare for a prediction, evaluation and mitigation session

✓ Book room(s), ensure that there are enough tables and chairs.
✓ Leave enough time. For a purely qualitative (+/–) analysis of statements like Statement L or Objective B, leave 20 minutes per statement. The first 2–3 statements will take much longer – say an hour each – as people get used to the process. Also leave 20 minutes in the beginning for introductions, settling in, latecomers, coffee, etc.
✓ Bring plenty of blank assessment forms (eg Tables 8.3–8.5, 8.13).
✓ Bring one copy of the strategic action per person. Where different SEA teams are looking at different parts of the strategic action, the teams only need the alternatives or statements they are assessing.
✓ If the assessment is being carried out by different SEA teams, bring a list of who is on which team (don't assume that anyone will have read your perfectly designed, previously circulated list).
✓ Bring coffee/tea and biscuits. This is not an exercise in martyrdom.

---

a major difficulty appears to be to encourage decisionmakers to integrate the findings from [SEA] into the process of decision-making. Although a comprehensive [SEA] report will highlight potential environmental problems, there is uncertainty (and considerable debate) about the importance that the environmental impacts should assume in relation to economic, social, and cultural impacts, and decisionmakers do not always consider the environmental information provided sufficiently (Curran et al, 1998).

Clearly the win–win–win or fully integrated approaches to dealing with environmental, social and economic issues discussed in Chapter 6 are the ideal way forward. However, this is not always possible. Different user groups may have very different ideas about what is appropriate integration: one person's cycle lane is another person's obstruction; one person's wildlife area is another person's haven for drug users. Table 8.14 discusses other ways of ensuring that issues are integrated. Compatibility assessment (Appendix C) can help to ensure that different measures do not pull against each other.

Box 8.6 Questions to ask when predicting, assessing and mitigating impacts

Ask 'What will this statement look like on the ground? Does the statement say what its author wants it to say?' If not, it should be rewritten to be clearer. This rewrite is a mitigation measure. Where the decision-maker will definitely change the statement so as to make it clearer, then the new improved statement should be used for the subsequent stages of assessment; otherwise the original statement should be used.

Discuss what impact the statement will have on each environmental component. The precise symbol that goes in the table is not the important thing. Answering the following questions is!

- If the statement is likely to have a negative impact, can this be avoided, reduced, repaired or compensated for? If so, rewrite the statement accordingly, add other statements, etc. These changes are mitigation measures.
- If the statement is likely to have a negative impact that cannot be mitigated, are its benefits so important that they override this negative impact? If so, justify why. If not, consider deleting the statement or giving it a major overhaul. The deletion or overhaul is a mitigation measure.
- Can positive impacts of the statement be enhanced? Try rewriting it to do this: this is a mitigation measure.
- If it is unclear what type of impact the statement will have, how can this be determined? What additional information is needed? Get that information, or consider setting up a monitoring system to collect it for the next SEA.
- Where the impact depends on how the statement is implemented, use the symbol I (for 'depends on implementation') and try to set measures in place to ensure that the implementation is done 'right'. The measures are a mitigation measure.

Document all of these changes: they 'prove' that the appraisal process has influenced the plan-making process.

Conclusions

We started this chapter with draft alternatives, options and/or statements. We leave it with preferred alternative(s); options and statements that have been analysed and possibly changed to make them clearer and more sustainable; and possibly additions to the strategic action in the form of new statements or links to subsequent SEAs or EIAs. The strategic action should also be more coherent.

As a result of the prediction, evaluation and mitigation stages, the strategic action authors should not only get ideas for how to improve their strategic action, but should also have a much clearer

---

Box 8.7 Examples of mitigation measures: Changes made to strategic action statements

Clarify wording

> The number of *long-term public* car parking spaces *in town centres* will be reduced.

Reduce negative impacts

> The general locational strategy is to concentrate development at settlements A, B, C and D. *Development will not be permitted on important open land within these settlements (see Map X).*

Enhance positive impacts

> In new developments *and redevelopments*, the council will require consideration to be given to measures to
> i)   conserve energy and the use of other resources
> ii) *use solar hot water and/or photovoltaic panels*
> iii) *use passive solar design (layout, design, orientation and shelter of buildings)*
> iv) *use energy-efficient technologies*
> v)   *conserve the use of water.*

Ensure good implementation

> *Planning applications for major development will only be permitted where accompanied by a transport assessment identifying the transport impacts of the proposal.*

Note: Phrases in italics are the changes/mitigation measures.

Source: adapted from Speight et al (2003)

---

understanding of their strategic action so that they can better explain, defend and implement it. The other people involved in the SEA should also have a better understanding of the decision-making process and how their work relates to it.

The prediction, evaluation and mitigation stages are often the most fun part of SEA. It is at this stage that grand plans for putting wind turbines on the tops of electricity pylons (you heard it here first...), insulating skyscrapers with straw bales, and installing ski lifts that pull bikes up long hills are hatched. My personal favourite assessment session was held in a hotel with erotic Japanese etchings in the ladies' room: the women in the group had a hard time concentrating on the SEA with such an interesting alternative topic of conversation.

Table 8.14 *Possible types of integration in SEA*

Type of integration	How it works	Example from Tooton Rush (notes in italics explain the types of mitigation measures)
Win–win–win	Solutions which meet some social, economic and/or environmental objectives without harming any others	Cycle lanes (*technical, reduce impacts of car use*) are installed parallel to major roads in Standstill. They cost little, slightly reduce traffic thus improving efficiency and reducing costs to businesses, and improve conditions for people who do not have access to a car.
Net gain/no net loss	Advances in some social, economic or environmental aspects outweigh losses in others	Congestion charging (*fiscal, reduce impacts of car use and enhance public transport*) in Standstill reduces urban traffic by 20%. The revenue is used to improve public transport services. People who continue to drive have to pay but have a faster journey: poorer people, and people whose jobs are car-based suffer more than others. People who use public transport benefit. Overall Standstill's residents agree that the benefits of congestion charging outweigh its costs.
Conflict minimization	Solutions which reduce the potential conflict between different objectives	The council wants to develop use of Park and Ride sites (*technical, reduce impacts of car use*) so as to reduce traffic in Standstill. However, people are concerned about the safety of their cars and the price of the Park and Ride service. The council installs security cameras at the Park and Ride sites, and makes the price of parking there considerably cheaper than parking in Standstill city centre.
Policy compatibility	Components of a strategic action are not working against each other	Tooton Rush's transport plan includes the provision of cycle lanes in Standstill to encourage people to travel by bike. The plan also reduces the number of parking spaces in Standstill (*regulatory, reduce impacts of car use*) to discourage car use and encourage car users to cycle instead.
Strategic coordination	Strategic actions covering the same area support each other	Tooton Rush's housing plan promotes high density housing, working from home, and mixed residential–commercial areas (*spatial, avoid car use*). This supports Tooton Rush's transport plan which aims to reduce the need to travel and promotes alternatives to the car.

Type of integration	How it works	Example from Tooton Rush (notes in italics explain the types of mitigation measures)
Addressing all three themes separately	Promoting social, economic and environmental objectives separately within one strategic action	Tooton Rush's transport plan promotes freight transfer facilities (*technical, reduce impacts of lorry use*) with consequent economic benefits; subsidized bus fares for the elderly (*fiscal, enhance accessibility afforded by bus*) with consequent social benefits; and requirements to carry out an air quality assessment for all large new transport-generating developments (*procedural, avoid impacts*) with benefits for air quality.

Source: adapted from CAG (2000)

Anyway, this is the time for the usual self-check, based on the quality assurance criteria of Box 4.3:

- Have the likely significant impacts on the environment and sustainability been identified and evaluated?
- Have the strategic action's likely indirect and cumulative impacts and impact interactions been identified and evaluated?
- Have appropriate impact prediction and evaluation techniques been used?
- Has impact evaluation been carried out in relation to relevant, accepted standards, regulations and thresholds?
- Have the environmental and sustainability impacts of each alternative been identified and compared?
- Have measures been identified to avoid, reduce, repair compensate and/or enhance any significant impacts of implementing the strategic action?
- Have links to project EIA been made explicit?

Chapter 9 discusses the final steps in SEA: documentation of the process, implementation of the strategic action, and monitoring of the strategic action's impacts.

Chapter 9

Documentation, Implementation and Monitoring

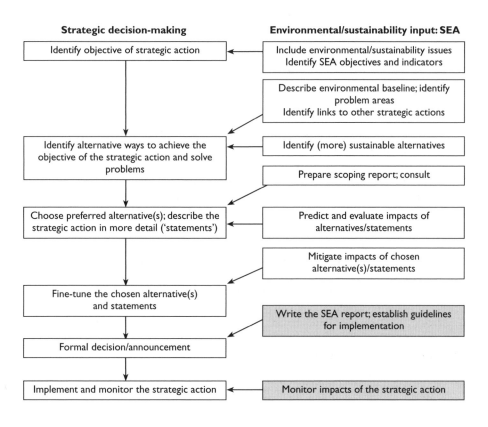

Strategic decision-making	Environmental/sustainability input: SEA
Identify objective of strategic action	Include environmental/sustainability issues Identify SEA objectives and indicators
	Describe environmental baseline; identify problem areas Identify links to other strategic actions
Identify alternative ways to achieve the objective of the strategic action and solve problems	Identify (more) sustainable alternatives
	Prepare scoping report; consult
Choose preferred alternative(s); describe the strategic action in more detail ('statements')	Predict and evaluate impacts of alternatives/statements
	Mitigate impacts of chosen alternative(s)/statements
Fine-tune the chosen alternative(s) and statements	Write the SEA report; establish guidelines for implementation
Formal decision/announcement	
Implement and monitor the strategic action	Monitor impacts of the strategic action

SEA stage	What to decide	What to record
Write the SEA report; establish guidelines for implementation	How to present the data from the previous stages of SEA	Prepare the SEA report
Consult	Whom to consult; how to respond to consultation results	How consultation results were addressed
Monitor environmental/sustainability impacts of the strategic action	How to deal with any negative impacts of the strategic action	How the strategic action's impacts will be monitored and significant effects dealt with

This chapter considers the last stages of an SEA process: documenting the process, consulting on the SEA report, ensuring that the report findings are used in decision-making, and setting up a system to monitor the actual effects of the plan.

Documentation

Hopefully by now it should be clear that the SEA report that accompanies the draft strategic action is not the important thing: what *is* important is the process that precedes it. The role of the SEA report is to document the SEA process so that readers can follow how environmental and sustainability considerations have been taken into account in decision-making. A report is not an effective way to convince decision-makers to make changes to their strategic action.

The SEA documentation will have several audiences:

- the public, who will want to see why certain alternatives were chosen and how major impacts will be mitigated, but will *not* be interested in massive, horrid assessment tables, or complex models;
- the organization(s) responsible for quality control, who will want to see the same, but will also want to ensure that the SEA has been rigorous: they will look at the SEA methodology, and at changes made to the strategic action as a result of the SEA; and
- consultants, academics and other authorities who will be interested in the SEA methodology.

None of them, in all honesty, will be interested in whether the North Pinksey Lane allotments provide + or ++ benefits to health. All of them will want to know what alternatives were considered to the statement that says that all new energy for Tooton Rush will come from nuclear power stations. So here are some rules for documenting SEA findings:

- DO focus on the big issues.
- DO focus on changes made to the strategic action as a result of the SEA. This will show that the SEA has been carried out well, and that a range of alternatives/ideas have been considered in decision-making.
- DO explain what alternatives and mitigation measures were considered, and why the preferred alternative was chosen. This provides an audit trail of decisions, and shows the role that sustainability issues played in the decisions.
- DO explain the SEA methodology used: who was involved, how long it took, etc. This shows that the SEA was carried out well.

- DO NOT feel obliged to include every single incredibly long and dreary assessment table.

Documentation of the SEA process can take various forms. It can be one big report near the end of the decision-making process; or (better) several smaller ones at various stages of the process which can be brought together into a final report if necessary; or information bulletins; or a website.

The information that must be covered in the SEA report(s) will vary according to legal requirements. For instance Annex I of the SEA Directive and Annex IV of the SEA Protocol specify the minimum SEA report requirements for countries that they apply to. Table 9.1 proposes a structure for a final SEA report: different parts of it could be presented in smaller reports instead.

It would definitely be worthwhile writing the SEA report in parallel with the SEA process, rather than in one big effort at the end. People move, die, forget: institutional memory gets lost. By the end of an SEA process, the entire SEA team may have changed, and nobody may remember why a particular alternative was chosen or environmental criterion rejected. Make notes as you go along!

Implementation plan

The SEA report(s) should include a plan which ensures that the strategic action is implemented in the most sustainable manner possible. This brings together the findings of different stages of the SEA process into an action plan, for instance:

- where other strategic actions conflict with the strategic action in question and need to be changed: who needs to be contacted and what might be done;
- what other actions need to be taken, for instance encouraging bus companies to provide more buses on route X, or asking the neighbouring authority to revise its parking policies;
- what further guidance needs to be written, eg guidance on energy efficiency standards, maximum parking standards or wildlife-friendly design; and
- what needs monitoring.

The plan could identify who is responsible for each action, by when, how one can tell whether it has been put in place and whether it is effective, and what to do if it is not put in place or is not effective.

Table 9.1 *Possible structure for final SEA report*

Structure of report	Information to include	Which chapter in this book discusses this
Summary and outcomes	• Non-technical summary of the SEA report • What difference the SEA process has made	8, 10
Methodology used	• Who carried out the SEA, when, who was consulted, etc	5
Background	• Purpose of the SEA • Strategic action objectives • Links to other strategic actions • Baseline environmental/sustainability data • Environmental/sustainability visions and problems • Difficulties in collecting data and limitations of the data	2, 5, 6
Plan issues and alternatives	• Significant environmental/sustainability impacts of the strategic action. This may be done for different 'levels' of the strategic action: strategic objectives, alternatives, detailed statements, individual sites, etc • Why the preferred alternative(s) were chosen, including how environmental/sustainability considerations were taken into account in the choice • Other alternatives considered, and why these were rejected • Mitigation measures that have been taken on board. • Where proposed mitigation measures have not been taken on board, the reasons why not	7, 8
Implementation	• Links to project EIA, design guidance, implementation plan, etc • Proposed monitoring	9

Consultation on the SEA report(s)

The most important aspects of public participation and the involvement of experts should already have taken place during the SEA process. Consultation on the SEA report(s) – note the deliberate use of that word rather than 'participation', since commenting on reports can be nothing else – will have a limited effect at best in improving the strategic action. Its main aim is to present information about the SEA process.

Table 9.2 *Summary of responses to SEA report consultation*

Consultee	Consultation response	How the strategic action was changed to take the consultation response on board or ...	... Why the strategic action was not changed
Landscape Agency	More emphasis needed on preservation of sensitive, but non-designated landscapes	Policy L3 amended to include reference to sensitive non-designated as well as designated landscapes	
M Beechey	Proposed extension of North Pinksey School is inappropriate because it would cause increased traffic in the lane		Children are currently being driven to Rotley School further away. Expansion of North Pinksey School should reduce the need to travel by car
...			

The final SEA report should be published in parallel with the draft strategic action, and should be made available for public consultation as part of the strategic action consultation process. It should also be made available for comment to the environmental and other authorities, and to other countries whose environment is likely to be significantly affected by the strategic action. SEA reports can be placed on the Web as well as being made available in hard copy: this is not only an increasingly common way to disseminate information to the public, but an invaluable tool for others carrying out SEA who can get ideas about report structure, data sources, etc from such reports.

According to the SEA Directive and Protocol, the views of the public, environmental and other authorities, and other countries where appropriate, on the SEA report must be 'taken into (due) account' in the final strategic action. Changes made to the strategic action as a result of this consultation should be documented. Where consultation responses are not taken on board, reasons should be given for why not. Table 9.2 shows a possible way of documenting this.

Monitoring

The SEA team should propose an SEA monitoring system. SEA monitoring allows the actual impacts of the strategic action to be tested

Table 9.3 *Possible format for a monitoring programme*

Objective	What to monitor	Who provides the data?	How often?	At what point should additional action be considered?	What could be done if a problem is identified?
Protect biodiversity at ecosystem, species and genetic levels	Condition of designated sites and other sites of nature conservation importance	Planners	Every 2 years	Condition gets worse	Consider ways of improving biodiversity protection and enhancement, eg provision of wildlife corridors
Protect human health and amenity	Number of accidents per person-kilometre travelled by car, foot, bike	Police	Annual	Any of these gets 10% worse	Improvements to pedestrian and cycling facilities, traffic calming, new road layout to reduce accidents
Promote positive health-related behaviour	% children walking or cycling to school	Environmental health authority	Every 2 years	10% decreases	Liaise with cycling officer; establish walking and cycling routes
...					

against those that were predicted, major problems to be identified and dealt with, and environment/sustainability baseline information to be gathered for future strategic actions. It helps to ensure that the proposed mitigation measures are carried out, and than no unforeseen impacts occur.

Monitoring should be carried out using the indicators/objectives used for describing the baseline environment and making SEA predictions. The table of baseline information (eg Tables 4.1 and 6.4) should already have identified some of the types of monitoring needed. The impact prediction and evaluation stage may have identified additional gaps in the data that require monitoring. By focusing on outcome measures (as do the indicators for the baseline environment), monitoring will help to take account of cumulative and indirect as well as direct impacts. Where it makes sense to do so, SEA monitoring can be linked to monitoring of the strategic action or other monitoring systems, but such monitoring often focuses on inputs, not outcomes, and could thus be inappropriate for SEA.

Table 9.3 shows a possible format for a monitoring programme. It includes possible actions to reduce impacts if they emerge: this is a form of mitigation of environmental/sustainability effects.

Conclusions

If an SEA process has been carried out well, writing the SEA report should be a straightforward process of recording what has been done, most of the consultation will already have been done before the draft strategic action is published, and devising the implementation and monitoring measures will simply be a way of tying up the loose ends. Otherwise this is the time to panic.

Here is the last self-check, based on the quality assurance criteria of Box 4.3:

- Has the SEA been conducted as an integral part of the decision-making process, starting when the strategic action objectives were developed and continuing throughout the decision-making process?
- Does the SEA report
  - identify the decision-maker and who carried out the SEA, and their competences?
  - have a clear and concise layout and presentation; is it presented as an integrated whole, and does it use maps and other illustrations where appropriate?
  - use simple, clear language and avoid technical jargon?
  - describe the methodology used in the SEA, including who was consulted and how?
  - focus on the big issues?
  - acknowledge external sources of information, including expert judgement and matters of opinion?
  - contain a non-technical summary which includes an explanation of the overall approach to the SEA; the objectives of the strategic action; the main alternatives considered, and how the strategic action was changed by the SEA?
  - avoid bias and is it presented in an impartial and open manner?
- Is an explanation given of how environmental/sustainability considerations are integrated into the strategic action, what changes (if any) were made to the strategic action as a result of the SEA, and the reasons for choosing the strategic action as adopted, in the light of other reasonable alternatives dealt with?
- Have the draft strategic action and SEA report been made available for consultation to the public and all relevant bodies/countries?
- Has the range of environmental and other authorities and the public consulted been appropriate?

- Have the environmental and other authorities and the public been given an early and effective opportunity within appropriate timeframes to express their opinion on the draft strategic action and SEA report before adoption of the strategic action?
- Have the public's and relevant bodies/countries' views been summarized and responded to?
- Have measures for monitoring been made explicit?
- Is monitoring linked to provision of future baseline information?

The next and final chapter discusses how to ensure that SEA is done well.

Part III

Assuring SEA Quality

Chapter 10

Ensuring that the SEA is Done Well and Resourcing It

This last chapter pulls together the material from the rest of the book. It considers what makes a 'good' SEA and how to ensure that an SEA is done well. It revisits some of the case studies discussed previously to reflect on the SEA process in its entirety. It then discusses the resources needed for SEA. Three SEA models are presented – SEA in 1, 10 and 100 person-days – to give an indication of what is feasible, and what can most usefully be prioritized. Capacity building for SEA is then discussed. The chapter concludes with a brief discussion of future directions in SEA.

Ensuring SEA quality

How does one ensure that an SEA has been done 'well'? What is a 'good' SEA process? This section aims to unpick the concept of SEA quality and identify ways of ensuring good SEA.

What is a good SEA process?

Returning to Chapter 2, the aim of SEA is to help to protect the environment and promote sustainability by helping to integrate environmental or sustainability issues in decision-making. One way of testing the quality of SEA is to check whether it has accomplished this aim. Unless a strategic action is perfectly sustainable or environmentally benign to begin with, which would be very nice but also very unlikely, one way of testing SEA quality is thus to compare the strategic action before and after SEA, noting any sustainability- or environment-related changes.

To get to such changes, shown as Box B in Figure 10.1, several criteria need to be met. First, the SEA has to identify the strategic action's sustainability or environmental impacts, and suggest possible

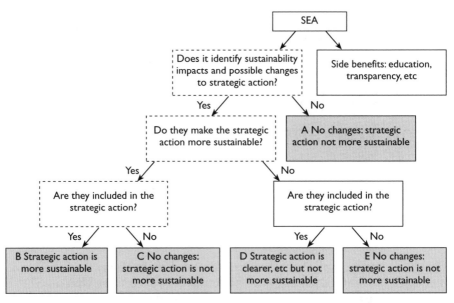

Source: adapted from Therivel and Minas (2002)

Figure 10.1 *Getting to improved strategic actions through SEA*

changes. Such changes could be simple amendments, clearer wording, or improvements to the internal consistency of the strategic action, or they could involve a totally new approach to the strategic action. Second, the changes must make the strategic action more sustainable or environmentally benign. Since SEA highlights environmental or sustainability impacts, subsequent changes to the strategic action could be expected to incorporate these concerns. However an SEA could also identify changes that improve the strategic action (for instance clearer wording or structure) but do not necessarily improve its sustainability or environmental aspects. Third, the changes have to be incorporated in the strategic action. Suggested changes may not be incorporated where, for instance, the SEA is carried out too late, other factors outweigh sustainability considerations, or the changes are not politically acceptable (Therivel and Minas, 2002).

However, even where the strategic action remains unchanged after the SEA, the SEA may still be useful because it has side benefits or 'indirect outcomes' (Thissen, 2000). For instance it may provide a better understanding of the environment, the strategic action or the SEA process; it may allow the decision-making process to be more transparent and publicly accountable; or it may provide ideas for how to improve the strategic action in the next round of decision-making. Indeed, although incorporating the SEA results into the strategic action is important from a *sustainability* perspective, it is not the only criterion by which to judge its effectiveness as a *decision-making* tool.

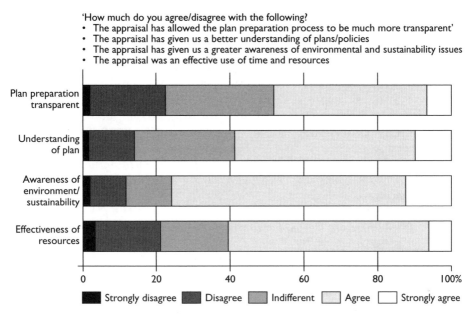

'How much do you agree/disagree with the following?
- The appraisal has allowed the plan preparation process to be much more transparent'
- The appraisal has given us a better understanding of plans/policies
- The appraisal has given us a greater awareness of environmental and sustainability issues
- The appraisal was an effective use of time and resources

Source: Therivel and Minas (2002)

Figure 10.2 *Side benefits of sustainability appraisal*

Figure 10.2 shows how UK planners perceive some of the side benefits of sustainability appraisal (Box 3.1). It is based on a questionnaire survey sent to all local authorities in England and Wales in autumn 2001, with 281 responses (68 per cent response rate). Interestingly, about 60 per cent of respondents felt that sustainability appraisal gave them a better understanding of their plans. In addition, 59 per cent of respondents disagreed with the statement '[SEA] is only worthwhile if it changes the plan/policy', presumably due to the recognition of these side benefits (Minas, 2002; Therivel and Minas, 2002).

Ensuring a good SEA process

Chapter 2 suggested several 'rules' for achieving an SEA process that improves the strategic action and optimizes 'indirect outcomes':

- start early;
- involve the decision-maker;
- focus on key environmental/sustainability constraints, thresholds and limits;
- consider alternatives;
- apply the precautionary principle;
- aim to minimize negative impacts, optimize positive ones, and compensate for the loss of valuable features and benefits; and

- be transparent and promote public participation in decision-making.

Several of these 'rules' come from four surveys of UK planners spanning eight years (Therivel 1995, 1996, 1998; Therivel and Minas, 2002). Planners' responses to the open question 'What advice would you give to others carrying out an appraisal?' have been remarkably consistent over the years:

- *[SEA] should be started early in the plan preparation process, in order to maximise the contribution it can make to guiding the plan process.*
- *Plan it into the timetable for plan preparation.*
- *[SEA] needs to be simple in order to be transparent. It is a tool not a panacea.*
- *Don't underestimate the amount of work involved.*
- *Just get on with it – we tried to employ consultants and realised it was huge time and money – and we would still have to do the work!.*
- *Always discuss issues and reach conclusions between at least two people to minimise subjectivity.*

The most recent of these questionnaire surveys focused on those factors that could lead to sustainability appraisals changing plans, and having side benefits such as those shown in Figure 10.2. The survey asked who had carried out the appraisal, how many person-days it took, and whether it was carried out early in the plan-making or near the end. From this, several factors were identified which improve the likelihood of a plan being changed in response to sustainability appraisal (and presumably SEA):

Appraisal carried out by groups of planners, possibly with consultant support: Plans were least likely to change when only one person in the local authority carried out the appraisal. When more than one planner was involved, plans were twice as likely to change. They were most likely to change when consultants worked with local authority planners. Appraisals carried out jointly between local authority personnel and consultants were also most likely to increase the planners' understanding of environmental/sustainability issues (suggesting a skills transfer) and of the plan.

Those authorities with more experience in undertaking appraisals were more likely to change the plan: 50 per cent of authorities that had completed one appraisal changed their plan, rising to 69 per cent for four or more. This suggests that, as planners become familiar with SEA techniques, they start using SEA as a way of improving, rather than just analysing, the plan.

Appraisal carried out early in decision-making: The survey showed that, for those plans *not* changed as a result of sustainability appraisal, nearly

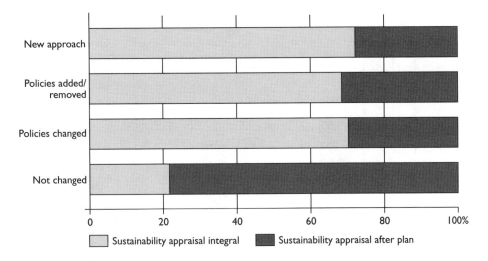

Figure 10.3 *Changes to the plan with sustainability appraisal carried out as an integral part of plan-making v. after the plan was completed*

80 per cent of the appraisals were carried out after the plan was largely completed. In contrast, for those plans that *were* changed as a result of sustainability appraisal, 70 per cent of appraisals were integral to the plan-making process (Figure 10.3). Appraisals undertaken as an integral part of plan-making were also more frequently associated with an improvement in planners' awareness of sustainability issues and the plan, and were much more likely to be perceived as an effective use of resources (Figure 10.4). This reflects the easier integration of appraisal results when the appraisal is carried out early: changing the plan when it is nearly completed will present greater barriers.

More resources, but with commitment to use the appraisal results positively: On average roughly twice as much time was spent on appraisals that resulted in changes to the plan compared with those that did not: about 60 person-days compared to about 30. Appraisals that were an integral part of the plan-making process also took on average longer than post-hoc appraisals. This suggests that a minimum amount of effort is needed before an appraisal is of a standard that can reveal the need for change. It could also suggest that, in a supportive institutional context where enough resources are put into the appraisal, there is also a willingness to take on board proposed changes from the appraisal process. On the other hand, of those appraisals that took 10 days or less, almost 40 per cent led to changes to the plan, suggesting that even rapid SEAs can be effective (Therivel and Minas, 2002). The survey of 1997 (Therivel, 1998) showed no link between resource use and changes to the plan: shorter appraisals were as likely to improve the plan as longer ones.

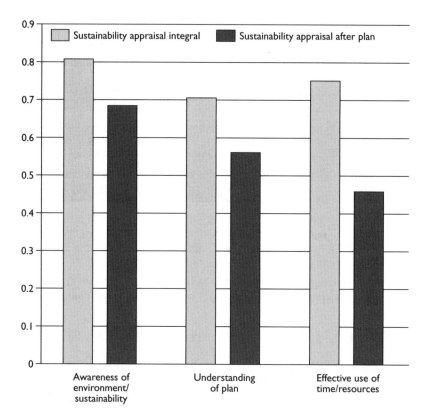

Figure 10.4 *Timing of appraisal v. indirect benefits and resource-efficiency*

All three factors together – group appraisal, an early start to appraisal and enough resources – are a particularly potent mixture. Of the appraisals that involved more than one person *and* were integral to plan-making *and* took more than 15 person-days, 95 per cent resulted in some change to the plan (Therivel and Minas, 2002).

Ensuring a bad SEA process

Just to hammer these points home, here is a five-step programme showing how to spend a lot of resources on SEA with minimal benefit:

1   Find out that you need an SEA when the strategic action is almost completed; alternatively 'forget' that you need an SEA until then. Decide that none of your staff can do the SEA because they are too busy putting final touches on the strategic action.
2   Hire the cheapest consultant you can find, who happens to live far away and be unfamiliar with the area: justify this by saying that you need 'independent' assessment of the strategic action.

Alternatively, get your most junior planner to do the SEA: explain that this will be 'a good introduction to our strategic action'.

3 Put the consultant/junior planner into a room with the strategic action and some blank tables on a computer. Give them detailed rules for filling out the tables, eg '?++ is totally different from +?+, and ++ / ? has a completely different meaning again. When adding the assessment symbols up, subtract 0.5 for each '?' which comes after a '+' but multiply the total of +s by 0.667 where the '?' comes before'. Forget about them for three weeks while you put further finishing touches on the strategic action. Rebuff attempts to involve you or any other member of your team in the SEA process.

4 When the bleary-eyed consultant/planner has filled in all the tables, pay the consultant lots of money. Expect the planner to either quit at the first opportunity (with consequent costs in terms of hiring someone new), or else press in an annoying manner for changes to the strategic action that simply cannot be accommodated before it is due at the printer's (wasting their own time and that of the other planners).

5 Print out the SEA tables, wrap them in a handsome cover that says 'SEA report', and place this on a prominent shelf. When the strategic action is put out to consultation and people ask where the SEA report is, let them look at the report only at limited and variable times, and provide only the corner of a cramped desk for them to do so.

Then the inspector, or judge, or audit commission asks for the SEA, prompted by public comments about the poor quality and lack of accessibility of the SEA report. The inspector decides that the SEA report does not provide the required information, and that the SEA process (as described – or not – in the SEA report) does not inspire confidence. She wants to know why you chose the preferred alternative that you did, and why you did not consider several alternatives and mitigation measures suggested by the public and other consultees. The inspector sends the strategic action back to you and asks you to re-do the SEA, getting it right this time. Several months and lots of resources after you started the SEA, you start again ...

Testing the quality of the SEA report

In the end, we want a strategic action that is as sustainable as possible. So the ultimate test of decision-making is to check the sustainability of the strategic action itself. Box 10.1 presents sustainability principles for strategic actions: if the strategic action fulfils these principles, decision-makers can feel justifiably proud.

Box 10.1 Is the strategic action sustainable? The Bellagio Principles

Does the strategic action...

1 Guiding vision and goals
   - have a clear vision of sustainable development and goals that define that vision?

2 Holistic perspective
   - include review of the whole system as well as its parts?
   - consider the well-being of social, ecological and economic sub-systems, and interactions?
   - consider all wider positive and negative consequences of human activity, in money and non-money terms?

3 Essential elements
   - consider equity and disparity within the current population and between present and future generations (resource use, over-consumption and poverty, human rights, access to services, etc)?
   - consider the ecological conditions on which life depends?
   - consider economic development and other, non-market activities that contribute to human/social well-being?

4 Adequate scope
   - use time horizons which cover short-term and future generations?
   - set boundaries to encompass local and remote impacts on people and ecosystems?
   - anticipate future conditions from past and current situations?

5 Practical focus
   - have an organizing framework linking vision and goals to indicators and criteria?
   - have a limited number of key issues for analysis?
   - use standardized units for comparison purposes?
   - compare indicator values to targets, ranges, thresholds, etc?

6 Openness
   - make methods and data accessible to all?
   - make judgements, assumptions and uncertainties explicit?

7 Effective communication
   - address the needs of the audience and the set of users?
   - find ways of engaging decision-makers with tools and indicators?
   - aim for simple structure and clear language?

8 Broad participation
   - obtain a broad representation of views to ensure recognition of diverse and changing values?
   - ensure participation of decision-makers to ensure a firm link to policies and action?

9   Ongoing assessment
  • develop a capacity for repeated measurement to determine trends?
  • have an iterative, adaptive and responsive approach to change and uncertainty?
  • adjust goals, frameworks and indicators as new insights are gained?
  • promote development of collective learning and feedback to decision-making?

10 Institutional capacity
  • clearly assign responsibilities and provide ongoing support in the decision-making process?
  • provide institutional capacity for data collection, maintenance and documentation?
  • support development of local assessment capacity?

Source: Hardi and Zdan (1997)

In SEA terms, although it is the process that matters, a post-hoc check of the SEA report can help to indirectly test whether the SEA process has been carried out well. There is already a tradition of testing the quality of environmental impact statements (eg European Commission, 2001; Glasson et al, 1999; Lee and Colley, 1990), and a similar approach can be used for SEA reports.

Box 4.3 presented a quality assurance checklist for SEA. Such a checklist can be used by government officials, inspectors/auditors, organizations carrying out SEA or members of the public. In carrying out an SEA review, reviewers would normally do the following:

• familiarize themselves with the content of the SEA report;
• identify whether the quality assurance questions are relevant to the strategic action under review;
• carry out the review using the grades described in Box 10.2;
• identify:
  – major omissions: shortcomings of the SEA report so serious that they require immediate correction in the form of a supplement to the report or a new SEA,
  – significant omissions: shortcomings that can be rectified fairly easily by means of explanations and conditions, and
  – secondary omissions: shortcomings that are not worth remedying immediately but should be kept in mind for the next SEA;
• decide what corrective action is needed if the report fails to meet the standards required.

Box 10.2 SEA review grades

A   well performed, no important tasks left incomplete
B   satisfactory and complete, only minor omissions and inadequacies
C   just satisfactory despite omissions and/or inadequacies
D   parts well attempted but must, on the whole be considered just unsatisfactory because of omissions and/or inadequacies
E   unsatisfactory, significant omissions or inadequacies
F   very unsatisfactory, important task(s) poorly done or not attempted
N/A   not applicable, the review topic is not applicable in the context of the strategic action

Source: Lee and Colley (1990)

The case studies revisited: Was SEA effective?

Throughout this book a range of examples from different case studies have been presented. At this stage it might be worthwhile stepping back and re-examining the SEA processes of three of the main case studies, each with a different scale, level of strategic-ness, and approach to SEA. The point here is not to criticize individual cases, but rather to extract messages about what makes SEA effective.

Case study 1: National policy on food and farming

In mid 2001, in response to a crisis in British agriculture – plummeting farmers' incomes, foot and mouth disease, changing European subsidies – the UK government set up a commission charged with developing a strategy for the future of farming and food. The commission published a discussion document in January 2002, held many meetings with the public and key stakeholders during spring/summer 2002, and received over 1000 responses.

The Sustainable Development Commission (SDC), a separate government commission responsible for promoting sustainability, took 16 of these responses – those of the most influential farming, retail and environmental organizations – and assessed the sustainability of each response in a sustainability appraisal. Essentially the appraisal treated each response/submission as a different alternative for the future of food and farming.

The SEA was carried out by consultants over two months, using the criteria of Table 6.2 to appraise the submissions. No stakeholders were involved in the appraisal, nor was the commission on farming and food. The resulting SEA report discussed the assessment methodology, the choice of submissions to appraise, the key benefits and costs of each submission – in the form of Tables 8.3 and 8.4, plus a few introductory paragraphs for each submission – and broad issues raised by the SEA.

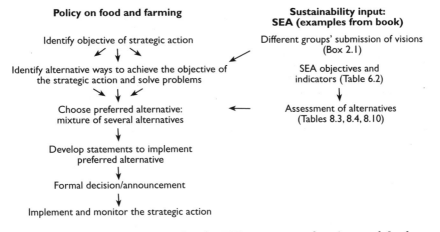

Figure 10.5 *SEA process for the UK strategy on farming and food*

The SEA highlighted the constraints imposed by current World Trade Organization rules on trade policy; the concentration of power to the giant supermarket chains which limited farmers' flexibility and incomes; that subsidies for agricultural production were failing to deliver value for money; and public ignorance about food production, purchase and use. It also noted that the submissions showed no real sensitivity to regional differences or different farming practices, made little mention of rural culture or recreation, and rarely discussed how farming could be made more resilient to change, for example to climate change or changes in subsidies.

The SEA (SDC, 2001) was published and sent to the commission on farming and food in December 2001. A year later the government published its *Strategy for Sustainable Farming and Food: Facing the Future* (DEFRA, 2002). The strategy was published alongside a report which considers how economic instruments can be used to promote environmental goals, and a proposal for monitoring which includes monitoring of some environmental effects. The strategy makes no mention of the SEA. Figure 10.5 summarizes this process.

So was it a good SEA process? The SEA criteria used were good, and incorporated equity and resilience issues. The use of different organizations' submissions as visions for the future of farming and food was novel and effective. But it is doubtful that the SEA had any real influence on the decision-makers: not only were they not actively involved in the assessment process, but they did not even commission the SEA. On the other hand, the commission on farming and food included several experts with very robust sustainability credentials, and the extensive consultation meetings would have raised many sustainability issues. Arguably these factors were more effective than any SEA could have been in integrating sustainability considerations in the final strategy.

Case study 2: Regional Economic Strategy

The South West of England Regional Development Agency (RDA) was formed in April 1999, and published its first Regional Economic Strategy (RES) in late 1999. In mid 2002, the RDA started reviewing the RES by identifying changes in circumstances that would require changes to the RES, and inviting stakeholders to comment on the existing RES. The respondents were generally happy with the existing RES, but suggested changes including a clearer focus on regional priorities and targets, a long-term economic vision expressed in an economic manner (eg GDP growth), better promotion of the region, a clearer vision for rural economic development and delivery of affordable housing, and greater emphasis on the importance of infrastructure to the region's prosperity.

These comments informed the development of a new draft RES. This was published in September 2002 along with a 'context' report which provided baseline economic data and a discussion of related policies.

The RDA also asked one of the consultees who had sustainability expertise to carry out a sustainability appraisal of the RES using the principles of the South West Regional Sustainable Development Framework as criteria. The sustainability appraisal considered the RES's sub-components in terms of key sustainability opportunities and threats and related Regional Sustainable Development Framework principles, and made recommendations for how the RES could be *implemented* in a sustainable manner. It did not discuss how the RES itself could be changed to become more sustainable because this was felt to be too detailed and concrete a level of appraisal for a strategy. The consultee included the appraisal as part of their consultation comments.

The consultation comments informed the development of the Ministerial Draft of the RES which was published in December 2002. Figure 10.6 summarizes the process.

Was it a good SEA process? The sustainability appraisal itself was very brief: more of a snapshot than an input to decision-making. It also remained at a very strategic level while the RES supports some quite specific development projects: as discussed in Box 8.4, these probably merit much more detailed assessment. On the other hand, several members of the South West RDA involved in developing the RES have strong sustainability credentials and have actively tried to ensure that the RES is as sustainable as possible, and hope to make subsequent versions of the RES still more sustainable. Again, these factors are at least as important as a formal SEA process would be in integrating sustainability in the RES.

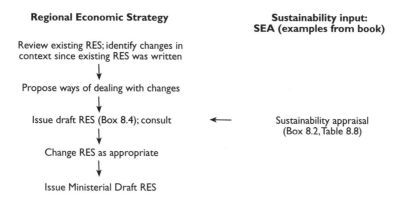

Figure 10.6 *SEA process for the Regional Economic Strategy for the South West*

Case study 3: UK local development plans

Local development plans – which will be superseded by Local Development Frameworks in 2004 (DTLR, 2001) – consist of perhaps half a dozen general statements of intention followed by roughly 50–250 more detailed statements of how those intentions will be implemented ('plan policies'). They were reviewed every 5–10 years (Local Development Frameworks will be rewritten more often).

When reviewing its development plan, a local authority would normally publish an Issues and Options paper, consult on this, publish a draft plan, consult on this, and publish a final plan. (This is a gross simplification: different levels of local authority, depths of review, levels of involvement by inspectors, regions, etc, all complicate things enormously. But the broad stages hold true.) Sustainability appraisals as described in Box 3.1 have traditionally been carried out on the draft plan – and, where the plan was being completely rewritten, increasingly at the earlier stages. The sustainability appraisal findings (if they weren't too late) were incorporated in the final plan. Figure 10.7 summarizes this.

Sustainability appraisals are not viewed with great warmth and enthusiasm by local authority planners. They are perceived as yet another thing that the poor beleaguered planners have to do as part of the plan-making process. But many planners have carried out several appraisals, there is plenty of guidance and many good practice examples of sustainability appraisal, quick appraisals at key decision times are increasingly carried out because such appraisals are perceived as a way of making sure that the plan is robust, and plan policies are routinely changed to take account of the findings of the sustainability appraisal.

Is this a good SEA process? Yes. UK local authority planners are starting to fully integrate the principles and process of SEA into their

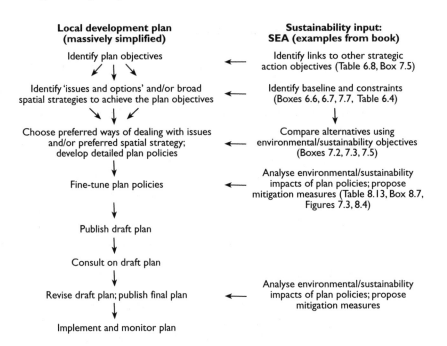

Figure 10.7 *SEA process (massively simplified) for local development plans*

daily work. They are writing policies that automatically integrate sustainability principles, are voluntarily starting their SEA early, and are perceiving it as an integral part of plan-making. Of course there is room for improvement, but the key principles of SEA are being applied.

Lessons from the case studies

SEA aims to integrate environmental and sustainability issues in decision-making. Something does not have to be called 'SEA', or follow a specific process, or even be documented to do so. In the first two case studies above, SEA reports were written but they had no visible effect. The thing that ensured that the policy on farming and food and the Regional Economic Strategy for the South West are (relatively) sustainable was the choice of, and skills of, the people writing them: the *people* ensured that *SEA-type thinking* was integrated into the decision-making process. In the third case study, the SEA process has primarily acted as an educational tool: it is the *different way of thinking* engendered in planners by going through the sustainability appraisal that really ensures that a plan is as sustainable as possible.

How to do SEA in 1, 10 and 100 person-days

Most of the effectiveness of SEA comes from decision-makers being prepared to take on board the SEA findings. A short SEA process can be effective, and in contrast even a huge commitment of time and energy can be wasted if decision-makers are unwilling to take account of the SEA findings.

As such, asking how long it takes to do an SEA is like asking how long a piece of string is. An SEA can take 10 years to carry out but this does not guarantee that it will improve the decision-making process. Conversely, the rudiments of a good SEA can be carried out in a day. Legal SEA requirements influence the minimum amount of work needed (more than a day, I'm afraid), but even then an efficiently run SEA can be carried out in a fraction of the time taken by an inefficient SEA. An SEA that fulfils the requirements of the SEA Directive or Protocol should normally be able to be completed in less than 100 person-days.

Factors that affect how long SEA takes include when the SEA is started in the decision-making cycle; the amount and quality of baseline data that already exists; whether stakeholders are willing to share data and/or collaborate in collecting data; whether there is consensus on key environmental/sustainability constraints; whether lists of relevant strategic actions and their requirements already exist; and what consultation processes already exist. A good scoping stage can vastly reduce the time spent on an SEA. In the UK, planners faced with implementing the SEA Directive (but who have not yet done so) have been most concerned about the time involved in collecting baseline data, consulting on the SEA, and considering alternatives.

To illustrate some of these points, three models of SEA are presented below: 1-day, 10-day and 100-day SEA. All of them include fundamentals of good SEA practice: involvement of the decision-makers, group assessment and a focus on improving the strategic action. The first one is primarily of use as a training exercise, so that decision-makers can get a feel for the kind of thinking and process involved in SEA. However, even such a short SEA can lead to improvements in some aspects of the strategic action. The second one is a 'quick-and-dirty' but effective process that would identify key issues: for a larger SEA, it could act as a scoping stage. The third one conforms to the requirements of the SEA Directive or Protocol. Note that all of them are in person-days, not time elapsed. Also note that the main purpose of this section is to suggest a rough allocation of what time should be spent on what SEA stages, not to act as a definitive work schedule.

SEA in 1 person-day

What this process will do:

- give initial ideas for possible improvements (if appropriate) to 4–6 statements or alternatives of the strategic action; and
- give a rough feel for several stages of SEA and an indication of what an entire SEA process feels like, as an educational process for the decision-makers involved.

The process can be carried out at any stage of the strategic action decision making process where alternatives or strategies are developed in enough detail so that they can be assessed. One planner – the SEA coordinator 📄 – spends slightly over an hour getting ready for the assessment. She and the author of the strategic action statements/alternatives 📄👥 – then spend another three hours each carrying out the assessment. There is no formal documentation of the process.

9:00 📄 Coffee (get the priorities right)

9:02 📄 Adapt the SEA objectives of Table 6.1 to the circumstances of the strategic action: take out objectives that are not appropriate to the context, and integrate any relevant other objectives currently used (as long as they deal with outcomes not inputs). Aim for 6–12 objectives.

9:30 📄 Brainstorm: what are worst environmental problems in the area? Put stars (*) next to the SEA objectives that symbolize the worst problems.

9:40 📄 Identify 6 statements that are most likely to cause significant environmental/sustainability impacts; alternatively identify up to 6 alternative approaches to a given issue or constraint. You only have one day to do all of this, so don't agonize. The aim is to focus on more, rather than less, important parts of the strategic action.

10:10 📄 Draw up a table like Table 4.2, with the 6 statements or alternatives in the first column, and the SEA objectives in the first row. Make sure to include a column on comments and proposed changes to the strategic action. Make enough copies of the table so that everyone involved in the SEA has a copy.

10:15 📄👥 Gather together the strategic action author. Give them coffee.

10:20 📄👥 Take the first statement/alternative. Fill in the table using the process outlined in Box 8.6. Focus particularly on any changes to the statement/alternative that would help to minimize negative impacts: the idea is to identify ways in which the strategic action could be improved. Focus particularly on those SEA objectives that you put a * next to.

11:10 🖹 ⁙ Now that you know how to do it, do the same thing for the other statements/alternatives, spending 20–25 minutes on each. If you are assessing alternatives, spend the last 10 minutes thinking about which alternative is best in terms of the environment or sustainability (using the SEA findings, focusing particularly on those objectives with * next to them).

13:00 Done!

SEA in 10 person-days

What this process will do:

- identify, in a rough-and-ready manner, key environmental/sustainability constraints to a strategic action;
- suggest some alternative approaches for dealing with these constraints;
- give ideas for possible improvements (if appropriate) to up to 60 statements or alternatives;
- result in an SEA report; and
- start ensuring that the SEA report findings are implemented.

The process should be begun early in the development of the strategic action, and involve all the plan authors.

Day 1:
- 🖹 ⁙ , 1–2 hours: Agree on how the SEA will be carried out. Agree SEA objectives and an initial list of key environmental/sustainability problems.
- 🖹, 1 hour: Document findings.

Day 2:
- 🖹, all day: Telephone local authority, environmental authority, etc officials; and do a web-search to confirm key environmental/sustainability problems and get data on them if available. If appropriate, in light of this work, suggest which SEA objectives are most important. Document the findings. (*Variant: if the strategic action has many alternatives or possible statements, spend part of the day identifying those that are most likely to have significant impacts so that the rest of the assessment process can focus on these*).

Day 3:
- 📄 ⫯⫯ , 2 hours: Using Figure 7.1, brainstorm strategic action alternatives or options that deal with the environmental/ sustainability constraints. Eliminate those that are clearly not feasible or appropriate.
- 📄, 1 hour: Document findings.

At this stage, ⫯⫯ would elaborate the alternatives/options into statements as part of their normal decision-making functions. The SEA resumes once this has been done.

Days 4–8:
- 📄 ⫯⫯ , 2 days: In groups of 2–3 (strategic action author, sustainability expert, one other person who knows the area, subject or sustainability), using the SEA objectives agreed on Day 1 (focusing particularly on key objectives identified on Day 2), analyse the statements as in the 10:20 and 11:10 sessions of the 1-day SEA (*Variant: assess broad alternatives, and then a limited number of more detailed statements. Another variant: assess fewer statements but in more depth, using some of the techniques in Appendix C.*) Document the SEA findings and proposed changes to the strategic action as the assessment progresses.

Days 9 and 10:
- 📄, all day: Follow up the SEA findings: discuss the SEA results with key decision-makers, try to ensure that they are actively taken on board, document the SEA methodology, put together the previously written documents into an SEA report, get the report put on the organization's website.

SEA in 100 days

Table 10.1 is based on a real-life SEA of a development plan carried out in accordance with the requirements of the SEA Directive (Speight et al, 2003). It allows for generous timing if little quantification of impacts is done; tight timing if much quantification is done.

What this process will do:

- a full SEA process in accordance with the SEA Directive or Protocol;
- inform decision-makers about sustainability and environmental issues; and
- result in an SEA report capable of withstanding inquiry/audit.

Table 10.1 *The Full Monty: 100-day SEA process*

SEA stage	Person-days	Comments and advice
Early in the development of the strategic action		
SEA training for decision-makers	3	An SEA consultant/trainer gives the SEA team a half-day training course on SEA, focusing on legal requirements and a good practice SEA case study similar to that being worked on
Devise SEA objectives	2	Link SEA objectives to existing objectives where appropriate. Check whether other assessment requirements (eg appropriate assessment) apply and integrate them with SEA if appropriate. Carry out an internal compatibility appraisal (see Appendix C) of the SEA objectives
Quick SEA of the existing strategic action	5	The authors of the strategic action quickly assess the (old) existing strategic action, if one exists, using the agreed SEA objectives, Table 4.2 and Box 8.6 (as in the 1-day SEA). This provides a starting point for drafting the new version of the strategic action
Collect baseline data and identify environmental/ sustainability issues	20	Set a specific timeframe for this stage, as it can in theory take forever. Use a cyclical process: collect some data, identify key issues, collect more data on these issues, etc. Start discussions with consultees. Document the findings
Identify links to other relevant strategic actions	5	Use existing lists of strategic actions and their requirements where possible to save time. Document the findings (see Table 6.8)
Write draft scoping report	2	Documentation of the above stages as they are being carried out helps to ease this process, leaving only the following aspects: methodology, purpose of the SEA, difficulties, limitations, etc. Test the quality of the report so far by using the checklist in Box 4.3
Consult on, and agree the scoping report (this could also be done after alternatives are identified)	4–7	This could be done (preferably) in a meeting of key stakeholders, or by correspondence. The extra days are if the public is also consulted (eg through a website and newspaper announcement)

SEA stage	Person-days	Comments and advice
As the strategic action evolves ...		
Identify alternatives or options; test them against the SEA objectives; mitigate impacts; test whether preferred alternatives/ options are compatible with each other	10	This is done in small groups, definitely including the decision-makers but possibly also other officers from the authority, outside experts, politicians and/or members of the public. Figure 7.1 provides a starting point for identifying sustainable alternatives. Table 4.2 and Box 8.6 provide a template for assessing the alternatives. Check the cumulative impacts of the preferred alternatives/options (eg Table 8.6), and revisit the options if cumulative impacts are significant
Implement the SEA findings	2	The decision-makers put procedures in place to ensure that the early SEA findings are implemented
... preferred alternatives/options are chosen and evolved into detailed statements		
Screen statements	1	Use the questions in Box 8.3 to ensure that those statements with the most significant impacts are given the most attention and vice versa
Test statements against the SEA objectives; mitigate impacts	30	This could involve small group 'expert judgement' sessions again, but could also involve research and possibly quantification for issues that need more detail (Appendix C). Remember to keep documenting limitations and any problems or uncertainty encountered
Implement the SEA findings, propose a monitoring programme	3	The decision-makers put procedures in place to ensure that the SEA findings are implemented and monitored
Write the SEA Report	4	Use Table 9.1 as a template. Allow plenty of time for formatting and editing. Test the quality of the report using the checklist in Box 4.3
Consult on the SEA report; take consultation comments on board; document how this was done	6–8	Table 9.2 provides a template for this
Celebrate the completion of the SEA	0.5	

Capacity building, setting a supportive context

SEA legislation tries to achieve a substantive outcome (environmental protection, sustainability) through procedural means. The two are linked, but are not the same thing: SEA legislation allows organizations to be challenged in terms of whether they have prepared the right reports at the right times and consulted the right people, but not in terms of whether their decision is environment-friendly and sustainable.

It is the substantive, not the procedural aspects of SEA that are important. SEA should not become a lawyer's charter: procedural requirements should only be referred to where it is clear that this is the only way to achieve SEA's objectives. A supportive context of training, resources and government support is needed, not the threat of the big legal stick.

This section discusses possible ways of promoting a positive 'SEA culture' that helps to avoid the uncertainty and confrontational aspects of SEA through training, efficiencies of scale and central support. This section is heavily based on Levett-Therivel (2002).

Promoting a culture of 'doing SEA'

Where SEA is not (yet) legally required, as a way to improve experience and confidence with SEA, decision-makers could voluntarily carry out SEA as part of their decision-making. This could have multiple advantages:

- it produces more sustainable strategic actions as soon as possible;
- it gives more decision-makers hands-on experience and confidence;
- it allows problems to be identified and ironed out before SEA becomes mandatory, and thus reduces the risk of problems and challenges when it does;
- it helps to improve people's skills and establishes a new type of 'green business' sector; and
- it increases the chances that when local or small-scale strategic actions come up for statutorily required SEA, the higher-level strategic actions that constrain them will already have undergone SEA and are therefore less likely to limit sustainable options.

Early examples of SEAs can provide invaluable models for others who are (considering) carrying out SEAs themselves. For instance they can give examples of relevant related strategic actions, suggest sources of baseline data, give an indication of the amount of work required, and encourage organizations to collaborate in carrying out common SEA requirements such as provision of baseline data and identification of problems. 'SEA pioneers' should ideally make their SEA reports publicly available, possibly at a central website.

Economies of scale

Some aspects of SEA only need to be done once, well, for each authority and then periodically updated:

- the description of the baseline environment;
- identification of key issues/constraints;
- monitoring; and
- a comprehensive list of relevant strategic actions and their requirements from which decision-makers for individual strategic actions can pick and choose.

This information – possibly with slight variants – is required for each SEA within a given authority or region, though it will vary by level (national v. regional v. local) and between authorities at the same level (South Oxfordshire v. West Oxfordshire). It would make sense to collect it once (if need be, with joint funding from the departments that would gain most from economies of scale) and make it available to everyone within the authority, say through a regularly updated website with downloadable documents. Then any given SEA team would only need to cut and paste those data or those other strategic actions' requirements that apply to their strategic action, and not have to re-invent the wheel each time.

In particular, much duplication of effort could be avoided if, at each regional, county and district level, existing monitoring data were collated and presented in a form conducive to SEA. For instance, environmental monitoring groups could be encouraged to provide data which:

- cover at minimum all of the SEA issues;
- are outcome, not input data;
- are at an appropriate scale: for regional plans and programmes, data should be at the regional level, not a disparate collection of district-level data or disaggregated national-level data;
- include an analysis of future trends;
- identify key environmental issues and problems in the region, possibly based on the threshold-and-trend approach of Figure 6.4; and
- ideally identify environmental thresholds that should not be exceeded, or targets that should be achieved.

In authorities where many SEAs are carried out, it might be worthwhile appointing one officer who is responsible for SEA data provision, support and training.

Training

Planners, engineers, consultants, environmentalists and politicians will all need training on how to carry out effective SEAs. SEA courses will be needed, possibly tailor-made for different types of audiences:

- Planners and bureaucrats need information on basic SEA requirements, how these will affect their organization, and what strategic actions require SEA.
- Senior government officials, politicians and elected representatives need a basic understanding of legal SEA requirements, and how to take the results of an SEA into account in decision-making.
- Environmental/sustainability authorities and non-governmental organizations, who will generally be responsible for SEA quality assurance, will require some training but also an impetus and forum for deciding how they will deal with SEAs once they start to be formally carried out, for example preparation of internal guidance, review criteria/checklists, and contact points.
- Consultants and academics involved in plan-making, policy appraisal and law will need training on legal SEA requirements and ideas on SEA good practice techniques. Given the large amount of group work, consensus-building and community involvement required in many SEAs, training on negotiation skills is also likely to be useful.
- Consultants and academics involved in environmental impact assessment, engineering, economic and other 'technical' subjects will need training on the more 'strategic' aspects of SEA, for instance how to generate alternatives, deal with uncertainty, and keep SEA from being the compilation of lots of EIAs. Training on negotiation skills is also likely to be useful. I personally find these professionals hardest to train in SEA techniques because they are so good at detailed work that they find it difficult to deal with the subjective aspects and inevitable lack of rigour that accompany SEA.
- The public is unlikely to be interested in formal SEA training. A website explaining the SEA process and sources of further information might, however, be useful.

Evening, block and distance learning courses are likely to be particularly useful for busy practitioners. In the longer run, university courses on planning, policy, law and possibly environmental studies, economics and engineering should include training on SEA.

Central government support

UK experience suggests that central sources of government support are crucial for the effective implementation of legal SEA requirements.

A *nominated central SEA support centre* such as the Dutch EIA Commission could publish SEA guidance and case studies; prepare an SEA website and keep it updated; commission relevant studies; and ensure SEA quality. In particular, it could act as a cross-departmental coordinating body to ensure that different departments with different remits (agriculture, energy, etc) are aware of SEA requirements and good practice, and carry out SEAs in a consistent manner. A *central SEA website* could provide information on legal requirements and guidance documents on SEA, examples of SEA (pilots, case studies), how SEAs should link to other types of assessment such as health impact assessment or appropriate assessment, and information on further references, training courses, etc.

The complexity of the SEA Directive's screening requirements means that, in the UK at least, there has been great uncertainty about what strategic actions require SEA. Whether or not SEA is needed for a given plan or programme (and what exactly is a plan? a 'programme'? is a strategy a plan? aaaagh!) will undoubtedly give decision-makers nightmares, and will keep lawyers well fed, for years to come. A government *list of strategic actions that definitely require SEA, and/or definitely do not* will do much to alleviate this problem (though the lawyers might disagree that this is a problem).

To kick-start or speed up SEA practice, *SEA guidance* could be written for specific sectors, organizations, or impacts. For instance, in the UK guidance is being prepared for Local Development Frameworks, Local Transport Plans and Environment Agency plans: this allows specific guidance to be provided on reasonable alternatives to consider, what databases to look at for baseline information, etc.

Resources

SEA has up-front costs. A typical, reasonably brief and efficient SEA might take 50–100 person-days. Longer ones can take multiple person-years (though one must query whether such SEAs could not be done faster with the same effect). For environmental authorities, being consulted on an SEA might take roughly 2–15 person-days per SEA. SEA effectively shifts some of the burden of environmental data collection and analysis from the private (EIA) to the public sector.

SEA may be a good use of resources in the short term (Figure 10.4), and may well save money in the longer term by preventing costly delays and legal challenges. For instance, after a bruising public inquiry into the UK Ministry of Defence's proposed development of the Otterburn Training Area in the Northumberland National Park for training with heavy artillery, which had not been subject to SEA, the Secretary of State for Defence issued a policy statement committing the Ministry of Defence to 'carry[ing] out environmental policy appraisals of all new or revised policies and equipment acquisition programmes and environmental impact assessment of all new projects and training activities'. However, these longer-term savings do not obviate the need for the short-term resources needed to carry out SEA.

The future of SEA

Over the last 30 years, we have gone from a single formative sentence in the US National Environmental Policy Act – *'include in every recommendation or report on proposals for legislation and other major Federal actions significantly affecting the quality of the human environment, a detailed statement by the responsible official on the environmental impacts of the proposed action'* – via years of evolving EIA procedures, to legal requirements to carry out SEAs in several dozen countries. The European SEA Directive and UNECE SEA Protocol are huge steps forward in this evolution.

As more SEAs are carried out, they will increasingly expose the inconsistencies, duplications and simple lack of logic in many decision-making systems. In the UK, for instance, the Royal Commission on Environmental Pollution (2002) has recommended that plan-making should be rationalized, particularly because of SEA requirements. Such rationalization could not only reduce the administrative burden posed by SEA but help to improve and streamline decision-making.

Where does SEA go from here? Based on experience with project EIA, the number of SEAs carried out will now rise rapidly, and their quality will rise equally fast (Therivel and Minas, 2002). SEA will also expand to cover other strategic actions and other countries: for instance, national government decision-makers will feel pressure to carry out SEAs of their policies when local and regional level decision-makers start arguing that the un-SEAed national policies do not provide them with an acceptable, sustainable framework for their decisions. Those countries with SEA systems will start requiring other countries to have SEA systems in place before they provide funding or collaborate with them.

Most notably, decision-makers will start 'thinking SEA' while they develop their strategic actions. Instead of perceiving SEA as a separate process that is 'done on' their strategic actions, they will start integrating environmental and sustainability thinking into their strategic actions ... to the point where ultimately, hopefully, SEA will make itself (and this book) redundant.

Appendix A

European Union Directive 2001/42/EC

DIRECTIVE 2001/42/EC OF THE EUROPEAN PARLIAMENT AND OF THE COUNCIL

of 27 June 2001
on the assessment of the effects of certain plans and programmes on the environment

THE EUROPEAN PARLIAMENT AND THE COUNCIL OF THE EUROPEAN UNION,

Having regard to the Treaty establishing the European Community, and in particular Article 175(1) thereof,

Having regard to the proposal from the Commission,[1]

Having regard to the opinion of the Economic and Social Committee,[2]

Having regard to the opinion of the Committee of the Regions,[3]

Acting in accordance with the procedure laid down in Article 251 of the Treaty,[4] in the light of the joint text approved by the Conciliation Committee on 21 March 2001,

Whereas:

(1)   Article 174 of the Treaty provides that Community policy on the environment is to contribute to, *inter alia*, the preservation, protection and improvement of the quality of the environment, the protection of human health and the prudent and rational utilisation of natural resources and that it is to be based on the precautionary principle. Article 6 of the Treaty provides that environmental protection requirements are to be integrated into the definition of Community policies and activities, in particular with a view to promoting sustainable development.

(2)   The Fifth Environment Action Programme: Towards sustainability – A European Community programme of policy and action in relation to the environment and sustainable development,[5] supplemented by Council Decision No 2179/98/EC[6] on its review, affirms the importance of assessing the likely environmental effects of plans and programmes.

(3) The Convention on Biological Diversity requires Parties to integrate as far as possible and as appropriate the conservation and sustainable use of biological diversity into relevant sectoral or cross-sectoral plans and programmes.

(4) Environmental assessment is an important tool for integrating environmental considerations into the preparation and adoption of certain plans and programmes which are likely to have significant effects on the environment in the Member States, because it ensures that such effects of implementing plans and programmes are taken into account during their preparation and before their adoption.

(5) The adoption of environmental assessment procedures at the planning and programming level should benefit undertakings by providing a more consistent framework in which to operate by the inclusion of the relevant environmental information into decision making. The inclusion of a wider set of factors in decision making should contribute to more sustainable and effective solutions.

(6) The different environmental assessment systems operating within Member States should contain a set of common procedural requirements necessary to contribute to a high level of protection of the environment.

(7) The United Nations/Economic Commission for Europe Convention on Environmental Impact Assessment in a Transboundary Context of 25 February 1991, which applies to both Member States and other States, encourages the Parties to the Convention to apply its principles to plans and programmes as well; at the second meeting of the Parties to the Convention in Sofia on 26 and 27 February 2001, it was decided to prepare a legally binding protocol on strategic environmental assessment which would supplement the existing provisions on environmental impact assessment in a transboundary context, with a view to its possible adoption on the occasion of the 5th Ministerial Conference 'Environment for Europe' at an extraordinary meeting of the Parties to the Conventions, scheduled for May 2003 in Kiev, Ukraine. The systems operating within the Community for environmental assessment of plans and programmes should ensure that there are adequate transboundary consultations where the implementation of a plan or programme being prepared in one Member State is likely to have significant effects on the environment of another Member State. The information on plans and programmes having significant effects on the environment of other States should be forwarded on a reciprocal and equivalent basis within an appropriate legal framework between Member States and these other States.

(8) Action is therefore required at Community level to lay down a minimum environmental assessment framework, which would set out the broad principles of the environmental assessment system and leave the details to the Member States, having regard to the principle of subsidiarity. Action by the Community should not go beyond what is necessary to achieve the objectives set out in the Treaty.

(9) The Directive is of a procedural nature, and its requirements should either be integrated into existing procedures in Member States or

incorporated in specifically established procedures. With a view to avoiding duplication of the assessment, Member States should take account, where appropriate, of the fact that assessments will be carried out at different levels of a hierarchy of plans and programmes.

(10) All plans and programmes which are prepared for a number of sectors and which set a framework for future development consent of projects listed in Annexes I and II to Council Directive 85/337/EEC of 27 June 1985 on the assessment of the effects of certain public and private projects on the environment,[7] and all plans and programmes which have been determined to require assessment pursuant to Council Directive 92/43/EEC of 21 May 1992 on the conservation of natural habitats and of wild flora and fauna,[8] are likely to have significant effects on the environment, and should as a rule be made subject to systematic environmental assessment. When they determine the use of small areas at local level or are minor modifications to the above plans or programmes, they should be assessed only where Member States determine that they are likely to have significant effects on the environment.

(11) Other plans and programmes which set the framework for future development consent of projects may not have significant effects on the environment in all cases and should be assessed only where Member States determine that they are likely to have such effects.

(12) When Member States make such determinations, they should take into account the relevant criteria set out in this Directive.

(13) Some plans or programmes are not subject to this Directive because of their particular characteristics.

(14) Where an assessment is required by this Directive, an environmental report should be prepared containing relevant information as set out in this Directive, identifying, describing and evaluating the likely significant environmental effects of implementing the plan or programme, and reasonable alternatives taking into account the objectives and the geographical scope of the plan or programme; Member States should communicate to the Commission any measures they take concerning the quality of environmental reports.

(15) In order to contribute to more transparent decision making and with the aim of ensuring that the information supplied for the assessment is comprehensive and reliable, it is necessary to provide that authorities with relevant environmental responsibilities and the public are to be consulted during the assessment of plans and programmes, and that appropriate time frames are set, allowing sufficient time for consultations, including the expression of opinion.

(16) Where the implementation of a plan or programme prepared in one Member State is likely to have a significant effect on the environment of other Member States, provision should be made for the Member States concerned to enter into consultations and for the relevant authorities and the public to be informed and enabled to express their opinion.

(17) The environmental report and the opinions expressed by the relevant authorities and the public, as well as the results of any transboundary consultation, should be taken into account during the preparation of

the plan or programme and before its adoption or submission to the legislative procedure.

(18) Member States should ensure that, when a plan or programme is adopted, the relevant authorities and the public are informed and relevant information is made available to them.

(19) Where the obligation to carry out assessments of the effects on the environment arises simultaneously from this Directive and other Community legislation, such as Council Directive 79/409/EEC of 2 April 1979 on the conservation of wild birds,[9] Directive 92/43/EEC, or Directive 2000/60/EC of the European Parliament and the Council of 23 October 2000 establishing a framework for Community action in the field of water policy,[10] in order to avoid duplication of the assessment, Member States may provide for coordinated or joint procedures fulfilling the requirements of the relevant Community legislation.

(20) A first report on the application and effectiveness of this Directive should be carried out by the Commission five years after its entry into force, and at seven-year intervals thereafter. With a view to further integrating environmental protection requirements, and taking into account the experience acquired, the first report should, if appropriate, be accompanied by proposals for amendment of this Directive, in particular as regards the possibility of extending its scope to other areas/sectors and other types of plans and programmes.

HAVE ADOPTED THIS DIRECTIVE:

Article 1. Objectives

The objective of this Directive is to provide for a high level of protection of the environment and to contribute to the integration of environmental considerations into the preparation and adoption of plans and programmes with a view to promoting sustainable development, by ensuring that, in accordance with this Directive, an environmental assessment is carried out of certain plans and programmes which are likely to have significant effects on the environment.

Article 2. Definitions

For the purposes of this Directive:

(a) 'plans and programmes' shall mean plans and programmes, including those co-financed by the European Community, as well as any modifications to them:

• which are subject to preparation and/or adoption by an authority at national, regional or local level or which are prepared by an authority for adoption, through a legislative procedure by Parliament or Government, and

• which are required by legislative, regulatory or administrative provisions;

(b) 'environmental assessment' shall mean the preparation of an environmental report, the carrying out of consultations, the taking into account of the environmental report and the results of the consultations in decision making and the provision of information on the decision in accordance with Articles 4 to 9;

(c) 'environmental report' shall mean the part of the plan or programme documentation containing the information required in Article 5 and Annex I;

(d) 'The public' shall mean one or more natural or legal persons and, in accordance with national legislation or practice, their associations, organisations or groups.

Article 3. Scope

1. An environmental assessment, in accordance with Articles 4 to 9, shall be carried out for plans and programmes referred to in paragraphs 2 to 4 which are likely to have significant environmental effects.

2. Subject to paragraph 3, an environmental assessment shall be carried out for all plans and programmes,

(a) which are prepared for agriculture, forestry, fisheries, energy, industry, transport, waste management, water management, telecommunications, tourism, town and country planning or land use and which set the framework for future development consent of projects listed in Annexes I and II to Directive 85/337/EC, or

(b) which, in view of the likely effects on sites, have been determined to require an assessment pursuant to Article 6 or 7 of Directive 92/43/EEC.

3. Plans and programmes referred to in paragraph 2 which determine the use of small areas at local level and minor modifications to plans and programmes referred to in paragraph 2 shall require an environmental assessment only where the Member States determine that they are likely to have significant environmental effects.

4. Member States shall determine whether plans and programmes, other than those referred to in paragraph 2, which set the framework for future development consent of projects, are likely to have significant environmental effects.

5. Member States shall determine whether plans or programmes referred to in paragraphs 3 and 4 are likely to have significant environmental effects either through case-by-case examination or by specifying types of plans and programmes or by combining both approaches. For this purpose Member States shall in all cases take into account relevant criteria set out in Annex II, in order to ensure that plans and programmes with likely significant effects on the environment are covered by this Directive.

6. In the case-by-case examination and in specifying types of plans and programmes in accordance with paragraph 5, the authorities referred to in Article 6(3) shall be consulted.

7. Member States shall ensure that their conclusions pursuant to paragraph 5, including the reasons for not requiring an environmental assessment pursuant to Articles 4 to 9, are made available to the public.

8. The following plans and programmes are not subject to this Directive:

• plans and programmes the sole purpose of which is to serve national defence or civil emergency,

- financial or budget plans and programmes.

9. This Directive does not apply to plans and programmes co-financed under the current respective programming periods[11] for Council Regulations (EC) No 1260/1999[12] and (EC) No 1257/1999[13].

Article 4. General obligations

1. The environmental assessment referred to in Article 3 shall be carried out during the preparation of a plan or programme and before its adoption or submission to the legislative procedure.

2. The requirements of this Directive shall either be integrated into existing procedures in Member States for the adoption of plans and programmes or incorporated in procedures established to comply with this Directive.

3. Where plans and programmes form part of a hierarchy, Member States shall, with a view to avoiding duplication of the assessment, take into account the fact that the assessment will be carried out, in accordance with this Directive, at different levels of the hierarchy. For the purpose of, *inter alia*, avoiding duplication of assessment, Member States shall apply Article 5(2) and (3).

Article 5. Environmental report

1. Where an environmental assessment is required under Article 3(1), an environmental report shall be prepared in which the likely significant effects on the environment of implementing the plan or programme, and reasonable alternatives taking into account the objectives and the geographical scope of the plan or programme, are identified, described and evaluated. The information to be given for this purpose is referred to in Annex I.

2. The environmental report prepared pursuant to paragraph 1 shall include the information that may reasonably be required taking into account current knowledge and methods of assessment, the contents and level of detail in the plan or programme, its stage in the decision-making process and the extent to which certain matters are more appropriately assessed at different levels in that process in order to avoid duplication of the assessment.

3. Relevant information available on environmental effects of the plans and programmes and obtained at other levels of decision making or through other Community legislation may be used for providing the information referred to in Annex I.

4. The authorities referred to in Article 6(3) shall be consulted when deciding on the scope and level of detail of the information which must be included in the environmental report.

Article 6. Consultations

1. The draft plan or programme and the environmental report prepared in accordance with Article 5 shall be made available to the authorities referred to in paragraph 3 of this Article and the public.

2. The authorities referred to in paragraph 3 and the public referred to in paragraph 4 shall be given an early and effective opportunity within appropriate time frames to express their opinion on the draft plan or

programme and the accompanying environmental report before the adoption of the plan or programme or its submission to the legislative procedure.

3. Member States shall designate the authorities to be consulted which, by reason of their specific environmental responsibilities, are likely to be concerned by the environmental effects of implementing plans and programmes.

4. Member States shall identify the public for the purposes of paragraph 2, including the public affected or likely to be affected by, or having an interest in, the decision-making subject to this Directive, including relevant non-governmental organisations, such as those promoting environmental protection and other organisations concerned.

5. The detailed arrangements for the information and consultation of the authorities and the public shall be determined by the Member States.

Article 7. Transboundary consultations

1. Where a Member State considers that the implementation of a plan or programme being prepared in relation to its territory is likely to have significant effects on the environment in another Member State, or where a Member State likely to be significantly affected so requests, the Member State in whose territory the plan or programme is being prepared shall, before its adoption or submission to the legislative procedure, forward a copy of the draft plan or programme and the relevant environmental report to the other Member State.

2. Where a Member State is sent a copy of a draft plan or programme and an environmental report under paragraph 1, it shall indicate to the other Member State whether it wishes to enter into consultations before the adoption of the plan or programme or its submission to the legislative procedure and, if it so indicates, the Member States concerned shall enter into consultations concerning the likely transboundary environmental effects of implementing the plan or programme and the measures envisaged to reduce or eliminate such effects.

Where such consultations take place, the Member States concerned shall agree on detailed arrangements to ensure that the authorities referred to in Article 6(3) and the public referred to in Article 6(4) in the Member State likely to be significantly affected are informed and given an opportunity to forward their opinion within a reasonable time frame.

3. Where Member States are required under this Article to enter into consultations, they shall agree, at the beginning of such consultations, on a reasonable time frame for the duration of the consultations.

Article 8. Decision making

The environmental report prepared pursuant to Article 5, the opinions expressed pursuant to Article 6 and the results of any transboundary consultations entered into pursuant to Article 7 shall be taken into account during the preparation of the plan or programme and before its adoption or submission to the legislative procedure.

Article 9. Information on the decision

1. Member States shall ensure that, when a plan or programme is adopted, the authorities referred to in Article 6(3), the public and any Member State consulted under Article 7 are informed and the following items are made available to those so informed:

(a)   the plan or programme as adopted;

(b)   a statement summarising how environmental considerations have been integrated into the plan or programme and how the environmental report prepared pursuant to Article 5, the opinions expressed pursuant to Article 6 and the results of consultations entered into pursuant to Article 7 have been taken into account in accordance with Article 8 and the reasons for choosing the plan or programme as adopted, in the light of the other reasonable alternatives dealt with; and

(c)   the measures decided concerning monitoring in accordance with Article 10.

2. The detailed arrangements concerning the information referred to in paragraph 1 shall be determined by the Member States.

Article 10. Monitoring

1. Member States shall monitor the significant environmental effects of the implementation of plans and programmes in order, *inter alia*, to identify at an early stage unforeseen adverse effects, and to be able to undertake appropriate remedial action.

2. In order to comply with paragraph 1, existing monitoring arrangements may be used if appropriate, with a view to avoiding duplication of monitoring.

Article 11. Relationship with other Community legislation

1. An environmental assessment carried out under this Directive shall be without prejudice to any requirements under Directive 85/337/EEC and to any other Community law requirements.

2. For plans and programmes for which the obligation to carry out assessments of the effects on the environment arises simultaneously from this Directive and other Community legislation, Member States may provide for coordinated or joint procedures fulfilling the requirements of the relevant Community legislation in order, *inter alia*, to avoid duplication of assessment.

3. For plans and programmes co-financed by the European Community, the environmental assessment in accordance with this Directive shall be carried out in conformity with the specific provisions in relevant Community legislation.

Article 12. Information, reporting and review

1. Member States and the Commission shall exchange information on the experience gained in applying this Directive.

2. Member States shall ensure that environmental reports are of a sufficient quality to meet the requirements of this Directive and shall communicate to the Commission any measures they take concerning the quality of these reports.

3. Before 21 July 2006 the Commission shall send a first report on the application and effectiveness of this Directive to the European Parliament and to the Council.

With a view further to integrating environmental protection requirements, in accordance with Article 6 of the Treaty, and taking into account the experience acquired in the application of this Directive in the Member States, such a report will be accompanied by proposals for amendment of this Directive, if appropriate. In particular, the Commission will consider the possibility of extending the scope of this Directive to other areas/sectors and other types of plans and programmes.

A new evaluation report shall follow at seven-year intervals.

4. The Commission shall report on the relationship between this Directive and Regulations (EC) No 1260/1999 and (EC) No 1257/1999 well ahead of the expiry of the programming periods provided for in those Regulations, with a view to ensuring a coherent approach with regard to this Directive and subsequent Community Regulations.

Article 13. Implementation of the Directive

1. Member States shall bring into force the laws, regulations and administrative provisions necessary to comply with this Directive before 21 July 2004. They shall forthwith inform the Commission thereof.

2. When Member States adopt the measures, they shall contain a reference to this Directive or shall be accompanied by such reference on the occasion of their official publication. The methods of making such reference shall be laid down by Member States.

3. The obligation referred to in Article 4(1) shall apply to the plans and programmes of which the first formal preparatory act is subsequent to the date referred to in paragraph 1. Plans and programmes of which the first formal preparatory act is before that date and which are adopted or submitted to the legislative procedure more than 24 months thereafter, shall be made subject to the obligation referred to in Article 4(1) unless Member States decide on a case-by-case basis that this is not feasible and inform the public of their decision.

4. Before 21 July 2004, Member States shall communicate to the Commission, in addition to the measures referred to in paragraph 1, separate information on the types of plans and programmes which, in accordance with Article 3, would be subject to an environmental assessment pursuant to this Directive. The Commission shall make this information available to the Member States. The information will be updated on a regular basis.

Article 14. Entry into force

This Directive shall enter into force on the day of its publication in the *Official Journal of the European Communities*.

Article 15. Addressees

This Directive is addressed to the Member States.

Done at Luxembourg, 27 June 2001.

For the European Parliament, The President, N. FONTAINE
For the Council, The President, B. ROSENGREN

Annex I. Information referred to in Article 5(1)

The information to be provided under Article 5(1), subject to Article 5(2) and (3), is the following:

(a) an outline of the contents, main objectives of the plan or programme and relationship with other relevant plans and programmes;

(b) the relevant aspects of the current state of the environment and the likely evolution thereof without implementation of the plan or programme;

(c) the environmental characteristics of areas likely to be significantly affected;

(d) any existing environmental problems which are relevant to the plan or programme including, in particular, those relating to any areas of a particular environmental importance, such as areas designated pursuant to Directives 79/409/EEC and 92/43/EEC;

(e) the environmental protection objectives, established at international, Community or Member State level, which are relevant to the plan or programme and the way those objectives and any environmental considerations have been taken into account during its preparation;

(f) the likely significant effects[14] on the environment, including on issues such as biodiversity, population, human health, fauna, flora, soil, water, air, climatic factors, material assets, cultural heritage including architectural and archaeological heritage, landscape and the interrelationship between the above factors;

(g) the measures envisaged to prevent, reduce and as fully as possible offset any significant adverse affects on the environment of implementing the plan or programme;

(h) an outline of the reasons for selecting the alternatives dealt with, and a description of how the assessment was undertaken including any difficulties (such as technical deficiencies or a lack of know-how) encountered in compiling the required information;

(i) a description of the measures envisaged concerning monitoring in accordance with Article 10;

(j) a non-technical summary of the information provided under the above headings.

Annex II. Criteria for determining the likely significance of effects referred to in Article 3(5)

1. The characteristics of plans and programmes, having regard, in particular, to

• the degree to which the plan or programme sets a framework for projects and other activities, either with regard to the location, nature, size and operating conditions or by allocating resources,

• the degree to which the plan or programme influences other plans and programmes including those in a hierarchy,

- the relevance of the plan or programme for the integration of environmental considerations in particular with a view to promoting sustainable development,
- environmental problems relevant to the plan or programme,
- the relevance of the plan or programme for the implementation of Community legislation on the environment (eg plans and programmes linked to waste-management or water protection).

2. Characteristics of the effects and of the area likely to be affected, having regard, in particular, to

- the probability, duration, frequency and reversibility of the effects,
- the cumulative nature of the effects,
- the transboundary nature of the effects,
- the risks to human health or the environment (eg due to accidents),
- the magnitude and spatial extent of the effects (geographical area and size of the population likely to be affected),
- the value and vulnerability of the area likely to be affected due to:
  - special natural characteristics or cultural heritage,
  - exceeded environmental quality standards or limit values,
  - intensive land-use,
- the effects on areas or landscapes which have a recognised national, Community or international protection status.

Notes

1 OJ C 129, 25.4.1997, p14 and OJ C 83, 25.3.1999, p13.
2 OJ C 287, 22.9.1997, p101.
3 OJ C 64, 27.2.1998, p63 and OJ C 374, 23.12.1999, p9.
4 Opinion of the European Parliament of 20 October 1998 (OJ C 341, 9.11.1998, p18), confirmed on 16 September 1999 (OJ C 54, 25.2.2000, p76), Council Common Position of 30 March 2000 (OJ C 137, 16.5.2000, p11) and Decision of the European Parliament of 6 September 2000 (OJ C 135, 7.5.2001, p155). Decision of the European Parliament of 31 May 2001 and Decision of the Council of 5 June 2001.
5 OJ C 138, 17.5.1993, p5.
6 OJ L 275, 10.10.1998, p1.
7 OJ L 175, 5.7.1985, p40. Directive as amended by Directive 97/11/EC (OJ L 73, 14.3.1997, p5).
8 OJ L 206, 22.7.1992, p7. Directive as last amended by Directive 97/62/EC (OJ L 305, 8.11.1997, p42).
9 OJ L 103, 25.4.1979, p1. Directive as last amended by Directive 97/49/EC (OJ L 223, 13.8.1997, p9).
10 OJ L 327, 22.12.2000, p1.
11 The 2000–2006 programming period for Council Regulation (EC) No 1260/1999 and the 2000–2006 and 2000–2007 programming periods for Council Regulation (EC) No 1257/1999.

12 Council Regulation (EC) No 1260/1999 of 21 June 1999 laying down general provisions on the Structural Funds (OJ L 161, 26.6.1999, p1).

13 Council Regulation (EC) No 1257/1999 of 17 May 1999 on support for rural development from the European Agricultural Guidance and Guarantee Fund (EAGGF) and amending and repealing certain regulations (OJ L 160, 26.6.1999), p80.

14 These effects should include secondary, cumulative, synergistic, short-, medium- and long-term, permanent and temporary, positive and negative effects.

United Nations Economic Commission for Europe Protocol on Strategic Environmental Assessment

PROTOCOL ON STRATEGIC ENVIRONMENTAL ASSESSMENT TO THE CONVENTION ON ENVIRONMENTAL IMPACT ASSESSMENT IN A TRANSBOUNDARY CONTEXT

The Parties to this Protocol,

Recognizing the importance of integrating environmental, including health, considerations into the preparation and adoption of plans and programmes and, to the extent appropriate, policies and legislation,

Committing themselves to promoting sustainable development and therefore basing themselves on the conclusions of the United Nations Conference on Environment and Development (Rio de Janeiro, Brazil, 1992), in particular principles 4 and 10 of the Rio Declaration on Environment and Development and Agenda 21, as well as the outcome of the third Ministerial Conference on Environment and Health (London, 1999) and the World Summit on Sustainable Development (Johannesburg, South Africa, 2002),

Bearing in mind the Convention on Environmental Impact Assessment in a Transboundary Context, done at Espoo, Finland, on 25 February 1991, and decision II/9 of its Parties at Sofia on 26 and 27 February 2001, in which it was decided to prepare a legally binding protocol on strategic environmental assessment,

Recognizing that strategic environmental assessment should have an important role in the preparation and adoption of plans, programmes, and, to the extent appropriate, policies and legislation, and that the wider application of the principles of environmental impact assessment to plans, programmes, policies and legislation will further strengthen the systematic analysis of their significant environmental effects,

Acknowledging the Convention on Access to Information, Public Participation in Decision-making and Access to Justice in Environmental

Matters, done at Aarhus, Denmark, on 25 June 1998, and taking note of the relevant paragraphs of the Lucca Declaration, adopted at the first meeting of its Parties,

Conscious, therefore, of the importance of providing for public participation in strategic environmental assessment,

Acknowledging the benefits to the health and well-being of present and future generations that will follow if the need to protect and improve people's health is taken into account as an integral part of strategic environmental assessment, and recognizing the work led by the World Health Organization in this respect,

Mindful of the need for and importance of enhancing international cooperation in assessing the transboundary environmental, including health, effects of proposed plans and programmes, and, to the extent appropriate, policies and legislation,

Have agreed as follows:

Article 1. OBJECTIVE

The objective of this Protocol is to provide for a high level of protection of the environment, including health, by:

a) Ensuring that environmental, including health, considerations are thoroughly taken into account in the development of plans and programmes;

b) Contributing to the consideration of environmental, including health, concerns in the preparation of policies and legislation;

c) Establishing clear, transparent and effective procedures for strategic environmental assessment;

d) Providing for public participation in strategic environmental assessment; and

e) Integrating by these means environmental, including health, concerns into measures and instruments designed to further sustainable development.

Article 2. DEFINITIONS

For the purposes of this Protocol,

1.   'Convention' means the Convention on Environmental Impact Assessment in a Transboundary Context;

2.   'Party' means, unless the text indicates otherwise, a Contracting Party to this Protocol;

3.   'Party of origin' means a Party or Parties to this Protocol within whose jurisdiction the preparation of a plan or programme is envisaged;

4.   'Affected Party' means a Party or Parties to this Protocol likely to be affected by the transboundary environmental, including health, effects of a plan or programme;

5.   'Plans and programmes' means plans and programmes and any modifications to them that are:

(a) Required by legislative, regulatory or administrative provisions; and

(b) Subject to preparation and/or adoption by an authority or prepared by an authority for adoption, through a formal procedure, by a parliament or a government;

6.   'Strategic environmental assessment' means the evaluation of the likely environmental, including health, effects, which comprises the determination of the scope of an environmental report and its preparation, the carrying-out of public participation and consultations, and the taking into account of the environmental report and the results of the public participation and consultations in a plan or programme;

7.   'Environmental, including health, effect' means any effect on the environment, including human health, flora, fauna, biodiversity, soil, climate, air, water, landscape, natural sites, material assets, cultural heritage and the interaction among these factors;

8.   'The public' means one or more natural or legal persons and, in accordance with national legislation or practice, their associations, organizations or groups.

Article 3. GENERAL PROVISIONS

1.   Each Party shall take the necessary legislative, regulatory and other appropriate measures to implement the provisions of this Protocol within a clear, transparent framework.

2.   Each Party shall endeavour to ensure that officials and authorities assist and provide guidance to the public in matters covered by this Protocol.

3.   Each Party shall provide for appropriate recognition of and support to associations, organizations or groups promoting environmental, including health, protection in the context of this Protocol.

4.   The provisions of this Protocol shall not affect the right of a Party to maintain or introduce additional measures in relation to issues covered by this Protocol.

5.   Each Party shall promote the objectives of this Protocol in relevant international decision-making processes and within the framework of relevant international organizations.

6.   Each Party shall ensure that persons exercising their rights in conformity with the provisions of this Protocol shall not be penalized, persecuted or harassed in any way for their involvement. This provision shall not affect the powers of national courts to award reasonable costs in judicial proceedings.

7.   Within the scope of the relevant provisions of this Protocol, the public shall be able to exercise its rights without discrimination as to citizenship, nationality or domicile and, in the case of a legal person, without discrimination as to where it has its registered seat or an effective centre of its activities.

Article 4. FIELD OF APPLICATION CONCERNING PLANS AND PROGRAMMES

1.   Each Party shall ensure that a strategic environmental assessment is carried out for plans and programmes referred to in paragraphs 2, 3 and 4 which are likely to have significant environmental, including health, effects.

2.   A strategic environmental assessment shall be carried out for plans and programmes which are prepared for agriculture, forestry, fisheries, energy, industry including mining, transport, regional development, waste management, water management, telecommunications, tourism, town and country planning or land use, and which set the framework for future development consent for projects listed in annex I and any other project listed in annex II that requires an environmental impact assessment under national legislation.

3.   For plans and programmes other than those subject to paragraph 2 which set the framework for future development consent of projects, a strategic environmental assessment shall be carried out where a Party so determines according to article 5, paragraph 1.

4.   For plans and programmes referred to in paragraph 2 which determine the use of small areas at local level and for minor modifications to plans and programmes referred to in paragraph 2, a strategic environmental assessment shall be carried out only where a Party so determines according to article 5, paragraph 1.

5.   The following plans and programmes are not subject to this Protocol:

(a) Plans and programmes whose sole purpose is to serve national defence or civil emergencies;

(b) Financial or budget plans and programmes.

Article 5. SCREENING

1.   Each Party shall determine whether plans and programmes referred to in article 4, paragraphs 3 and 4, are likely to have significant environmental, including health, effects either through a case-by-case examination or by specifying types of plans and programmes or by combining both approaches. For this purpose each party shall in all cases take into account the criteria set out in annex III.

2.   Each Party shall ensure that the environmental and health authorities referred to in article 9, paragraph 1, are consulted when applying the procedures referred to in paragraph 1 above.

3.   To the extent appropriate, each Party shall endeavour to provide opportunities for the participation of the public concerned in the screening of plans and programmes under this article.

4.   Each Party shall ensure timely public availability of the conclusions pursuant to paragraph 1, including the reasons for not requiring a strategic environmental assessment, whether by public notices or by other appropriate means, such as electronic media.

Article 6. SCOPING

1.   Each Party shall establish arrangements for the determination of the relevant information to be included in the environmental report in accordance with article 7, paragraph 2.

2.   Each Party shall ensure that the environmental and health authorities referred to in article 9, paragraph 1, are consulted when determining the relevant information to be included in the environmental report.

3.   To the extent appropriate, each Party shall endeavour to provide opportunities for the participation of the public concerned when determining the relevant information to be included in the environmental report.

Article 7. ENVIRONMENTAL REPORT

1.   For plans and programmes subject to strategic environmental assessment, each Party shall ensure that an environmental report is prepared.

2.   The environmental report shall, in accordance with the determination under article 6, identify, describe and evaluate the likely significant environmental, including health, effects of implementing the plan or programme and its reasonable alternatives. The report shall contain such information specified in annex IV as may reasonably be required, taking into account:

(a) Current knowledge and methods of assessment;

(b) The contents and the level of detail of the plan or programme and its stage in the decision-making process;

(c) The interests of the public; and

(d) The information needs of the decision-making body.

3.   Each Party shall ensure that environmental reports are of sufficient quality to meet the requirements of this Protocol.

Article 8. PUBLIC PARTICIPATION

1.   Each Party shall ensure early, timely and effective opportunities for public participation, when all options are open, in the strategic environmental assessment of plans and programmes.

2.   Each Party, using electronic media or other appropriate means, shall ensure the timely public availability of the draft plan or programme and the environmental report.

3.   Each Party shall ensure that the public concerned, including relevant non-governmental organizations, is identified for the purposes of paragraphs 1 and 4.

4.   Each Party shall ensure that the public referred to in paragraph 3 has the opportunity to express its opinion on the draft plan or programme and the environmental report within a reasonable time frame.

5.   Each Party shall ensure that the detailed arrangements for informing the public and consulting the public concerned are determined and made publicly available. For this purpose, each Party shall take into account to the extent appropriate the elements listed in annex V.

Article 9. CONSULTATION WITH ENVIRONMENTAL AND HEALTH AUTHORITIES

1.   Each Party shall designate the authorities to be consulted which, by reason of their specific environmental or health responsibilities, are likely to be concerned by the environmental, including health, effects of the implementation of the plan or programme.

2.   The draft plan or programme and the environmental report shall be made available to the authorities referred to in paragraph 1.

3.   Each Party shall ensure that the authorities referred to in paragraph 1 are given, in an early, timely and effective manner, the opportunity to express their opinion on the draft plan or programme and the environmental report.

4.   Each Party shall determine the detailed arrangements for informing and consulting the environmental and health authorities referred to in paragraph 1.

Article 10. TRANSBOUNDARY CONSULTATIONS

1.   Where a Party of origin considers that the implementation of a plan or programme is likely to have significant transboundary environmental, including health, effects or where a Party likely to be significantly affected so requests, the Party of origin shall as early as possible before the adoption of the plan or programme notify the affected Party.

2.   This notification shall contain, inter alia:

(a) The draft plan or programme and the environmental report including information on its possible transboundary environmental, including health, effects; and

(b) Information regarding the decision-making procedure, including an indication of a reasonable time schedule for the transmission of comments.

3.   The affected Party shall, within the time specified in the notification, indicate to the Party of origin whether it wishes to enter into consultations before the adoption of the plan or programme and, if it so indicates, the Parties concerned shall enter into consultations concerning the likely transboundary environmental, including health, effects of implementing the plan or programme and the measures envisaged to prevent, reduce or mitigate adverse effects.

4.   Where such consultations take place, the Parties concerned shall agree on detailed arrangements to ensure that the public concerned and the authorities referred to in article 9, paragraph 1, in the affected Party are informed and given an opportunity to forward their opinion on the draft plan or programme and the environmental report within a reasonable time frame.

Article 11. DECISION

1.   Each Party shall ensure that when a plan or programme is adopted due account is taken of:

(a) The conclusions of the environmental report;

(b) The measures to prevent, reduce or mitigate the adverse effects identified in the environmental report; and

(c) The comments received in accordance with articles 8 to 10.

2.   Each Party shall ensure that, when a plan or programme is adopted, the public, the authorities referred to in article 9, paragraph 1, and the Parties consulted according to article 10 are informed, and that the plan or programme is made available to them together with a statement summarizing how the environmental, including health, considerations have been integrated

into it, how the comments received in accordance with articles 8 to 10 have been taken into account and the reasons for adopting it in the light of the reasonable alternatives considered.

Article 12. MONITORING

1.   Each Party shall monitor the significant environmental, including health, effects of the implementation of the plans and programmes, adopted under article 11 in order, inter alia, to identify, at an early stage, unforeseen adverse effects and to be able to undertake appropriate remedial action.

2.   The results of the monitoring undertaken shall be made available, in accordance with national legislation, to the authorities referred to in article 9, paragraph 1, and to the public.

Article 13. POLICIES AND LEGISLATION

1.   Each Party shall endeavour to ensure that environmental, including health, concerns are considered and integrated to the extent appropriate in the preparation of its proposals for policies and legislation that are likely to have significant effects on the environment, including health.

2.   In applying paragraph 1, each Party shall consider the appropriate principles and elements of this Protocol.

3.   Each Party shall determine, where appropriate, the practical arrangements for the consideration and integration of environmental, including health, concerns in accordance with paragraph 1, taking into account the need for transparency in decision-making.

4.   Each Party shall report to the Meeting of the Parties to the Convention serving as the Meeting of the Parties to this Protocol on its application of this article.

Article 14. THE MEETING OF THE PARTIES TO THE CONVENTION SERVING AS THE MEETING OF THE PARTIES TO THE PROTOCOL

1.   The Meeting of the Parties to the Convention shall serve as the Meeting of the Parties to this Protocol. The first meeting of the Parties to the Convention serving as the Meeting of the Parties to this Protocol shall be convened not later than one year after the date of entry into force of this Protocol, and in conjunction with a meeting of the Parties to the Convention, if a meeting of the latter is scheduled within that period. Subsequent meetings of the Parties to the Convention serving as the meeting of the Parties to this Protocol shall be held in conjunction with meetings of the Parties to the Convention, unless otherwise decided by the meeting of the Parties to the Convention serving as the Meeting of the Parties to this Protocol.

2.   Parties to the Convention which are not parties to this Protocol may participate as observers in the proceedings of any session of the Meeting of the Parties to the Convention serving as the Meeting of the Parties to this Protocol. When the Meeting of the Parties to the Convention serves as the Meeting of the Parties to this Protocol, decisions under this Protocol shall be taken only by the Parties to this Protocol.

3.   When the Meeting of the Parties to the Convention serves as the Meeting of the Parties to this Protocol, any member of the Bureau of the Meeting of the Parties representing a Party to the Convention that is not, at that time, a Party to this Protocol shall be replaced by another member to be elected by and from amongst the Parties to this Protocol.

4.   The Meeting of the Parties to the Convention serving as the Meeting of the Parties to this Protocol shall keep under regular review the implementation of this Protocol and, for this purpose, shall:

(a) Review policies for and methodological approaches to strategic environmental assessment with a view to further improving the procedures provided for under this Protocol;

(b) Exchange information regarding experience gained in strategic environmental assessment and in the implementation of this Protocol;

(c) Seek, where appropriate, the services and cooperation of competent bodies having expertise pertinent to the achievement of the purposes of this Protocol;

(d) Establish such subsidiary bodies as it considers necessary for the implementation of this Protocol;

(e) Where necessary, consider and adopt proposals for amendments to this Protocol; and

(f) Consider and undertake any additional action, including action to be carried out jointly under this Protocol and the Convention, that may be required for the achievement of the purposes of this Protocol.

5.   The rules of procedure of the Meeting of the Parties to the Convention shall be applied mutatis mutandis under this Protocol, except as may otherwise be decided by consensus by the Meeting of the Parties serving as the Meeting of the Parties to this Protocol.

6.   At its first meeting, the Meeting of the Parties to the Convention serving as the Meeting of the Parties to this Protocol shall consider and adopt the modalities for applying the procedure for the review of compliance with the Convention to this Protocol.

7.   Each Party shall, at intervals to be determined by the Meeting of the Parties to the Convention serving as the Meeting of the Parties to this Protocol, report to the Meeting of the Parties to the Convention serving as the Meeting of the Parties to the Protocol on measures that it has taken to implement the Protocol.

Article 15. RELATIONSHIP TO OTHER INTERNATIONAL AGREEMENTS

The relevant provisions of this Protocol shall apply without prejudice to the UNECE Conventions on Environmental Impact Assessment in a Transboundary Context and on Access to Information, Public Participation in Decision-making and Access to Justice in Environmental Matters.

Article 16. RIGHT TO VOTE

1.   Except as provided for in paragraph 2 below, each Party to this Protocol shall have one vote.

2.   Regional economic integration organizations, in matters within their competence, shall exercise their right to vote with a number of votes equal to the number of their member States which are parties to this Protocol. Such organizations shall not exercise their right to vote if their member States exercise theirs, and vice versa.

Article 17. SECRETARIAT

The secretariat established by article 13 of the Convention shall serve as the secretariat of this Protocol and article 13, paragraphs (a) to (c), of the Convention on the functions of the secretariat shall apply mutatis mutandis to this Protocol.

Article 18. ANNEXES

The annexes to this Protocol shall constitute an integral part thereof.

Article 19. AMENDMENTS TO THE PROTOCOL

1.   Any Party may propose amendments to this Protocol.

2.   Subject to paragraph 3, the procedure for proposing, adopting and the entry into force of amendments to the Convention laid down in paragraphs 2 to 5 of article 14 of the Convention shall apply, mutatis mutandis, to amendments to this Protocol.

3.   For the purpose of this Protocol, the three fourth of the Parties required for an amendment to enter into force for Parties having ratified, approved or accepted it, shall be calculated on the basis of the number of Parties at the time of the adoption of the amendment.

Article 20. SETTLEMENT OF DISPUTES

The provisions on the settlement of disputes of article 15 of the Convention shall apply mutatis mutandis to this Protocol.

Article 21. SIGNATURE

This Protocol shall be open for signature at Kiev (Ukraine) from 21 to 23 May 2003 and thereafter at United Nations Headquarters in New York until 31 December 2003, by States members of the Economic Commission for Europe as well as States having consultative status with the Economic Commission for Europe pursuant to paragraphs 8 and 11 of Economic and Social Council resolution 36(IV) of 28 March 1947, and by regional economic integration organizations constituted by sovereign States members of the European Commission for Europe to which their member States have transferred competence over matters governed by this Protocol, including the competence to enter into treaties in respect of these matters.

Article 22. DEPOSITARY

The Secretary-General of the United Nations shall act as the Depositary of this Protocol.

Article 23. RATIFICATION, ACCEPTANCE, APPROVAL AND ACCESSION

1.   This Protocol shall be subject to ratification, acceptance or approval by signatory States and regional economic integration organizations referred to in article 21.

2.   This Protocol shall be open for accession as from 1 January 2004 by the States and regional economic integration organizations referred to in article 21.

3.   Any other State, not referred to in paragraph 2 above, that is a Member of the United Nations may accede to the Protocol upon approval by the Meeting of the Parties to the Convention serving as the Meeting of the Parties to the Protocol.

4.   Any regional economic integration organization referred to in article 21 which becomes a Party to this Protocol without any of its member States being a Party shall be bound by all the obligations under this Protocol. If one or more of such an organization's member States is a Party to this Protocol, the organization and its member States shall decide on their respective responsibilities for the performance of their obligations under this Protocol. In such cases, the organization and its member States shall not be entitled to exercise rights under this Protocol concurrently.

5.   In their instruments of ratification, acceptance, approval or accession, the regional economic integration organizations referred to in article 21 shall declare the extent of their competence with respect to the matters governed by this Protocol. These organizations shall also inform the Depositary of any relevant modifications to the extent of their competence.

Article 24. ENTRY INTO FORCE

1.   This Protocol shall enter into force on the ninetieth day after the date of deposit of the sixteenth instrument of ratification, acceptance, approval or accession.

2.   For the purposes of paragraph 1 above, any instrument deposited by a regional economic integration organization referred to in article 21 shall not be counted as additional to those deposited by States members of such an organization.

3.   For each State or regional economic integration organization referred to in article 21 which ratifies, accepts or approves this Protocol or accedes thereto after the deposit of the sixteenth instrument of ratification, acceptance, approval or accession, the Protocol shall enter into force on the ninetieth day after the date of deposit by such State or organization of its instrument of ratification, acceptance, approval or accession.

4.   This Protocol applies to plans, programmes, policies and legislation for which the first formal preparatory act is subsequent to the date on which this Protocol enters into force. Where the Party under whose jurisdiction the preparation of a plan, programme, policy or legislation is envisaged is one for which paragraph 3 applies, this Protocol shall apply to plans, programmes, policies and legislation for which the first formal preparatory act is subsequent to the date on which this Protocol comes into force for that Party.

Article 25. WITHDRAWAL

At any time after four years from the date on which this Protocol has come into force with respect to a Party, that Party may withdraw from the Protocol by giving written notification to the Depositary. Any such withdrawal shall take effect on the ninetieth day after the date of its receipt by the Depositary. Any such withdrawal shall not affect the application of articles 5 to 9, 11 and 13 with respect to a strategic environmental assessment under this Protocol which has already been started, or the application of article 10 with respect to a notification or request which has already been made, before such withdrawal takes effect.

Article 26. AUTHENTIC TEXTS

The original of this Protocol, of which the English, French and Russian texts are equally authentic, shall be deposited with the Secretary-General of the United Nations.

IN WITNESS WHEREOF the undersigned, being duly authorized thereto, have signed this Protocol.

DONE at Kiev (Ukraine), this twenty-first day of May, two thousand and three.

Annex I. LIST OF PROJECTS AS REFERRED TO IN ARTICLE 4, PARAGRAPH 2

1. Crude oil refineries (excluding undertakings manufacturing only lubricants from crude oil) and installations for the gasification and liquefaction of 500 metric tons or more of coal or bituminous shale per day.

2. Thermal power stations and other combustion installations with a heat output of 300 megawatts or more and nuclear power stations and other nuclear reactors (except research installations for the production and conversion of fissionable and fertile materials, whose maximum power does not exceed 1 kilowatt continuous thermal load).

3. Installations solely designed for the production or enrichment of nuclear fuels, for the reprocessing of irradiated nuclear fuels or for the storage, disposal and processing of radioactive waste.

4. Major installations for the initial smelting of cast iron and steel and for the production of non-ferrous metals.

5. Installations for the extraction of asbestos and for the processing and transformation of asbestos and products containing asbestos: for asbestos-cement products, with an annual production of more than 20,000 metric tons of finished product; for friction material, with an annual production of more than 50 metric tons of finished product; and for other asbestos utilization of more than 200 metric tons per year.

6. Integrated chemical installations.

7. Construction of motorways, express roads[1] and lines for long-distance railway traffic and airports[2] with a basic runway length of 2,100 metres or more.

8. Large-diameter oil and gas pipelines.

9. Trading ports and also inland waterways and ports for inland-waterway traffic which permit the passage of vessels of over 1,350 metric tons.

10. Waste-disposal installations for the incineration, chemical treatment or landfill of toxic and dangerous wastes.

11. Large dams and reservoirs.

12. Groundwater abstraction activities in cases where the annual volume of water to be abstracted amounts to 10 million cubic metres or more.

13. Pulp and paper manufacturing of 200 air-dried metric tons or more per day.

14. Major mining, on-site extraction and processing of metal ores or coal.

15. Offshore hydrocarbon production.

16. Major storage facilities for petroleum, petrochemical and chemical products.

17. Deforestation of large areas.

Annex II. ANY OTHER PROJECTS REFERRED TO IN ARTICLE 4, PARAGRAPH 2

1. Projects for the restructuring of rural land holdings.

2. Projects for the use of uncultivated land or semi-natural areas for intensive agricultural purposes.

3. Water management projects for agriculture, including irrigation and land drainage projects.

4. Intensive livestock installations (including poultry).

5. Initial afforestation and deforestation for the purposes of conversion to another type of land use.

6. Intensive fish farming.

7. Nuclear power stations and other nuclear reactors[3] including the dismantling or decommissioning of such power stations or reactors (except research installations for the production and conversion of fissionable and fertile materials whose maximum power does not exceed 1 kilowatt continuous thermal load), as far as not included in annex I.

8. Construction of overhead electrical power lines with a voltage of 220 kilovolts or more and a length of 15 kilometres or more and other projects for the transmission of electrical energy by overhead cables.

9. Industrial installations for the production of electricity, steam and hot water.

10. Industrial installations for carrying gas, steam and hot water.

11. Surface storage of fossil fuels and natural gas.

12. Underground storage of combustible gases.

13. Industrial briquetting of coal and lignite.

14. Installations for hydroelectric energy production.

15. Installations for the harnessing of wind power for energy production (wind farms).

16. Installations, as far as not included in annex I, designed:
    - For the production or enrichment of nuclear fuel;
    - For the processing of irradiated nuclear fuel;
    - For the final disposal or irradiated nuclear fuel;
    - Solely for the final disposal of radioactive waste;
    - Solely for the storage (planned for more than 10 years) of irradiated nuclear fuels in a different site than the production site; or
    - For the processing and storage of radioactive waste.
17. Quarries, open cast mining and peat extraction, as far as not included in annex I.
18. Underground mining, as far as not included in annex I.
19. Extraction of minerals by marine or fluvial dredging.
20. Deep drillings (in particular geothermal drilling, drilling for the storage of nuclear waste material, drilling for water supplies), with the exception of drillings for investigating the stability of the soil.
21. Surface industrial installations for the extraction of coal, petroleum, natural gas and ores, as well as bituminous shale.
22. Integrated works for the initial smelting of cast iron and steel, as far as not included in annex I.
23. Installations for the production of pig iron or steel (primary or secondary fusion) including continuous casting.
24. Installations for the processing of ferrous metals (hot-rolling mills, smitheries with hammers, application of protective fused metal coats).
25. Ferrous metal foundries.
26. Installations for the production of non-ferrous crude metals from ore, concentrates or secondary raw materials by metallurgical, chemical or electrolytic processes, as far as not included in annex I.
27. Installations for the smelting, including the alloyage, of non-ferrous metals excluding precious metals, including recovered products (refining, foundry casting, etc.), as far as not included in annex I.
28. Installations for surface treatment of metals and plastic materials using an electrolytic or chemical process.
29. Manufacture and assembly of motor vehicles and manufacture of motor-vehicle engines.
30. Shipyards.
31. Installations for the construction and repair of aircraft.
32. Manufacture of railway equipment.
33. Swaging by explosives.
34. Installations for the roasting and sintering of metallic ores.
35. Coke ovens (dry coal distillation).
36. Installations for the manufacture of cement.
37. Installations for the manufacture of glass including glass fibre.

38. Installations for smelting mineral substances including the production of mineral fibres.

39. Manufacture of ceramic products by burning, in particular roofing tiles, bricks, refractory bricks, tiles, stoneware or porcelain.

40. Installations for the production of chemicals or treatment of intermediate products, as far as not included in annex I.

41. Production of pesticides and pharmaceutical products, paint and varnishes, elastometers and peroxides.

42. Installations for the storage of petroleum, petrochemical, or chemical products, as far as not included in annex I.

43. Manufacture of vegetable and animal oils and fats.

44. Packing and canning of animal and vegetable products.

45. Manufacture of dairy products.

46. Brewing and malting.

47. Confectionery and syrup manufacture.

48. Installations for the slaughter of animals.

49. Industrial starch manufacturing installations.

50. Fish meal and fish-oil factories.

51. Sugar factories.

52. Industrial plants for the production of pulp, paper and board, as far as not included in annex I.

53. Plants for the pre treatment or dyeing of fibres or textiles.

54. Plants for the tanning of hides and skins.

55. Cellulose-processing and production installations.

56. Manufacture and treatment of elastomer-based products.

57. Installations for the manufacture of artificial mineral fibres.

58. Installations for the recovery or destruction of explosive substances.

59. Installations for the production of asbestos and the manufacture of asbestos products, as far as not included in annex I.

60. Knackers' yards.

61. Test benches for engines, turbines or reactors.

62. Permanent racing and test tracks for motorized vehicles.

63. Pipelines for transport of gas or oil, as far as not included in annex I.

64. Pipelines for transport of chemicals with a diameter of more than 800 mm and a length of more than 40 km.

65. Construction of railways and intermodal transshipment facilities, and of intermodal terminals, as far as not included in annex I.

66. Construction of tramways, elevated and underground railways, suspended lines or similar lines of a particular type used exclusively or mainly for passenger transport.

67. Construction of roads, including realignment and/or widening of any existing road, as far as not included in annex I.

68. Construction of harbours and port installations, including fishing harbours, as far as not included in annex I.

69. Construction of inland waterways and ports for inland-waterway traffic, as far as not included in annex I.

70. Trading ports, piers for loading and unloading connected to land and outside ports, as far as not included in annex I.

71. Canalization and flood-relief works.

72. Construction of airports[4] and airfields, as far as not included in annex I.

73. Waste-disposal installations (including landfill), as far as not included in annex I.

74. Installations for the incineration or chemical treatment of non-hazardous waste.

75. Storage of scrap iron, including scrap vehicles.

76. Sludge deposition sites.

77. Groundwater abstraction or artificial groundwater recharge, as far as not included in annex I.

78. Works for the transfer of water resources between river basins.

79. Waste-water treatment plants.

80. Dams and other installations designed for the holding-back or for the long-term or permanent storage of water, as far as not included in annex I.

81. Coastal work to combat erosion and maritime works capable of altering the coast through the construction, for example, of dykes, moles, jetties and other sea defence works, excluding the maintenance and reconstruction of such works.

82. Installations of long-distance aqueducts.

83. Ski runs, ski lifts and cable cars and associated developments.

84. Marinas.

85. Holiday villages and hotel complexes outside urban areas and associated developments.

86. Permanent campsites and caravan sites.

87. Theme parks.

88. Industrial estate development projects.

89. Urban development projects, including the construction of shopping centres and car parks.

90. Reclamation of land from the sea.

Annex III. CRITERIA FOR DETERMINING OF THE LIKELY SIGNIFICANT ENVIRONMENTAL, INCLUDING HEALTH, EFFECTS REFERRED TO IN ARTICLE 5, PARAGRAPH 1

1. The relevance of the plan or programme to the integration of environmental, including health, considerations in particular with a view to promoting sustainable development.

2. The degree to which the plan or programme sets a framework for projects and other activities, either with regard to location, nature, size and operating conditions or by allocating resources.

3. The degree to which the plan or programme influences other plans and programmes including those in a hierarchy.

4. Environmental, including health, problems relevant to the plan or programme.

5. The nature of the environmental, including health, effects such as probability, duration, frequency, reversibility, magnitude and extent (such as geographical area or size of population likely to be affected).

6. The risks to the environment, including health.

7. The transboundary nature of effects.

8. The degree to which the plan or programme will affect valuable or vulnerable areas including landscapes with a recognized national or international protection status.

Annex IV. INFORMATION REFERRED TO IN ARTICLE 7, PARAGRAPH 2

1. The contents and the main objectives of the plan or programme and its link with other plans or programmes.

2. The relevant aspects of the current state of the environment, including health, and the likely evolution thereof should the plan or programme not be implemented.

3. The characteristics of the environment, including health, in areas likely to be significantly affected.

4. The environmental, including health, problems which are relevant to the plan or programme.

5. The environmental, including health, objectives established at international, national and other levels which are relevant to the plan or programme, and the ways in which these objectives and other environmental, including health, considerations have been taken into account during its preparation.

6. The likely significant environmental, including health, effects[5] as defined in article 2, paragraph 7.

7. Measures to prevent, reduce or mitigate any significant adverse effects on the environment, including health, which may result from the implementation of the plan or programme.

8. An outline of the reasons for selecting the alternatives dealt with and a description of how the assessment was undertaken including difficulties encountered in providing the information to be included such as technical deficiencies or lack of knowledge.

9. Measures envisaged for monitoring environmental, including health, effects of the implementation of the plan or programme.

10. The likely significant transboundary environmental, including health, effects.

11. A non-technical summary of the information provided.

Annex V. INFORMATION REFERRED TO IN ARTICLE 8, PARAGRAPH 5

1.   The proposed plan or programme and its nature.

2.   The authority responsible for its adoption.

3.   The envisaged procedure, including:

    (a)   The commencement of the procedure;

    (b)   The opportunities for the public to participate;

    (c)   The time and venue of any envisaged public hearing;

    (d)   The authority from which relevant information can be obtained and where the relevant information has been deposited for examination by the public;

    (e)   The authority to which comments or questions can be submitted and the time schedule for the transmittal of comments or questions; and

    (f)   What environmental, including health, information relevant to the proposed plan or programme is available.

4.   Whether the plan or programme is likely to be subject to a transboundary assessment procedure.

Notes

1   For the purposes of this Protocol:
- 'Motorway' means a road specially designed and built for motor traffic, which does not serve properties bordering on it, and which:
  (a) Is provided, except at special points or temporarily, with separate carriageways for the two directions of traffic, separated from each other by a dividing strip not intended for traffic or, exceptionally, by other means;
  (b) does not cross at level with any road, railway or tramway track, or footpath; and
  (c) Is specially sign posted as a motorway.
- 'Express road' means a road reserved for motor traffic accessible only from interchanges or controlled junctions and on which, in particular, stopping and parking are prohibited on the running carriageway(s).

2   For the purposes of this Protocol, 'airport' means an airport which complies with the definition in the 1944 Chicago Convention setting up the International Civil Aviation Organization (annex 14).

3   For the purposes of this Protocol, nuclear power stations and other nuclear reactors cease to be such an installation when all nuclear fuel and other radioactively contaminated elements have been removed permanently from the installation site.

4   For the purposes of this Protocol, 'airport' means an airport which complies with the definition in the 1944 Chicago Convention setting up the International Civil Aviation Organization (annex 14).

5   These effects should include secondary, cumulative, synergistic, short-, medium- and long-term, permanent and temporary, positive and negative effects.

SEA Prediction and Evaluation Techniques

The aim of this appendix is not to make the reader an expert on different types of SEA prediction and evaluation techniques: that would require at least one book of this size per technique. Rather, it aims to give an introduction to a range of techniques, an understanding of the circumstances under which their use might be appropriate in SEA, and sources of further information.

This appendix starts with the least technical and most commonly used qualitative techniques, then discusses techniques for mapping and simple spatial analysis, then techniques for ensuring that all impacts are identified and for quantifying them, and finally evaluation techniques and compatibility assessment. Table 8.11 summarized how these techniques could be used in SEA.

For each technique, information is given on what the technique aims to do, what doing it involves, what the outputs look like, advantages and disadvantages of the technique, and some sources of further information where appropriate (these do not purport to be the best ones, but only aim to give a starting point for further reading). Some of the techniques partly overlap, for instance overlay maps can be done using GIS; vulnerability assessment involves multi-criteria analysis and GIS.

I have included some techniques despite my personal doubts about them – which will emerge quickly enough in the 'advantages and disadvantages' sections – because they are widely advocated as ways of improving the robustness of SEA, and thus its ability to withstand critique (eg in lawsuits and inquiries).

Expert judgement

What the technique aims to do

Expert judgement can be used for a wide range of applications: collecting data, developing alternatives from the most strategic policy level to the very detailed site level, analysing and ranking them, predicting impacts, and suggesting mitigation measures.

What doing it involves

One or preferably several experts whose specialisms cover the range of impacts of the strategic action brainstorm/discuss/consider the relevant issue. This has been formalized in some situations, for instance through the Delphi Technique which uses consecutive cycles of questionnaires of expert participants until agreement on a subject is reached.

What the outputs look like

'Expert' data, ideas, decisions.

Advantages

- quick and cheap
- requires no specialist equipment
- can take unquantifiable, partial, political, etc information on board
- can lead to innovative, win–win solutions
- fosters information sharing and education between the expert participants
- the level of uncertainty of the results is not necessarily higher than that of much more complex techniques

Disadvantages

- potential for bias depending on the experts involved
- non-replicable, not scientific

Quality of Life Assessment

What the technique aims to do

QoLA aims to identify what matters and why in an area, so that the quality of life consequences (both good and bad) of strategic actions can be better taken into account. The core idea of QoLA is that the environment, the economy and society provide a range of benefits for people, and that it is these benefits that need to be protected and/or enhanced. For example a small woodland on the edge of a town does not matter because it provides x hectares of woodland, but rather because it provides recreation, a habitat for rare species, carbon 'fixing', jobs for foresters etc. Analysing these benefits gives an indication of how the area should be managed in the future.

What doing it involves

QoLA involves six steps (A–F). Having identified the purpose of the assessment (A) and described the area to be studied (B), the benefits/disbenefits that the area offers to present and future generations are identified (C). The technique then asks (D): how important is each benefit or disbenefit, to whom, and why? on current trends, will there be enough of each of them? what (if anything) could substitute for the benefits? The answers to these questions lead to a series of management implications (E) which allow a 'shopping list' to be

Table C.1 *Part of Quality of Life Assessment for major new development proposal west of the A1(M) at Stevenage*

Feature (B)	Benefit (C)	Reason it matters/to whom it matters	Answers to evaluation questions (D)			Substitutability	Management implications (E)
			Scale at which it matters	Importance	Trend relative to target		
Rights of way network (including bridleways)	Circular routes/choice of routes	Recreation, links to west of valley. Cross-country fixtures and training, eg 'pony riding route'	Local	High	From public consultation exercise not enough	Substitute with other non-vehicular access	Ensure footpaths lead to and connect with area beyond development. Give access from Stevenage without going through the new development. Bridleways to connect to Stevenage 'pony riding route'. Allow electrical buggies (for physically challenged people) but not motorbikes
	Alignment associated with historic movement and ancient boundary patterns	Historians, specialist interest	Local	?	?	Cannot replace historic features	Retain alignment and existing character, improve signage and information for users

Source: CPM (2001)

devised of things that any development/management of that area should achieve, how they could be achieved, and their relative importance. The 'shopping list' stipulates the benefits that any development would have to provide before it was considered acceptable and, as a corollary, indicates where development would not be appropriate. Monitoring of the benefits (F) should be carried out to ensure that they are actually provided.

What the outputs look like

The main output of a QoLA exercise is a list of management implications for the area in questions. Stages B–E are normally documented as a table such as Table C.1.

Advantages

- sets a context for development proposals by stipulating benefits that any development should provide to an area
- offers flexibility for developers in terms of *how* they provide the benefits
- encourages public participation; enhances public ownership and transparency of decision-making
- acknowledges the complementary role of experts and local residents
- focuses on management and enhancement of an area, rather than just minimizing impacts on it
- values the uniqueness, scarcity and diversity of assets affected, not just quality: goes beyond just protecting a limited number of 'best' areas
- most effectively protects those sites that provide the most benefits
- provides an equitable basis for comparing sites in terms of the benefits they offer and the degree to which those benefits can be substituted

Disadvantages

- not well understood or widely used
- does not compare alternative types of development, ie does not consider potential benefits

Further information

Countryside Agency et al (2002)

Overlay maps

What the technique aims to do

Overlay maps identify areas that would be appropriate or inappropriate for development.

What doing it involves

Maps of areas of constraint, for instance areas of importance for landscape, wildlife and groundwater protection, are superimposed using transparencies.

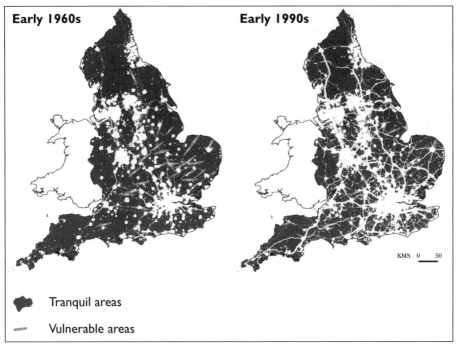

Source: CPRE/Countryside Commission (1995)

Figure C.1 *Example of overlay maps: tranquil areas*

What the outputs look like

A map showing constraints (or lack of constraints) to development. For instance Figure C.1 shows two maps of 'tranquil areas' in England. The maps superimpose (in white):

*   4km radius from the largest power stations,
*   3km buffers from the most heavily used roads and from major industrial areas,
*   2km buffers from other heavily used roads and from the edge of smaller towns,
*   1km buffers from roads with medium disturbance, some main line railways, 400KV and 275KV power lines,
*   noise lozenges from military and civil airfields, and
*   areas of very extensive opencast mining.

The dark tranquil areas are those in which special efforts should be made to preserve tranquillity. Note the impact that development has had on tranquil areas between the early 1960s and early 1990s!

Advantages

*   gives easily understandable results that can be used in public participation exercises

- can be carried out by non-experts
- applicable at all scales

Disadvantages

- can only be used with impacts/developments that have a spatial component (that are 'mappable'), and so are unlikely to be useful at the policy level
- can be time-consuming and expensive, especially if done through GIS
- can be difficult to keep up to date if *not* done through GIS

Further information

Hyder (1999)

Land use partitioning analysis

What the technique aims to do

Linear infrastructure cuts across land and divides it into smaller parcels. This has effects on nature conservation because it fragments habitats; landscape because it reduces the scale of the landscape; tranquillity because it reduces the size of tranquil areas; the viability of agricultural businesses because it reduces the cost-effectiveness of large field sizes; peoples' ability to move from one area to another, etc. Land use partitioning aims to identify, assess and record this fragmentation.

What doing it involves

Land use partitioning analysis analyses the size and quality of areas of non-fragmentation before and after a programme of linear infrastructure construction. It involves, for both the before (baseline without the infrastructure) and after (with the infrastructure) scenario:

- identifying non-fragmented areas
- identifying areas of high nature conservation/landscape/etc by overlaying various designations and land uses, eg national parks, woodland
- grading the areas of non-fragmentation according to their surface area and quality
- representing the gradings on a map.

A comparison of the gradings before and after proposed infrastructure developments indicates the impact of the infrastructure on land use partitioning. The impacts can also be shown in a graph of the number of land units versus their cumulative area: this shows how the same cumulative area (eg 1000 hectares) would be formed by more individual land units after the strategic action than before.

What the outputs look like

Figure C.2 shows the results of a land use partitioning exercise.

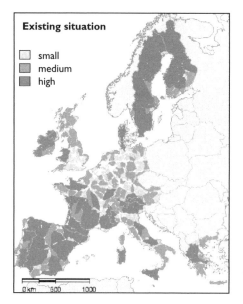

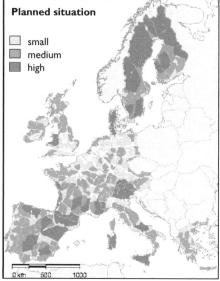

High

More than 50% of the area is designated by international conventions and more than 50% of the area is forest or semi-natural habitat.

Small

Less than 50% of the area is designated by international conventions and less than 50% of the area is forest or semi-natural habitat.

Medium

Intermediate ranking.

Source: European Environment Agency (1998)

Figure C.2 *Example of land use partitioning analysis for biodiversity: European Trans-European Network*

Advantages

- deals with a topic that would otherwise be poorly (or not) considered
- gives a good visual representation of impacts

Disadvantages

- requires GIS
- requires much data
- is expensive and time-consuming
- its application is limited to only a few subjects: it supports other techniques rather than being a 'main' SEA technique

Further information

BCEOM (1994), European Environment Agency (1998)

Geographical Information Systems

What the technique aims to do

GISs are support tools for other SEA techniques. They are often only used to map data. However, they are also valuable analytical tools. They can, for instance, calculate areas, calculate distances (straight line and sometimes also along a network), identify viewing areas from a point, construct buffer zones around features, draw contour lines using interpolated values between points, and superimpose maps of the above to produce combined maps.

What doing it involves

GISs link attribute data to map data. Map data (spatial reference points) are essentially points or lines on a map. Attribute data are characteristics of map features, for instance land use of an area or slope of a road. GISs thus are a combination of a computerized cartography system that stores map data, and a database management system that stores attribute data. Links between map data and attribute data allow maps of the attribute data to be displayed, combined and analysed with relative speed and ease.

GISs require an appropriate computer system, compilation or purchase of map data and related attribute data, and analysis of these data. Specialist skills are required.

What the outputs look like

Figure C.3 shows an example where GIS was used in association with a decision tree (eg 'if a site with land use X is close to deciduous woodland then convert it to...') to identify potential sites for expansion of UK Biodiversity Action Plan priority habitats in the Chiltern Natural Area (Lee et al, 2002).

Advantages

- Relatively easy manipulation of large amounts of data
- Allows location-specific impacts to be clearly visualized
- Its zoning features and its ability to consider several layers of information at a time can be used in sensitivity mapping
- Long-term cost-savings in map-making
- Results can easily be used in public participation exercises, sometimes in an interactive manner

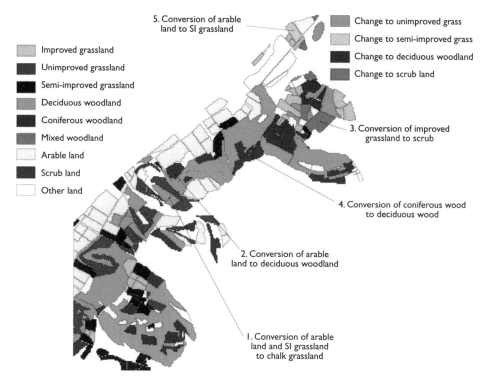

Source: Lee et al (2002)

Figure C.3 *Example of GIS: Potential sites for expansion of UK Biodiversity Action Plan priority habitats in the Chiltern Natural Area*

Disadvantages

- Carries out only a limited range of analytical tasks: essentially it provides data description rather than real spatial analysis
- Can be expensive with high start-up costs
- Requires considerable technical expertise
- Limited to impacts that have a direct spatial component

Further reading

European Environment Agency (1998), Rodriguez-Bachiller (2001)

Network analysis

(also called cause-effect analysis, consequence analysis, or causal chain analysis)

What the technique aims to do

Network analysis explicitly recognizes that environmental systems consist of a complex web of relationships, and that many activities' impacts occur at several stages removed from the activity itself. It aims to identify the key cause-effect links which describe the causal pathway from initial action to ultimate environmental outcome. In doing so, it can also identify assumptions made in impact predictions, unintended consequences of the strategic action, and possible measures to ensure effective implementation. It is particularly useful for identifying cumulative impacts.

What doing it involves

Network analysis involves, through expert judgement, drawing the direct and indirect impacts of an action as a network of boxes (activities, outcomes) and arrows (interactions between them).

What the outputs look like

Figure 8.4 showed an example of a network analysis.

Advantages

- easy to understand, transparent, good for public participation
- rapid and not cost-intensive
- identifies main impacts on environmental receptors, makes mechanisms of cause and effect explicit
- identifies cumulative and indirect impacts
- identifies constraints to effective implementation of a strategic action
- useful input to other SEA techniques, eg modelling

Disadvantages

- not quantitative, not replicable
- can miss important impacts if not done well
- does not deal with spatial impacts or impacts that vary over time
- diagram can become very complex

Further reading

Hyder (1999)

Modelling

(also called forecasting)

What the technique aims to do

Modelling techniques aim to predict likely future environmental conditions with and without the strategic action (the strategic action's impacts are the difference between the two).

What doing it involves

Modelling involves making a series of assumptions about future conditions under various scenarios, and calculating the resulting impacts. Models typically deal with quantifiable impacts: air pollution, noise, traffic, etc. For instance, the likely noise and air pollution impacts of a proposed road network can be calculated based on assumptions about expected traffic volumes on the network, the ratio of heavy goods vehicles, average speeds along the network, and noise recipients. Most models used in SEA have evolved from EIA techniques. Many are computerized.

What the outputs look like

Numbers (possibly with ranges to denote uncertainty) or graphs that show future air, noise, etc levels under different scenarios. Box 8.2 shows a simple example. Another example is an accident modelling exercise carried out for a network of high-speed roads in Poland. This used as inputs information about road length for eight different categories of road, accident rates for these categories, and costs of accidents. Future accident rates were expected to be lower than current ones because it was expected that Poland would reach Western European standards of road network hierarchization, signing, and quality of pavements. The study concluded that:

> *Transferring a large part of the [vehicle-kilometres onto] motorways and expressways, i.e. roads with lower accident rates will decrease [the] number of accidents. According to moderately optimistic prediction for [2025] the number of accidents will be reduced by 17,000, number of injured by 22,000 persons and killed by 360–380 persons, and reduction in costs of about 3.6–3.9 billions nzl* (Tracz, 1999).

(Note that uncertainty has been shown as ranges for deaths and costs, but not for the number of accidents).

Advantages

- objective, scientific, rigorous (as rigorous as possible given uncertainties)
- can deal with cumulative and indirect impacts

Disadvantages

- limited to impacts that can be quantified/modelled
- can require large amounts of expensive or unreliable data
- many models are 'black boxes': technocratic, complex and not transparent. They generally do not encourage participation or ownership by those people affected by the strategic action
- many models are based on untested assumptions, and have not been verified/ monitored on the ground, particularly over longer timeframes. For instance, UK traffic models assumed for many years that new roads merely dispersed existing traffic: monitoring later showed that new roads also generate new traffic. The current assumptions on which models are based (eg height of 1 in 100 year flood) may also not be appropriate in the future
- because most models used in SEA were initially used in EIA, they promote project-level rather than strategic thinking

- many models can only compare like with like (eg road with road, not road with rail)

Further information

The whole June 1998 issue of *Impact Assessment and Project Appraisal* (Vol. 16, No. 2) is on modelling, though primarily in the context of EIA. Also Hyder (1999).

Scenario/sensitivity analysis

What the technique aims to do

Often the impacts of a strategic action, or the relative benefits and disbenefits of different options depend on variables outside the strategic action's control. For instance the benefits provided by flood prevention measures could change depending on future weather conditions; or future air pollution levels could depend in part on whether a new power station is built. Scenarios can be used to describe a range of future conditions. The impact of a strategic action can be forecast and compared for different scenarios – sensitivity analysis – to test the strategic action's robustness to different possible futures.

What doing it involves

Forecasts based on current trends and/or scenarios representing trends outside the decision-makers' control are generated and the strategic action's impacts are predicted based on these forecasts/scenarios. Sensitivity analysis measures the effect on predictions of changing one or more key input values about which there is uncertainty.

What the outputs look like

The following are examples of scenarios and sensitivity analyses.

The SEA of the Dutch waste management plan 1992–2002 was based on two *scenarios* for future waste production. The 'policy scenario' assumed that national objectives regarding waste prevention, reduction etc would be fully achieved. The 'headwind scenario' assumed that they would not be fully achieved, and that therefore more waste would have to be dealt with (Verheem, 1996).

An SEA for oil extraction could estimate the annual probability of an oil spill per vessel under various scenarios, including the *worst case scenario*, the likely (and worst case) volume of an oil spill, the impact of such a spill on biodiversity etc.

The economic impact of a road construction programme depends on issues such as future traffic, the percentage of heavy goods vehicles using the road, travel time savings, the 'value' of a life, and discount rates. Different assumptions for each of these would lead to different results. *Sensitivity analysis* could predict and compare the economic costs and benefits of the programme using different values for each of these inputs.

Advantages

- Gives more realistic data which reflects uncertainties
- Gives ideas for reducing uncertainties, leads to more robust strategic actions
- Supports the precautionary principle

Disadvantages

- Can be time- and resource-intensive

Further information

Finnveden et al (2003)

Cost-benefit analysis

What the technique aims to do

CBA compares the monetary value of a strategic action's benefits with the monetary value of its costs. It aims to help decision-makers by translating environmental and social costs into a single, well-understood and widely used unit of measure: money. In theory this allows all impacts to be put on the same footing.

What doing it involves

The two broad approaches to doing CBA involve identifying stated preferences – preferences stated by a respondent to a question – and revealed preferences – preferences inferred from an individual's behaviour.

Stated preference techniques include:

- contingent valuation: asks individuals about their willingness to pay and/or accept compensation for changes in environmental resources, and
- contingent ranking: asks individuals to rank several alternatives.

Revealed preference techniques include:

- replacement cost approach: estimates the cost of restoring the environment to its original state if it were damaged,
- avertive expenditures: measures expenditures undertaken by individuals to offset some environmental risk (eg noise abatement),
- travel cost method: surveys visitors to a site (eg a nature area) to determine how they value the (mainly recreational) characteristics of the site and how much time they spent travelling to the site,
- hedonic price methods (house prices approach): cross-sectional data on house prices are assembled, together with data on factors likely to influence these prices (eg noise, views). Links between factors and prices are analysed using multiple regression techniques,
- hedonic price methods (wage risk premiums): uses multiple regression to relate wages/salaries to the factors which influence them (eg morbidity and mortality risks), and
- dose-response approach: determines the links between pollution (dose)

Table C.2 *Example of part of a CBA*

Journey times and vehicle operating costs	Overall, public transport should enjoy reduced journey times, as general congestion will be reduced. A new bus lane in Wellington Road will benefit buses travelling inbound to the bus station	Trunk road journey time savings: 2.46 minutes	Low growth: present value of benefits (PVB) £7.99m High growth: PVB £8.98m
Cost	The cost to Railtrack of maintaining and operating the level crossing barriers and signalling would be negated	Not applicable	present value of costs (PVC) £4.023m
Local air quality	Slight decrease in air quality with the opening of the bridge. Slight improvement to air quality in town centre	No. properties experiencing: better air quality: 747 worse air quality: 1685	Neutral to slight adverse effects

Low Growth PVB £7.99m; PVC £4.02m; net present value £3.97m

High Growth PVB £8.98m; PVC £4.02m; net present value £4.96m

Source: adapted from Somerset County Council (2000)

and its impacts (response), and predicts the costs of the impacts (eg cost of crop/forest damage from air pollution).

What the outputs look like

Table C.2 shows a partial CBA of a local transport plan. Note that the last row only adds up the monetary values, not the other values such as landscape.

Advantages

- is widely accepted by economists and decision-makers
- allows all impacts to be considered on the same footing: 'integrates' different types of impact appraisal
- makes transparent the value of things that have not traditionally been considered in economic analyses
- may be the only way that environmental values can be taken into account in some decision-making processes

Disadvantages

- many CBA techniques are very indirect – for instance house values in a given neighbourhood may have little to do with air pollution levels – and the techniques used can greatly affect the results
- it is unclear over what time period costs and benefits should be compared: the impact on jobs may last for 20 years, on climate change for hundreds of years

- the discount rate – the reduced cost of future impacts – used can have a large impact on the CBA's results. There is no agreement on what discount rates to use. Anything other than no discount rate – future impacts given the same cost as today's – contradicts the intra-generational principle of sustainable development
- economic efficiency is not the only principle which matters in decision-making and efficiency is not value-free: placing an economic value on nature or a human life is seen by many as an alien, reductionist approach
- does not consider who wins and who loses. For instance it does not distinguish whether the noise increases are borne by people with already high noise levels or not
- can be perceived as unethical. It relies on individuals' judgements about their personal interests, which is arguably not an appropriate approach to decision-making about public goods
- probably limited to projects and programmes
- requires much data, and takes much time/resources

Further information

DoE (1991), Economics for the Environment (1999), Pearce et al (1992), UK Treasury (1997), Weiss (1998)

Multi-criteria analysis

(also called multiple attribute analysis or multi-objective trade-off)

What the technique aims to do

MCA analyses and compares how well different alternatives achieve different objectives, and identifies a preferred alternative.

What doing it involves

MCA involves choosing relevant assessment criteria/impacts and alternatives; scoring how each alternative affects each criterion; assigning a weight (value of importance) to the impact; and aggregating the score and weight of each alternative. Table C.3 shows different scoring systems, using noise as the criterion.

Weighting of the criteria aims to reflect the fact that different criteria can have different relative importance. For instance, noise may have been identified in the SEA baseline stage as being much more important than air pollution and landscape: it could be given a weighting of, say, 3 compared to the other weightings of 1. Weighting would normally be carried out by a panel of experts or public participation.

The scores and weightings are then multiplied and the results added up for each alternative. The alternative that scores most highly 'wins'. Table C.4 shows a hypothetical example of this, using the 'value' approach to scoring from Table C.3. In Table C.4, alternative B 'wins'; despite very good scores for air and landscape, alternative D comes out poorly because of the significance of the noise criterion.

Table C.3 *Scoring systems for MCA*

Scoring method	Alternatives				Basis of the score
	A	B	C	D	
Absolute	65	62	71	75	Measured L_{10}dBA levels
Interval	0	−3	+6	+10	Difference in L_{10}dBA levels compared to alternative A
Ordinal	B	A	C	D	Ranking according to ascending L_{10}dBA levels
Binary	0	0	1	1	0 = less than 70 L_{10}dBA; 1 = more than 70 L_{10}dBA
'Value'	0	+1	−2	−3	+1 = good, -3 = very poor

Source: Lee (1987)

What the outputs look like

A choice of preferred alternative(s) underpinned by a table similar to Table C.4. For instance Tkach and Simonovic (1998) used MCA to explore four alternative floodplain management strategies for the Red River Valley in Manitoba, Canada.

Advantages

- acknowledges that society is composed of diverse stakeholders with different goals and values, and makes these views transparent
- reflects the fact that some issues 'matter' more than others
- is simple and can be used in a variety of settings, including public participation
- can compare alternatives
- can be used with both quantifiable and unquantifiable data

Disadvantages

- can be used to 'twist' data; can lead to very different results depending on who establishes the weightings and scoring systems
- generally does not cope well with irreversible/critical limits; 'show stoppers' which mean that no matter how important other aspects are, they cannot outweigh the adverse implications of one factor.

Further information

Economics for the Environment (1999), Finnveden et al (2003), Glasson et al (1999)

Life cycle analysis

What the technique aims to do

LCA analyses the entire impacts of a strategic action throughout its 'life', from

Table C.4 *Ranking of alternatives based on weighted scores*

Criterion	Weight (w)	Alternative							
		A		B		C		D	
		score (a)	a x w	a	a x w	a	a x w	a	a x w
Noise	3	0	0	+1	+3	-2	-6	-3	-9
Landscape	1	+2	2	-2	-2	+1	+1	+2	+2
Biodiversity	1	-2	-2	0	0	0	0	+3	+3
Total			0		+1		-5		-4

initial development ('cradle') to implementation ('grave'). It considers not only the strategic action's direct impacts, but also its impacts up and down the line: for instance, where the aggregates needed for road construction would come from, or how the wastes from an energy generation programme would be disposed of.

What doing it involves

LCA involves four main steps:

1 Agreement on objectives, the alternatives to be assessed, system boundaries, etc: for instance comparison of landfilling versus recycling in the UK over the next 10 years;
2 Compilation of an inventory of relevant inputs (eg materials, energy) and outputs (eg emissions to air, water and soil) associated with each alternative (landfilling, recycling);
3 Evaluation of the magnitude and significance of potential environmental impacts associated with those inputs and outputs. This may involve grouping the data into impact categories (eg global warming, soil pollution); assigning the inventory data to the impact categories; and quantifying the alternatives' impacts on the impact categories; and
4 Interpretation of the results to identify the preferred alternative, ways of improving the strategic action, etc.

What the outputs look like

Information about the impacts of different alternatives and a choice of preferred alternative. LCA has been applied to the development of the Dutch Ten Year Waste Management Programme 1995–2005 (Commission for Environmental Impact Assessment, 1994), and to three policy scenarios for a waste incineration tax in Sweden (Björklund et al, 2003). Most examples have been for products (eg disposable v reusable nappies) or sites.

Advantages

*   comprehensive, deals with all impacts from a strategic action
*   can be used to compare alternatives

Disadvantages

- agreement/standardization has not yet been reached on many aspects of LCA, for instance what is 'cradle' and 'grave', or whether to consider second generation impacts such as the energy needed to produce building materials
- requires judgements that balance apples and oranges, eg impacts on water v on air
- because of this, LCAs to date have not been particularly replicable: LCAs have reached different and sometimes contradictory conclusions about similar products because they used different assumptions
- probably limited to programme SEA
- requires large amounts of detailed data

Further information

Economics for the Environment (1999), International Organization for Standardization (1997), Tukker (2000)

Vulnerability analysis

What the technique aims to do

Vulnerability analysis allows different development scenarios to be evaluated in terms of how they affect the vulnerability of the receiving environment.

What doing it involves

Vulnerability analysis combines GIS and multi-criteria analysis to assess the impacts of a planned activity on the vulnerability of an area. Vulnerability in this context is the combination of sensitivity and a valuation of the system. A typical vulnerability analysis follows the following steps:

1.   Definition of the impacts and targets for which the vulnerability assessment will be carried out. For instance for a motorway network, one might have the following impact groups:

impact:	*affecting which targets:*
habitat destruction	flora and fauna
desiccation	flora and fauna
barrier impact	fauna, people (local transport)
disturbance	fauna
noise disturbance	people
fragmentation	landscape, flora and fauna

2.   Preparation of vulnerability maps that show, for each target, 1. the sensitivity of the target with relation to the impacts, and 2. evaluation criteria used to valuate the system, standardized as classes (0 = not vulnerable, 1 = somewhat vulnerable etc up to 4 = very vulnerable, percentages (0–100), or some other unit).

3.   Integration of the different vulnerability maps to maps of all the factors that affect a target. This involves overlaying several vulnerability maps using GIS and MCA. For instance all of the vulnerability maps for flora and fauna (habitat destruction, dessication, barrier impact etc) can be 'added' together using weightings based on the standardized classes (eg very vulnerable has four times the weight of somewhat vulnerable; habitat destruction is twice as important as desiccation). The weighted overlays allow areas of high vulnerability to be identified.

4.   Finally, using GIS, the expected noise increase, groundwater decline etc associated with different development options is overlaid onto the vulnerability maps. This indicates the expected locations of negative environmental impacts regarding different targets and/or impacts. The GIS can then be used to add together the weighted impacts to identify those alternatives with the least impacts.

What the outputs look like

Maps showing the vulnerability of areas overlaid with possible developments. Graphs comparing alternatives in terms of their (weighted) types of impacts.

Advantages

*   allows quantitative expression of spatial impacts, which is useful in comparing alternatives
*   because vulnerability analysis uses the local (geographical) characteristics of the environment, it is also useful for site-specific EIA

Disadvantages

*   can be costly and time-intensive
*   only works with impacts that can be mapped
*   the concept of vulnerability involves value judgements, but these are 'hidden' in the final analysis
*   not much used to date

Further information

van Straaten (1996, 1999)

Carrying capacity, ecological footprints

What the technique aims to do

Identify limits to growth, ie where human activities go beyond the capacity of the environment to support them.

What doing it involves

The concepts of carrying capacity and ecological footprinting take as a basis that:

total human impact on an area = the area's population x
per capita impact.

Carrying capacity analysis aims to determine the human population that can
be 'carried' by a particular area based on given per capita consumption levels.
Carrying capacity analysis has a long history, for instance in tourism planning
('how many tourists should be allowed on this island each year so that its
quality as a tourism destination does not decline?') or to determine whether a
given city can cope with more houses. However it has been mired in
controversies over what exactly 'capacity' is, how land can be managed to
increase capacity, whether a few more people can't be snuck in after all etc.

Ecological footprinting looks at the equation from the other side. It
identifies how much productive land and water area is required to support a
given area's population indefinitely at current consumption levels (if the
required land/water area is larger than that which exists, then the area is over
capacity); *or* the maximum rate of resource consumption and waste discharge
that can be sustained indefinitely by a given population in a given area.

What the outputs look like

- Carrying capacity: the maximum number of people/households/etc that
  can be sustained by an area; *or*
- Ecological footprint: the average amount of productive land and sea
  required per person (or for a given population) to maintain a particular
  consumption level. For instance Wackernagel and Rees (1996) have
  calculated that the average American's footprint in 1991 was 5.1 hectares,
  compared to the average Indian's 0.4 hectares; *or*
- 'Earthshares': the average amount of productive land and sea available
  globally per capita. For instance Chambers et al (2000) calculate that
  worldwide 'earthshares' were 2.1 hectares in 2000 but, because of
  increases in human population, will only be 1.4 hectares in 2050.

Advantages

- directly linked to concepts of sustainability
- can be carried out at any scale
- results can be easily understood
- educational: can help to trigger behavioural change

Disadvantages

- complicated process which can only really be done by experts
- makes huge assumptions, not easily replicable

Further information

Chambers et al (2000), Jacobs (1997), RSPB (1994), TCPA (1998),
Wackernagel and Rees (1996)

Risk assessment

What the technique aims to do

Risk assessment estimates the risk that products and activities cause to human health, safety and ecosystems.

What doing it involves

It involves identifying possible hazards (eg oil spills), identifying and analysing their consequences (eg on birds, on the local economy), and estimating their frequency. It may also translate these risks into costs, for instance by multiplying likely risks (frequency x consequences) by the nominal value of a human life or a clean beach.

What the outputs look like

Statements about the probability of a specified event, eg 1 in 10,000 chance of an oil spill in area X in a given year; 1 in 250,000 chance of human death from particulates per year; or about consequences, eg 5 oil spills on UK shores per year, 35 human deaths due to particulates per year.

For instance, a post-conflict SEA of depleted uranium in Kosovo (UNEP, 2001) included a (horror-inducing in its 'neutrality') assessment of the risks to 7–12 year old children of picking up solid pieces of depleted uranium (DU):

> *The only significant exposure may be by external beta radiation... The surface radiation dose rate is about 2 mSv [per hour]. If the piece of DU is put in the pocket the beta radiation is somewhat reduced, 50% is assumed. The exposed skin area will be quite small each time and from day to day it may shift a little making the skin dose smaller. By keeping the piece of DU in the pocket for several weeks it might be possible that the skin dose will exceed values corresponding to the limit for the public (50 mSv/year) and workers (500 mSv/year). It is out of the question that there will be any deterministic effects (skin burns)... The gamma dose rate at different distances from a penetrator, about 300 g DU, has been measured at the approximate dose rates are...*

external dose rate (μSv/h)	distance from the penetrator (m)
2.7	0.05
0.85	0.1
0.25	0.2

Advantages

- can be used to compare alternatives on the basis of the risk that they cause
- can incorporate the precautionary principle

Disadvantages

- only considers one aspect of the 'environment', namely risk/safety
- often extrapolates the risks at high dose levels of a pollutant to low dose levels, with consequent uncertainties
- results can vary enormously depending on the assumptions made

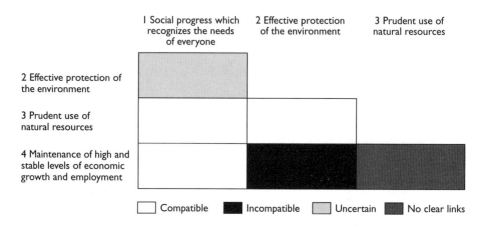

Figure C.4 *Example of an internal compatibility matrix*

- where it is used in cost-benefit assessment, values placed on human life or ecosystems can be highly contentious and possibly not politically acceptable

Further information

Economics for the Environment (1999), Finnveden et al (2003)

Compatibility appraisal

What the technique aims to do

Compatibility appraisal aims to ensure that the strategic action is internally coherent and consistent with other strategic actions. This is not strictly an SEA function, more one associated with good planning.

What doing it involves

Normally this is done using two types of matrices.

An internal compatibility matrix plots different components/ statements of the strategic action on one axis and the same strategic actions on the other axis. Matrix cells are filled in by asking 'is this statement compatible with that statement (tick) or not (cross)?'. Where incompatibility is found, one or both statements may need to be changed.

An external compatibility matrix plots the strategic action (normally as a whole) against other relevant (normally higher- and equal-level) strategic actions. Matrix cells are filled in by listing those statements of the strategic action that fulfil the requirements of the other strategic actions, or explaining how the evolving strategic action should take the requirements into account. Where no statements in the strategic action fulfil the others' requirements, or where they conflict, then this may need to be redressed.

What the outputs look like

Figure C.4 shows an example of an internal compatibility matrix. It tests the internal compatibility of the four UK objectives for sustainable development (DETR, 2001): the results help to explain some of the stresses and strains involved in implementing 'sustainable' development! Table 6.8 showed an example of an external compatibility matrix.

Advantages

- Helps to ensure that a strategic action is internally coherent and consistent with other strategic actions
- Clarifies trade-offs, eg between social benefits and environmental costs
- Is easy to understand

Disadvantages

- Is subjective
- Can be time-intensive
- Outputs can look daunting

References

Alberta Energy and Utilities Board, Alberta Environment, and Natural Resources Conservation Board (2002) *Cumulative Effects Assessment in Environmental Impact Assessment Reports Required under the Alberta Environmental Protection and Enhancement Act*, www3.gov.ab.ca/env/protenf/documents/cea.pdf

ANSEA Team (TAU Consultora Ambiental et al) (2002) *Towards an Analytical Strategic Environmental Assessment*, Madrid

Audit Commission (1999) *Listen Up! Effective Community Consultation*, www.audit-commission.gov.uk/reports

BCEOM (1994) *Etude strategique d'impact sur l'environnement: Essai méthodologique*, Ministère de l'Environnement, Direction de la Nature et du Paysage, Sous-direction de l'Aménagement et du Paysage, Paris

Bedfordshire County Council (1995) *Bedfordshire Structure Plan 2011, Technical Report 5, Targets and Indicators*, Bedford

Bishop, J (2001) *Working Paper 2: Participation in Development Plan Preparation*, www.planning.odpm.gov.uk/gpppmdpp/02.htm

Björklund, A, J Johansson, M Nilsson, P Eldh and G Finnveden (2003) *Environmental Assessment of a Waste Incineration Tax: Case Study and Evaluation of a Framework for Strategic Environmental Assessment*, Forskningsgruppen för Miljöstrategiska Studier, Stockholm

Brown, A L (1997) 'The environmental overview in development project formulation', *Impact Assessment* 15(1), pp73–78

Brown, A L (1998) 'The environmental overview as a realistic approach to strategic environmental assessment in developing countries', in A Porter and J Fittipaldi, eds, *Environmental Methods Review: Retooling Impact Assessment for the New Century*, US Army Environmental Policy Institute, The Press Club, Fargo, USA, pp127–134

CAG Consultants (2000) *Integrating Policies in Development Plans, Phase 1*, report to Countryside Agency, Cheltenham

CAG Consultants (2003) *SEA pilot 5: Newcastle City Council UDP review*, report to the Office of the Deputy Prime Minister, Manchester

Canadian Environmental Assessment Agency (1999) *Addressing Cumulative Environmental Effects*, www.ceaa-acee.gc.ca/0011/0001/0008/guide1_e.htm

Chambers, N, C Simmons and M Wackernagel (2000) *Sharing Nature's Interest*, Earthscan, London

Cobb C, and J Cobb (1994) *The Green National Product*, University of Americas Press, Lanham, Maryland, USA

Commission for Environmental Impact Assessment (1994) *Advisory Guidelines for the Environmental Impact Statement on Ten Years Programme Waste of the Waste Management Council 1995–2005*, The Hague, Netherlands, www.eia.nl/english/projects

Commission of the European Communities (CEC) (1985) 'Council Directive on the assessment of the effects of certain private and public projects on the environment (85/337/EEC)', *Official Journal of the European Communities* L175/40, Brussels

CEC (1993) *Checklist for Review of Environmental Information Submitted under EIA Procedures*, DGXI, Brussels

CEC (1997a) 'Proposal for a Council Directive on the assessment of the effects of certain plans and programmes on the environment', *Official Journal of the European Communities* C129, 25.4.1997, pp14–18

CEC (1997b) 'Council Directive 97/11/EC amending Directive 85/337/EEC on the assessment of the effects of certain public and private projects on the environment', *Official Journal of the European Commission* L073/5-21, Brussels, http://europa.eu.int/comm/environment/eia

CEC (1999) 'Amended proposal for a Council Directive on assessment of the effects of certain plans and programmes on the environment', COM (1999) 73, Brussels

CEC (2001) 'Directive 2001/42/EC on the assessment of the effects of certain plans and programmes on the environment', http://europa.eu.int/comm/environment/eia

Council for the Protection of Rural England (CPRE) and Countryside Commission (1995) *Tranquil Areas*, London

Council on Environmental Quality (1997) *Considering Cumulative Effects Under the National Environmental Policy Act*, http://ceq.eh.doe.gov/nepa/ccenepa/exec.pdf

Countryside Agency, Environment Agency, English Nature and English Heritage (2002) *Quality of Life Capital*, www.qualityoflifecapital.org.uk

CPM (1999) *The Results of the Environmental Capital Approach for Land West of the A1(M)*, Coln St Aldwyns

Curran, J M, C Wood and M Hilton (1998) 'Environmental appraisal of UK development plans: Current practice and future directions', *Environment and Planning B: Planning and Design* 25, pp411–433

Dalal-Clayton, B and B Sadler (2003) *The Status and Potential of Strategic Environmental Assessment*, International Institute for Environment and Development, London

Dalkmann, H (2001) 'Future perspective of SEA: Transport case study in Germany', presented at NECTAR Conference No 6, European Strategies in the Globalising Markets, 16–18 May 2001, Espoo, Finland

Daly, H and J Cobb (1989) *For the Common Good: Redirecting the Economy Towards Community, the Environment and Sustainable Development*, Beacon Press, Boston

Department of the Environment (DoE) (1991) *Policy Appraisal and the Environment*, HMSO, London

DoE (1992) *Planning Policy Guidance Note 12, Development Plans and Regional Guidance*, HMSO, London

DoE (1993) *Environmental Appraisal of Development Plans: A Good Practice Guide*, HMSO, London

Department of Environment, Food and Rural Affairs (DEFRA) (2001) *Digest of Environmental Statistics*, www.defra.gov.uk/environment/statistics/des

DEFRA (2002) *Strategy for Sustainable Farming and Food: Facing the Future*, www.defra.gov.uk/farm/sustain

Department of Environment, Transport and the Regions (DETR) (1998) *A New Deal for Transport: Better for Everyone*, www.dft.gov.uk/itwp/paper

DETR (1999a) *Good Practice Guide on Sustainability Appraisal of Regional Planning Guidance*, www.planning.dtlr.gov.uk/gpgsarpg

DETR (1999b) *Planning Policy Guidance Note 12, Development Plans*, HMSO, London

DETR (2001) *Quality of Life Counts. Indicators for a Strategy for Sustainable Development for the UK: A Baseline Assessment*. The Government Statistical Service, www.sustainable-development.gov.uk/sustainable/quality99

Department of Finance and Personnel (Northern Ireland) (2002) *Developing Policy on the Location of Civil Service Jobs: An Equality Impact Assessment*, Belfast

Department for Transport (DfT) (2002) *Transport Statistics*, www.transtat.dft.gov.uk

Department for Transport, Local Government and the Regions (DTLR) (2001) *Planning Green Paper: Planning: Delivering a Fundamental Change*. HMSO, London

DHV Environment and Infrastructure BV (1994) *Existing Strategic Environmental Assessment Methodology*, report prepared for the European Commission DGXI, Brussels

Economics for the Environment Consultancy (1999) *Review of Technical Guidance on Environmental Appraisal*, report to the Department of the Environment, Transport and the Regions, www.defra.gov.uk/environment/economics/rtgea

Ekins, P, ed (1986) *The Living Economy*, Routledge, London

European Commission (2000) *Managing Natura 2000 sites: The provisions of Article 6 of the 'Habitats' Directive 92/43/EEC*, Brussels

European Commission (2001a) *Assessment of Plans and Projects Significantly Affecting Natura 2000 Sites: Methodological Guidance on the Provisions of Article 6(3) and 6(4) of the Habitats Directive 92/43/EEC*, Brussels

European Commission (2001b) *Guidance on EIA: EIS Review*, Brussels

European Commission (2003) *Implementation of Directive 2001/42 on the Effects of Certain Plans and Programmes on the Environment*, Brussels

European Environment Agency (1998) *Spatial and Ecological Assessment of the TEN: Demonstration of Indicators and GIS Methods*, Environmental Issues Series No 11, Copenhagen, http://reports.eea.eu.int/GH-15-98-318-EN-C/en/seaoften.pdf

Feldmann, L (1998) 'The European Commission's proposal for a strategic environmental assessment directive: Expanding the scope of environmental impact assessment in Europe', *Environmental Impact Assessment Review* 18(1), pp4–15

Feldmann, L, M Vanderhaegen and C Pirotte (2001) 'The European Union's Strategic Environmental Assessment Directive: Status and links to integration and sustainable development', *Environmental Impact Assessment Review* 21(3), pp203–222

Finnveden, G, M Nilsson, J Johansson, A Persson, A Moberg and T Carlsson (2003) 'Strategic environmental assessment methodologies: Applications within the energy sector', *Environmental Impact Assessment Review* 23, pp91–123

Firat, A F and N Dholakia (1998) *Consuming People: From Political Economy to Theatres of Consumption*, Routledge, London

Friends of the Earth and New Economics Foundation (2003) personal communication, London

Gauthier, M, L Simard, and J-P Waaub (2000) *Participation du Public à l'Evaluation Environnementale Stratégique*, Cahier de recherche de l'Institut des sciences de l'environnement, Université du Québec a Montréal, Montreal

Glasson, J, R Therivel and A Chadwick (1999) *Introduction to Environmental Impact Assessment*, 2nd edition, UCL Press, London

Hadley Centre (2003) *Predictions of Future Climate Change*, www.meto.gov.uk/research/hadleycentre/pubs

Halcrow Group Ltd (2002) *Ashford's Future: The Overarching Report*, prepared for Ashford Borough Council, London

Hales, R (2000) 'Land-use development planning and sustainable development', *Journal of Environmental Planning and Management* 43(1), pp99–121

Hardi, P and T Zdan (1997) 'Assessing sustainable development: Principles in practice', presented at conference held by International Institute for Sustainable Development, Bellagio, Italy

Hyder (1999) *Guidelines for the Assessment of Indirect and Cumulative Impacts as well as Impact Interactions*, report prepared for European Commission DG XI, Brussels

Impacts Assessment Unit, Oxford Brookes University (2001) *Assessment of Plans and Projects Significantly Affecting Natura 2000 Sites*, prepared for the European Commission, Brussels, www.europa.eu.int/comm/environment/nature/natura_2000_assess_en.pdf

Institute of Environmental Management and Assessment (IEMA) (2002) *Perspectives: Guidelines on Participation in Environmental Decision-making*, Lincoln

International Association for Impact Assessment and Vereniging van Milieukundigen (2002) *Assessing the Impact of Impact Assessment*, 22nd annual conference abstracts volume, The Hague, Netherlands

International Organization for Standardization (1997) *Life Cycle Assessment: Principles and Framework, ISO 14040*, Geneva

International Union for the Conservation of Nature (IUCN) (1991) *Caring for the Earth: A Strategy for Sustainable Living*, Geneva

Jackson, T and N Marks (1994) *Measuring Sustainable Economic Welfare – A Pilot Index: 1950–1990*, Stockholm Environment Institute in cooperation with the New Economics Foundation, Stockholm

Jacobs, M (1997) *Making Sense of Environmental Capacity*, report prepared for the Council for the Protection of Rural England, London

Jansson, A (1999) 'Transport SEA: A Nordic perspective', presented at the OECD/ECMT conference on SEA of transport, Warsaw, 14–15 October

Kleinschmidt, V and D Wagner, eds (1998) *Strategic Environmental Assessment in Europe: Fourth European Workshop on Environmental Impact Assessment*, Kluwer Academic Publishers, Dordrecht, The Netherlands

Land Use Consultants (1994) *National Forest Environmental Statement*, report prepared for the National Forest Office, London

Land Use Consultants (2003) *SEA pilot 3: Hampshire, Portsmouth and Southampton Minerals Local Plan Review*, report to the Office of the Deputy Prime Minister, London

Lee, J, G Griffiths, S Warnock, N Bailey, J Bayliss, I Vogintzakis and S Thompson (2002) *Development of a Biodiversity and Landscape Map for the Chilterns Using a GIS Based Model*, Chilterns Area of Outstanding Natural Beauty, English Nature, Forestry Commission and Oxford Brookes University, Oxford

Lee, N (1987) *Environmental Impact Assessment: A Training Guide*, 2nd edition, Occasional Paper 18, Department of Planning and Landscape, University of Manchester, Manchester

Lee, N and R Colley (1990) *Reviewing the Quality of Environmental Statements*, Occasional Paper 24, EIA Centre, University of Manchester, Manchester

Lee, N and C Wood (1987) 'EIA: A European perspective', *Built Environment* 4, pp101–110

Levett, R, with I Christie, M Jacobs and R Therivel (2002) *A Better Choice of Choice?*, report to the Sustainable Development Commission, London

Levett-Therivel (2002) *Implementing the SEA Directive: Analysis of Existing Practice*, report for the South West Regional Assembly, Taunton, www.southwest-ra.gov.uk

Levett-Therivel (2003a) *Implementing the SEA Directive: Five Pilot Studies*, report for the South West Regional Assembly, Taunton, www.southwest-ra.gov.uk

Levett-Therivel (2003b) *SEA Pilot 7: Taunton Urban Extension*, report to the Office of the Deputy Prime Minister, London

Levett-Therivel and Land Use Consultants (2003) *What Matters and Why in Epping Forest*, report for the Corporation of London, London

Local Government Management Board (1994) *Sustainability Indicators Research Project: Report of Phase 1*, Luton

Lucas, K and R Simpson (2000) *Transport and Accessibility: The Perspectives of Disadvantaged Communities*, report for the Joseph Rowntree Foundation, Transport Studies Unit, University of Westminster, London

Lucht, J and L Jaubert (2001) *Rapid Site Assessment Guide*, Environmental Data Centre, University of Rhode Island, Providence

Mayo, E, A MacGillivray and D McLaren (1997) *The Index of Sustainable Economic Welfare for the United Kingdom*, www.icsu-scope.org/downloadpubs/scope58/box3w.html

McCold, L and J Holman (1995) 'Cumulative impacts in environmental assessments: How well are they considered?', *The Environmental Professional* 17(1), pp2–8

Minas, P (2002) 'The effectiveness of SEA at integrating environmental considerations into landuse development plans in England and Wales', MSc dissertation, Oxford Brookes University, Oxford

Morris, P and R Therivel, eds (2000) *Methods of Environmental Impact Assessment, 2nd edition*, Spon Press, London

Münster, M (2002) 'Mise au point d'une grille d'évaluation d'après les critères du développement durable pour les projets soumis au Conseil d'État vaudois', MSc work-study report, Ecole Polytechnique Federale de Lausanne, Lausanne

National Trust (2002) *In the National Interest? Government Proposals for Planning Major Infrastructure Projects*, report by Levett-Therivel, London

New Economics Foundation (1998) *Participation Works! 21 Techniques of Community Participation for the 21st Century*, www.neweconomics.org

Office of the Deputy Prime Minister (ODPM)(2002) *Draft Guidance on the Strategic Environmental Assessment Directive*, www.planning.odpm.gov.uk/consult/sea

ODPM (2003) *The Strategic Environmental Assessment: Guidance for Planning Authorities*, www.planning.odpm.gov.uk

Oxfordshire County Council (1995) *Oxfordshire County Council Structure Plan: Alternative Actions*, public consultation leaflet, Oxford

Partidario, M R (1992) *An Environmental Assessment and Review (EAR) Procedure: A Contribution to Comprehensive Land-use Planning*, PhD dissertation, University of Aberdeen, Aberdeen

Partidario, M R and R Clark, eds (2000), *Perspectives on Strategic Environmental Assessment*, Lewis Publishers, Boca Raton, pp29–43

Pearce, D et al (1992) *Blueprint for a Green Economy*, Earthscan, London

Piper, J M (2002) 'CEA and sustainable development: Evidence from UK case studies', *Environmental Impact Assessment Review* 22, pp17–36

Rodriguez-Bachiller, A (2001) in P Morris and R Therivel, eds, *Methods of Environmental Impact Assessment*, UCL Press, London

Royal Commission on Environmental Pollution (2002) *Environmental Planning*, CEP Twenty-third report, London

Royal Society for the Protection of Birds (RSPB) (1994) *Capacity Planning: A Practical Application of Sustainable Development Concepts in the Land Use Field*, Bedford

Sadler, B (2003) *Strategic Environmental Assessment at the Policy Level*, Proceedings of a workshop on SEA systems and applications to policy and legislation, Ministry of Housing, Spatial Planning and Development (VROM), The Hague, Netherlands

Sadler, B and R Verheem (1996) *SEA: Status, Challenges and Future Directions*, Report 53, Ministry of Housing, Spatial Planning and the Environment, The Hague, Netherlands

Secretariat Francophone de l'Association Internationale pour l'Évaluation d'Impacts et le Ministère de l'Aménagement du Territoire et de l'Environnement (2000) *5eme Colloque International des Spécialistes Francophones en Évaluation d'Impacts: Résumés des Conférences*, Centre international de conférences Kleber, Paris

Smith, S P and W R Sheate (2001a) 'Sustainability appraisal of English regional plans: Incorporating the requirements of the EU Strategic Environmental Assessment Directive', *Impact Assessment and Project Appraisal*, December, pp263–276

Smith, S P and W R Sheate (2001b) 'Sustainability appraisal of regional planning guidance and regional economic strategies in England: An assessment', *Journal of Environmental Planning and Management* 44(5), pp735–755

Somerset County Council (2000) *Local Transport Plan for Somerset 2001–2006, Annex 6 North West Taunton Package*, www.somerset.gov.uk/enprop/ltp

South West Ecological Surveys, Oxford Brookes University and Levett-Therivel (2003) *Strategic Environmental Assessment and Biodiversity: Guidance for Practitioners*, report for English Nature, Royal Society for the Protection of Birds and others, Peterborough

Speight, C, T Ibbotson, O Venn and B Rosedale (2003) *Strategic Environmental Assessment for Vale of White Horse Local Plan 2011*, report prepared as part of work towards MSc in Environmental Assessment and Management, Oxford Brookes University, Oxford

Stirling, A (1999) 'The appraisal of sustainability: Some problems and possible responses', *Local Environment* 4(2), pp111–135

Sustainable Development Commission (2001) *Sustainability Appraisal of Policies for Farming and Food*, www.sd-commission.gov.uk/pubs/pcfff

Swedish National Board of Housing, Building and Planning and Swedish Environmental Protection Agency (2000) *Planning with Environmental Objectives! A Guide*, Stockholm

Therivel, R (1995) 'Environmental appraisal of development plans: Current status', *Planning Practice and Research* 10(2), pp223–234

Therivel, R (1996) 'Environmental appraisal of development plans: Status in late 1995', *Report*, March, pp14–16

Therivel, R (1998) 'Strategic environmental assessment of development plans in Great Britain', *Environmental Impact Assessment Review*, 18, pp39–57

Therivel, R and L Brown (1999) 'Methods of strategic environmental assessment', in J Petts, ed, *Handbook of Environmental Impact Assessment, Vol. 1*, Blackwell Science, Oxford, pp441–464

Therivel, R and P Minas (2002) 'Ensuring effective SEA in a changing context', *Impact Assessment and Project Appraisal* 29(2), pp81–91

Therivel, R and M R Partidario, eds (1996) *The Practice of Strategic Environmental Assessment*, Earthscan, London

Therivel, R, E Wilson, S Thompson, D Heaney and D Pritchard (1992) *Strategic Environmental Assessment*, Earthscan, London

Thissen, W (2000) 'Criteria for evaluation of strategic environmental assessment', in M R Partidario and R Clark, eds, *Perspectives on Strategic Environmental Assessment*, Lewis Publishers, Boca Raton, pp113–127

Tkach, R J and S P Simonovic (1998) 'A new approach to multi-criteria decision making in water resources', *Journal of Geographic Information and Decision Analysis* 1(1), pp25–43

Town and Country Planning Association (1999) *Urban Housing Capacity: What can be done?*, London

Tracz, M (1999) 'SEA of planned network of motorways and expressways in Poland', OECD/ECMT conference on SEA for transport, Warsaw, 14–15 October, www1.oecd.org/cem/topics/env/SEA99/SEAtracz.pdf

TRL Ltd (2002) *Analysis of Baseline Data Requirements for the SEA Directive: Final Report*, Crowthorne

Tukker, A (2000) 'Life cycle assessment as a tool in EIA', *Environmental Impact Assessment Review* 20(4), pp435–456

UK Treasury (1997) *The Green Book*, http://greenbook.treasury.gov.uk

United Nations Economic Commission for Europe (2003) *The Protocol on Strategic Environmental Assessment*, www.unece.org/env/eia/sea_protocol.htm

United Nations Environment Programme (UNEP) (2001) *Depleted Uranium in Kosovo: Post-Conflict Environmental Assessment*, Kenya

van Straaten, D (1996) 'Methodological considerations to strategic environmental assessment', in R Verheyen and K Nagels, eds, *Methodology, Focalization, Evaluation and Scope of Environmental Assessment: Fourth Report: Strategic Environmental Assessment: Theory Versus Practice*, University of Antwerp, Wilrijk, Belgium, pp135–143

van Straaten, D (1999) 'Vulnerability maps as a tool for SEA and infrastructure planning', www.vista.gov.vn/VistaEnglish/VistaWeb/learn/Env.%20Planning/texts%20in%20English/P3Chap7.pdf

Verheem, R (1996) 'SEA of the Dutch ten-year programme on waste management', in R Therivel and M R Partidario, eds, *The Practice of Strategic Environmental Assessment*, Earthscan, London, pp86–94

Verheyen, R and K Nagels (1996) *Methodology, Focalization, Evaluation and Scope of EIA: Fourth Report: Strategic Environmental Assessment: Theory Versus Practice*, NATO/CCMS Pilot Study, University of Antwerp, Wilrijk, Belgium

von Seht, H and C Wood (1998) 'The proposed European Directive on Environmental Assessment: Evolution and evaluation', *Environmental Policy and Law* 28/5, pp242–249

Wackernagel, M and W Rees (1996) *Our Ecological Footprint: Reducing Human Impact on the Earth*, New Society Publishers, Gabriola Island, British Columbia

Weiss, J (1998) 'Cost-benefit analysis and assessing privatisation projects in transitional economies', *Impact Assessment and Project Appraisal* 16(4), pp289–294

Wood, C (1988) 'EIA in plan making', in P Wathern, ed, *Environmental Impact Assessment*, Unwin Hyman, London

Wood, C and M Djeddour (1991) 'Strategic environmental assessment: EA of policies, plans and programmes', *The Impact Assessment Bulletin* 10(1), pp3–22

World Bank (1996) *Participation Source Book*, www.worldbank.org/wbi/sourcebook/sb0001.htm

World Commission on Environment and Development (Brundtland Commission) (1987) *Our Common Future*, Oxford University Press, Oxford

Index